**LETTERS TO
TWO FRIENDS
1926-1952**

**PIERRE TEILHARD
DE CHARDIN**

Already Published

Moses Hadas—THE LIVING TRADITION

Theodosius Dobzhansky—THE BIOLOGY
OF ULTIMATE CONCERN

John A. T. Robinson, Bishop of Woolwich—
BUT THAT I CAN'T BELIEVE!

PERSPECTIVES
IN HUMANISM
Planned and Edited by
RUTH NANDA ANSHEN

Board of Editors

LETTERS TO TWO FRIENDS 1926-1952

PIERRE TEILHARD DE CHARDIN

 THE NEW AMERICAN LIBRARY

First Printing

Published by The New American Library, Inc.
1301 Avenue of the Americas, New York, New York 10019
Published simultaneously in Canada by
General Publishing Company, Ltd.
Library of Congress Catalog Card Number: 68-14357
Printed in the United States of America

CONTENTS

PERSPECTIVES IN HUMANISM
THE FUTURE OF TRADITION—ix
RUTH NANDA ANSHEN

PERSPECTIVES IN HUMANISM
THE FUTURE OF TRADITION
RUTH NANDA ANSHEN

Perspectives in Humanism is designed to affirm that the world, the universe, and man are remarkably stable, elementally unchanging. Protons remain protons, and the other known elements are themselves, even when their atoms are broken; and man remains, in his essence, man. Every form of nature possesses what Aristotle called its own law. The blade of grass does not exist to feed the cow; the cow does not exist in order to give milk to man; and man does not exist to be subdivided, for to subdivide him is to execute him. Man is an organism, a whole, in which segregation of any sort is artificial and in which every phenomenon is a manifestation of the whole. The lawfulness of nature, including man's nature, is a miracle defying understanding.

My Introduction to this Series is not of course to be construed as a prefatory essay for each individual book. These few pages simply attempt to set forth the general aim and purpose of the Series as a whole. They try to point to the humanistic significance of the respective disciplines as represented by those scholars who have been invited to participate in this endeavor.

Perspectives in Humanism submits that there is a constant process of continuity within the process of change. This process lies in the very nature of man. We ask ourselves: What is this constant? What is it that endures and is the foundation of our intellectual and moral civilization? What is it that we are able to call our humanistic tradition? What is it that must survive and be transmitted to the future if man is to remain human?

The answer is that this constant lies in recognizing what is changeless in the midst of change. It is that heritage of timeless and immutable values on which we can fix our gaze whenever the language of change and decline which history speaks seems to become too overwhelming for the human heart. It offers us the spectacle of the constancy of certain basic forms and ideas throughout a process of continuous social mutations, intellectual development, and scientific revolution. The constant is the original form maintaining itself by transformation and adapting itself to changing social conditions, the continuity which is the very medium of change.

It is the loss of awareness of this constant in our time, not through the failure but rather through the very success of our modern scientific and technological achievements that has produced a society in which it becomes increasingly difficult to live a life that is human.

Perspectives in Humanism tries to confront, and, if possible, show the way to the resolution of, the major dilemma of our epoch: the greatest affliction of the modern mind. This dilemma is created by the magnificent fruits of the industrial revolution on the one hand and by an inexorable technology on the other. It is the acceptance of power as a source of authority and as a substitute for truth and knowledge. It is the dilemma born out of a skepticism in values and a faith in the perfectibility of the mind. It accepts the results of scientific inquiry as carrying self-evident implications, an obvious error. And finally it defines knowledge as a product, accepting lines of force emptied of lines of will, rather than, as indeed it is, a process.

The authors in this Series attempt to show the failure of what has been called scientific humanism, to show the limitation of scientific method which determines only sequences of events without meaning and among these events none more meaningless than man. For modern science is not concerned with human experience, nor with human purposes, and its knowledge of ascertained natural facts can never represent the whole of human nature. Now man is crying out for the recognition of insights derived from other sources, from the awareness that the problem of mechanism and teleology is a legitimate problem, requiring a humanistic solution.

It has always been on the basis of the hypothesis that the world and man's place in it can be understood by reason that the world and man become intelligible. And in all the crises of the mind and heart it has been the belief in the possibility of a solution that has made a solution possible.

Studies of man are made in all institutions of research and higher learning. There is hardly a section of the total scholarly enterprise which does not contribute directly or indirectly to our knowledge of man's nature. Not only philosophy and theology, not only history and the other humanities, not only psychology, sociology, biology, and medicine investigate man's nature and existence, but also the natural sciences do so, at least indirectly, and even directly, whenever they reflect upon their own methods, limits, and purposes.

It is in the light of such considerations that *Perspectives in Humanism* endeavors to show the false antinomy between the scientist and the humanist and the Cartesian error of dualizing mind and body. This Series tries to point to the incoherence of our time which implies the breakdown of integrative relationships, and to demonstrate that in science, as in all other fields of human thought and action, humanism may be preserved only through channels of shared experience and through mutual hopes. Indeed, humanism in these volumes is defined as that force which may render science once more part of universal human discourse. In this, it is here proposed, lies the future of tradition. Our search is for the "ought" which does not derive from facts alone.

In many realms of scholarly work there is an awareness of the fragmentation of man. And there is an increasing recognition that the study of man-made and natural ecological systems is as necessary as the study of isolated particles and elementary reactions. Most impressive has been the reaction of many scientists to the problems of the "atomic age" created by the technical application of their own theories. They realize that the question of the human meaning of scientific research cannot be repressed any longer in view of the immensity of these problems.

In biology and medicine the qualitative uniqueness of every

life process, and especially the uniqueness of that process which is called human, has come into the foreground of investigation. And, above all, biology, psychology, and medicine have made parallel efforts to overcome the accepted but untenable split between the psychological and the physiological aspects of human nature, remembering with Aristotle that the soul is the meaning of the body.

Historical studies in all directions, including political, social, economic, cultural, and religious history, have begun to ask the question: What are the characteristics of man as they are manifested in history? The exclusively factual and causal approach to history generally, and its special divisions such as history of the arts, of literature, of societal forms, of religion, has been broken down in many places. The question of meaning has not replaced the question of fact but has given research another dimension and a direct relevance for man's self-interpretation.

This is the situation. No convincing picture of man has arisen in spite of the many ways in which human thought has tried to reach it. But one thing has been achieved: The problem has made itself felt with great force in many places in spite of considerable resistance. This alone would justify a concentrated attempt to seek for preliminary answers and new questions resulting from them. And this is the aim of *Perspectives in Humanism.*

There is, however, another rather serious reason for cooperation in the study of this new and enlarged meaning of humanism. It is the fact that, under the impact of these developments, a linguistic confusion in all important matters of man's existence has taken place in the Western world — a confusion which makes cooperation extremely difficult. Most concepts used in scholarly attempts to draw a picture of man are ambiguous, or obsolete, or fashionable clichés. It is impossible *not* to use them, but they mislead if they are used. This is not a recent development — although the methods of contemporary publicity have supported it and are one of the greatest impediments to healing it — but it is a result of the intellectual and social history of the last centuries. A change is possible only if this history in all its ramifications is studied from the point of view of the disintegration of the language concerning man which has taken place in the last centuries. Such a dialogue is formidable and must be done in terms of a continuous exchange between representatives of the different spheres of knowledge and of cultures. It is our hope that this Series will provide favorable conditions for such an exchange.

The historical approach must be done in interdependence with a systematic approach. Concepts developed in one sphere must show their relevance for other spheres. This also is being done in a casual way in contemporary literature. It must be done methodologically. The departmental boundaries must be trespassed continuously. It is ultimately impossible to make a true statement about the physiological dynamics of the human body without taking into consideration the spirit which forms the flesh. It is ultimately impossible to describe the self-destructive tendencies in a neurotic person without describing the structures of estrangement in man's social existence. These examples can be increased indefinitely. They show that the departmentalization of our knowledge of man, although it was and is a matter of expediency, is at the same time a cause for distortion. Here lies the main positive task of *Perspectives in Humanism.*

Humanism is the ideal pattern supposed to reveal the true nature of man and the task for which he was born — the task of shaping himself into a true man and thereby creating a society worthy of him to be transmitted to future generations. For humanism is a lasting truth, not merely a transitory historical phenomenon. Like the changeless *logos* of which Heraclitus spoke, it pervades the whole process of eternal flux, and may even be said to be like a divine fire that works in each of us whether we know it or not. There stands behind our Western tradition, just as behind the great traditions of the East, a common metaphysical faith which transcends all schisms and conflicts within it.

And just as humanism means that there exists a common humanity beyond all divisiveness, so humanism also means that a unitary nature unites scientist and humanist alike. It can no longer be said that man is either a scientist or a humanist. The knower and the known, the doubter and the doubt, are one. To identify the scientist with a single method, the scientific one, that is, with a single procedure, is a distortion of science. All the powers of the mind, of intuition, of observation (to which the observer brings his own perception), of discursive and non-discursive knowledge, are brought into play in the achievement of scientific interpretation. And the pre-analytic data of science, if called "facts," are in reality but problematic facts. The only facts initially given for exploration are the facts of humanistic relevance, facts laden or saturated with loose or crude interpretations and demanding therefore reinterpretations by procedures free from what Bacon described as idols of the mind.

The difference between humanistic and scientific meaning is a difference not of kind but of degree. Can it be seriously maintained that, prior to the advent of scientific knowledge, with its elaborate hypotheses and theories, all intent upon the search for the nature of things, men were acquainted merely with sense data, or meaningless impressions? Prescientific knowledge is also knowledge, involving in incipient or inchoate form most of the activities in which science is engaged, such as naming and classifying, numbering and measuring, describing and explaining. And all these aspects are but the humanistic yearning in man's nature to establish a legitimate place for himself in the cosmic scheme from which he feels that he has been estranged. However far-flung its hypotheses or comprehensive its theories, science has no objects for its application save such as can be known through a humanistic interpretation and therefore known through perception suffused with judgment and belief. Science plunges into the phenomena, isolated and apart from the wholeness of reality, interpreting with precision and even accuracy and by devices that make possible more adequate inferences, and sometimes even more reliable predictions, the very same world of things which are antecedently recognized through the implicit perceptions of humanistic insights.

What this Series hopes to demonstrate is that humanism by its nature is intent upon forcing the mind to make, since it is unable not to make, judgments of value. It is to accept once more the validity of the metaphysical hypothesis. What humanism desires and demands is an insight into the meaning of the universe of nature and of man as totality by the use of categories more general or pervasive than those required for the things segmented by a special science. The antihumanist prejudice, prevalent in certain quarters, can be explained only by the dogma that the universe and man in it are everlastingly divided among and by the special sciences, the synopsis of each being separate and exclusive so that a categorial synopsis of the total nature of the thing remains *a priori* precluded.

It is the endeavor of *Perspectives in Humanism* to show that there is no knowledge (knowledge which is synonymous with being) save by a humanistic perception of what we know. For we bring ourselves to every objective act of cognition, we are always intimately involved in every cognitive act. And we can no longer allow ourselves to separate thought from feeling nor to push our subjective experiences into the cognitively irrelevant corner of the emotions (of which poetry, religion, metaphysics, and morality are supposed to be expressions). Knowledge which is at the same time humanistic will then be seen to have a no less legitimate claim than that of any science.

In other words this Series attempts to affirm the truth that man's knowledge can be made relevant to life only by including a knowledge about knowledge. And therefore the humanist can no longer be isolated from the scientist nor can he defend, as he did in the Renaissance, his own studies against the claims of other disciplines. For the humanist even as the scientist has to face the problem of truth, a problem which may be treated in multiple ways, retaining the emphasis, however, on the quest for unity, for that which is constant, in the face of apparently divergent and incompatible doctrines. *Perspectives in Humanism* suggests that one of man's fundamental concerns, be he scientist, philosopher, theologian, artist, or political thinker is the humanist authority which derives from truth and not the technological authority which derives from power.

Humanism, it is shown here, differs from the specific humanisms of past history in that it forces the mind again and again to recognize wider and subtler relations, lifting seemingly unrelated patterns into a higher harmony. A knowledge of past humanisms is of course indispensable since some of this knowledge is intrinsically valid and true, and we are summoned to recognize this before we can make significant contributions to our own humanism. This is the heritage each generation is called upon to transmit to the future. It is the humanist heritage which is synonymous with a doctrine of man, explored, enriched, and enlarged for the benefit of mankind and society.

Humanism as presented in this Series affirms the dependence of cultural values on concrete realities. We cannot conceive the former apart from the latter any more than we can conceive a painting apart from its pigment and canvas. And the unity, the constant, in both instances belongs to the realm of values. Therein lie their essence, meaning, and reality. And it is no difficult task to show that those who reject such interpretations in the name of scientific method, of blood, of property, or of economic necessity, and are therefore scornful of humanism as an ineffective phantasm, are themselves actuated to this scorn by dogmas, ideologies, or other value-impregnated thought forms, which can come to terms with the former only in the eternal arena of humanistic ideas.

The socialist program of humanism as envisaged by the communists has failed, and henceforth we cannot speak of the problem of Man as having significance only after the collapse of capitalism. For to offer man only what is human is to betray him and to wish him ill, since by the principal part of him which is the mind and the heart man is called to something better than a merely historical or physical life. As Aristotle reminds us, "To propose to man a merely human end is to misunderstand nature."

It is clear that whoever uses the term humanism (and the term itself is ambiguous) brings into play at once an entire metaphysic, and the idea we form of humanism will have wholly different implications according to whether we hold or do not hold that there is in the nature of man a constant, an essence, something which breathes an air outside of time and a personality whose profoundest needs transcend time and space, and even the self.

The authors in this Series try to show that humanism is the

essence of all disciplines of the human mind. Humanism indeed tends to render man more truly human. It makes man's original greatness manifest itself by causing him to participate in all that can enrich him in nature and in history by concentrating the universe in man and by dilating man to the universe. This Series endeavors to show how, through humanism, man may make use of all the potentialities he holds within him, his creative powers and the life of reason, and how he may make the powers of the physical world the instruments of his freedom.

The question raised by the authors here is: Can humanism become aware of itself and significant to man only in those moments of despair, at a time of the dissipation of its own energies, of isolation, alienation, loss of identity, dissociation, and descent; only when pain opens man's eyes and he sees and finds his burden unendurable? Does this lead to the proliferation of that atomic anarchy of which Nietzsche has spoken and which Dostoevsky's Grand Inquisitor offers us as a picture of a threatening fate, the nihilism of our time? Is there a humanism conscious of itself and free, leading man to sacrifice and greatness, which is indeed transcendent because here human suffering and consciousness of responsibility open man's eyes? For it is on the humanist answer to this question (and the grounds on which it is decided) that the various positions men take in the face of the travail of history enacted before our eyes and the diverse practical decisions which they feel obliged to make, do in fact depend.

Perspectives in Humanism tries to work toward defining a sound and sane philosophy of modern history so desperately needed. The authors in this Series work to substitute for the inhuman system currently confronting us a new form of civilization which would outline and represent humanism both sacred and secular. *Perspectives in Humanism* tries to show that this humanism is all the more human since it does not worship man but has a real and effective respect for human dignity and for the rights of human personality.

Our age, like every other, is in the grip of its own changing and conflicting thought forms, but the scholar who deals with "facts" cannot achieve objectivity by denuding these "facts" of value, for if he treats them as nonvalues he does not treat them at all. The best he can aspire to is the catholic comprehension and the tolerance that find nothing alien in anything human. Humanism requires that we interpret in our own terms, in the terms of our culture, the total given reality, persistently evaluating it all, means and ends in one, together with the sustaining earth and the indifferent cosmos, and thereby transmuting fact not only into value but also into symbol. This is its necessity, its life, as well as its peril.

The Chinese ideograph, the symbol of humanism, on the jacket and binding of each volume in this Series is found on early Chinese bronzes in the year 1200 B.C. It reflects the vision and image not of an individual man but of all mankind. It is the symbol chosen for the ability of man to transcend his own isolated self, a quality fundamental to his humanity. The "objectivity" of science cannot help man in his present human predicament, since for science in this sense there can be no commitment. So that in the end we know everything but understand nothing. In fact, we would seek nothing, not being motivated by concern for any question. It is a symbol which is concise, not precise; it is reflective, not descriptive. It is the impersonal self, identical from man to man, and is even perhaps similar to the essence of all life in its manifold expressions in nature. This symbol* thereby shows us why, in our search for meaning, direction, historical unities, and experience in science or in life, we must give logical priority as well as metaphysical preeminence to what we call, for lack of a better term, humanism: that which has something in common with intellectual achievement, with moral action, and with love.

---

* I am indebted and grateful to Professor Chiang Yee, Professor of Art and Calligraphy at Columbia University. He has generously drawn my attention to this ideograph.

R.N.A.

PROLOGUE

BY RENÉ D'OUINCE, S. J.

Numerous letters by Father Pierre Teilhard de Chardin have already been published: letters to his parents, to his cousin Marguerite Teilhard-Chambon, to Léontine Zanta. Each of these correspondences covers a short period of time and could be published as a unit.

The present collection follows a different plan. At the request of Ruth Nanda Anshen, editor of the *Perspectives in Humanism* series, two of the Father's correspondents presently living in America have chosen from a long series of letters addressed to themselves those passages dealing with the author's daily life and the development of his thought. In this way they have succeeded in creating a kind of "Journal of Pierre Teilhard de Chardin," extending from 1926 to 1952, or almost throughout his life as a scientist and priest. In this "journal" the Father regularly notes his occupations, his plans, his meetings with a number of well-known figures, the vicissitudes of his health, the opposition and the support he encounters in his Order and in the Church. I myself, who was Father Teilhard's friend and for several years his religious superior, found in these letters numerous details that I undoubtedly knew once but had forgotten, which indicates the exceptional interest of this volume.

A concern for rigorous objectivity and discretion has inspired the choice of passages. When I received the letter asking me to present the book to the public, I confess I was very moved by the disinterestedness to which it attested: "By eliminating all personal reference, each of us has tried, insofar as possible, to efface the personalities of the recipients. For if the publication of these letters is useful, it will be so solely for what they reveal of the mind and thought of their author. It is for this reason that we have wished to remain anonymous." To such a desire the publisher could only respectfully accede.

The first group of letters was written by Father Teilhard in French, the second in English. A double edition — in English and in French — is appearing simultaneously in New York and Paris. In each case, therefore, a part of the text has been translated; the other part is published in its original form.

This correspondence contains several long periods of silence. These are sometimes the result of external circumstances, such as the difficulty of sending mail during a scientific exploration or during the years of the Japanese occupation. Usually, however, the silences are due to the epistolary habits of the author. All his life Teilhard, like many great workers, was economical of his time, knowing how to maintain a strict hierarchy among his various activities. The priority of "duties of state" was not an empty phrase for him. During periods of intense scientific activity and even more so of literary creation, he buried himself in his work like a miner. Always polite and affable to those around him, he nevertheless kept his distance, avoided long friendly conversations, and neglected his correspondence. Those who lived close to him guessed him to be prodigiously occupied and respected his reserve. A few months later he would emerge again, available for communication, ready to resume a correspondence or a conversation with the same spontaneity as if the previous interview had taken place the night before.

Despite a few lacunae, the "Journal of Pierre Teilhard de Chardin" permits us to follow the story of his inner life almost month by month. The spontaneity of the tone, the quality of the remarks — the Father speaks of what is really on his mind — make this collection a unique document.

The first letters date from 1926, when the Father left his professorship at the Catholic Institute in Paris to lead the life of an explorer in the Far East. This period was one of the most difficult of his life. It was not that his new assignment lacked interest for him; he himself had desired it a few years earlier. "I would prefer Tientsin to the Catholic Institute," he wrote to a friend at that time, and it was with a youthful ardor that he had embarked for China in 1923 and brought off his first exploration in the desert of Ordos. But this time his departure had something of the aspect of a disgrace. He had been removed from Paris by the prudence of his superiors, to whom he had been denounced for propagating dubious ideas, and who feared a censure that would be equally prejudicial to the career of the young scientist and the good name of the Order. Thus he was leaving France under a cloud for an indefinite time, and he saw the momentum of his influence broken just as it was beginning to prove fruitful. The penalty imposed on him seemed unjustified. It was hard for him to "bend." He obeyed in a spirit of faith, but without understanding.

At this same period a profound change took place in his scientific vision of the World, or more precisely in his relation to the World. He, who until now had been passionately interested in the study of prehistory, felt an insidious aversion invade him: he lost his taste for the past. Henceforth only the future of the Universe would interest him. Thus he doubted both his religious vocation and his scientific vocation. Was it a momentary weariness, or was it already the weight of age and the irreversible process of human erosion? Never, certainly, had he been so profoundly shaken.

But Teilhard had always held that "everything that happens is worthy of adoration." Since at the time no other activity was possible, he would continue to scrutinize the Earth's past. He applied himself to his "duties of state" with a kind of fierce determination: "I must return from this second voyage stronger in body and in soul. I owe this to God."

And in fact, once in the field, the charm of Asia did its work, the joy of discovery seized him once again, the contact with "Mother Earth" restored his relish for living. Gradually he was able to see his work as a geologist-priest as part of the evolution of the World and of the Church. Geology was to be the necessary scientific platform to attract the attention of those to whom he was called to deliver his message.

Moreover, the temptation to rebellion receded. He reduced

the incident that caused him to be removed from Europe to its true proportions; he experienced a new awareness of his devotion to the Church, his inevitable limitations, his irreplaceable mission. A Christian must be ready to suffer for the Church and by the Church. And in his pacified soul the song of creation — the hymn of the Universe — became once again audible. "Believe me, when one has penetrated to this axis of the Christian attitude, the ritual, disciplinary and theological encrustations matter little more than musical or acoustical theories matter to the enjoyment of a beautiful piece of music. Truly, there is a Christian *note* which makes the whole World vibrate like an immense gong, in the divine Christ."

Soon, in the form of a discreet word of advice, he reveals his own victory: "For you, as for everyone, there is only one road that can lead to God, and this is the fidelity to remain constantly true to yourself, to what you feel is highest in you. Do not worry about the rest. The road will open before you as you go." About ten months after his departure, the road opened before him again: "I have recovered that familiar and very precious state of mind which makes me see and grasp some vital and intoxicating element at the bottom (or more precisely, at the end) of everything that exists and everything that happens. This is that unique Note produced by the World that I mentioned in my last letter. . . . For if I am now in China and if I am to set off the day after tomorrow, I realize that it is solely to obey this mysterious Attraction of the World to serve and to make serve . . . I have confidence that my line of thought is essentially Christian. . . ."

Teilhard has regained a human and spiritual equilibrium, but it is a new equilibrium. The investigator bent on scrutinizing the past of the Earth has made a definitive about-face; he is oriented toward the future. It is no longer enough for him to enrich the patrimony of a science by the contribution of new data; he longs to communicate a spirit, "a certain enthusiastic vision of the immensity and promise of the World."

This is why his thoughts turn more and more frequently toward Paris, not only because his scientific roots are there, but because only there does he find a milieu disposed to hear him. It is for his friends in Europe that between two field trips, he writes his "pious book," *The Divine Milieu,* which he dedicates "to those who love the World." Europe remains for him the Promised Land, momentarily inaccessible: "In the end, if I have come to China, if I am burying myself in my masses of fossils, if I am playing the part of the 'Knight Errant,' it is in the hope of better feeding this inner flame at all the great sources of inspiration of the Earth, and of acquiring, through a bit of notoriety or foreignness, the power to make myself heard, if only for one brief moment, before I die."

In August 1927, after eighteen months in China, he obtained authorization to sail for France. He was to return there in 1930, 1932, 1937, and 1938 (when his stay was interrupted by a trip to the United States), maintaining this "seesaw motion," to use the picturesque expression of Claude Cuenot, his first biographer, up to the Second World War, which was to immobilize him in Peking for more than six years.

Each trip to Paris was an occasion for him not only to resume relations with scientific circles and with old friends, but to widen his influence and to compare his thought with the most diverse minds. Harassed by visits, invitations, requests for speeches and articles, he could not face the solicitations that besieged him. "The life I lead would be absurd if it went on very long . . . and yet I have the impression not of losing myself, but of finding myself." However, his growing prestige, although it was limited to narrow circles, aroused the concern of his Roman protectors, who exhorted him more and more earnestly to use caution. He was careful not to prolong his visits: after a few months in Paris (he was detained there longer in 1937 for reasons of health), he hurried back to China and obscurity. A difficult life, of which it is not enough to say that he adjusted himself as well as he could; he came to see its advantages: "We must to a certain extent look for a secure port; but if life keeps tearing us away, not letting us settle anywhere, this in itself may be a call and a benediction. The World is understood and may, perhaps, be saved . . . only by those who have no place to lay their heads. Personally, I ask God to let me die (metaphorically, at least) by the side of the road."

With the passing years, his spiritual life, refined by experience, ripened by fidelity, became simpler and calmer. In 1936, on the occasion of his fifty-fifth birthday, he wrote, "Decisive year: all I hope for is to feel closer to God." And again in 1940: "Without feeling any less close to the World, I feel closer to God. And without seeing any less clearly its rigidities and limitations, I realize that I am more wholeheartedly a member of the Christian movement — the phylum of the personal and of what must become the true charity."

During the Japanese occupation, Teilhard tried to continue his scientific activities as long as possible. With his friend and colleague, Pierre Leroy, he founded the Institute of Geobiology in Peking, and, in a series of articles and reports, presented the results of the Chou-kou-tien excavations, which were abruptly halted. Finally, he took advantage of his forced inactivity to write the final draft of his great work, *The Phenomenon of Man*, which he had begun in 1938: eight months of happy work, at the rate of one or two pages a day.

When the draft was finished, toward the end of summer, 1940, the Father was obliged, like every religious, to submit his book to the censure of his Order with a view to publication. Since he could not communicate with France, which was disorganized by the German invasion, he decided to address himself directly to his general superior. He wrote him at the beginning of November, requesting Roman consideration, and also asking for permission to participate in a conference that was to take place in New York the following year on "the relation between science and religion" and "the possibility for a human Credo."

Like Francis-Xavier, lost in his remote Indies, requesting the directives of Ignatius, Teilhard fully intended to remain, at all costs, "an obedient son." But his fidelity was to be severely put to the test. The reply, which reached him in March 1941, betrayed abiding reservations: a discreet promise to have the book examined by competent censors, and refusal to take part in the conference in New York, to which he was, however, permitted to send a written communication. The result is disappointing. Teilhard put a brave face on his ill fortune — "After all, I expected worse" — and armed himself with a fresh provision of courage.

He would need all of it. Soon afterwards a typewritten manuscript of *The Phenomenon of Man* (Teilhard possessed three copies) was entrusted to a traveler leaving for America. From there, through the offices of another friend, a diplomatic pouch forwarded it to Rome, where it arrived in April 1941. Under the circumstances, its arrival represents quite a feat. But the reply of the examiners, slower to arrive than in the age of caravels, would not reach him until 1944: publication judged untimely. In the interval, the Father's isolation worsened: the American colony among whom he numbered so many friends received orders to leave Peking; his ablest Chinese associates were recalled to the southern provinces; the French Embassy remained his great resource, but it was itself isolated from the metropolis.

With the help of the rare news reports that reached him, he tried to imagine the situation in Europe. He wanted to believe that so much suffering would not be in vain, that "something resembling a movement, a spirit" would come out of it. His letters to various friends show him more than ever turned toward the future. "The problem," he wrote, "is to sublimate force in the mind." "Peace cannot be the consequence of a general lassitude: it requires a passionate union of men with respect to common objectives." "I remain convinced that a flame is rising without our being able to see it from here." The apparent resignation of occupied France worried him: "Life is fire, not wisdom!" He hoped that from the pain and destruction of the war there would emerge a more complete type of man who, without repudiating his national ties, would feel himself at last a citizen of the Earth. But he lacked too many facts to be able to interpret events correctly, and his anticipations often took the form of dreams. Meanwhile he pursued his personal meditations, adding to the list of his "scientifico-philosophico-religious writings." "I work, I must confess, for Paris and for tomorrow."

On August 17, 1945, the Japanese troops called a cease-fire in China. Teilhard longed to return to Paris and wrote asking me to reserve a room at the Etudes, but he desired to do nothing save in obedience. A few months later he received from his new Provincial, who was also a friend, the long-awaited invitation. He sailed with a minimum of baggage on a military transport and arrived in Paris at the beginning of May 1946.

This time he had the sense of being overwhelmed: during his six years of absence the duplicated manuscripts intended for his friends had proliferated beyond his expectations. He was welcomed by a crowd of strangers, as a prophet.

"Paris is very interesting," he wrote. "Almost every day I make contact with new and curious personalities who are interested in the construction of a new World, a new economy, a new morality." He felt himself living in harmony with a World "that was seeking more light and more liberty." He had hoped that this war would deepen and transform the human conscience and he was convinced that he had been right. The formulas that he had meditated upon during his exile in Peking returned to his lips with an accent of victory: "And there are still people who do not see that Humanity is the collective subject of a veritable evolution!" "Something is in the process of rising and finding expression in the human conscience." "The Christian faith can survive and flourish only by incorporating faith in human progress." He even encouraged a few men of good will to form a group (short-lived, however) with the significant name of "the Human Front." These first months in Paris were probably the most exciting of his life.

Naturally because of his success he was more fiercely discussed, suspected, and denounced, and the recommendations of his Roman superiors became more imperious. He must stop circulating his typewritten essays and renounce articles and speeches on all subjects not strictly scientific, which sometimes raised psychologically insoluble problems for him. Hence, at the end of a "purely scientific" speech which he gave at the Ecole de Guerre, one of his listeners suddenly questioned him on Original Sin. Could he remain silent? "I answered," he writes, "trusting to God."

On June 2, 1947, a serious accident (infarctus of the myocardium) temporarily released him from these perplexities. Moved to the clinic of the Brothers of Saint John of God near the Etudes building, for two weeks he hovered between life and death, and then was obliged to take several months' rest at Saint-Germain-en-Laye with the Sisters of Mercy, whose attentive solicitude he celebrated in his letters.

The following year saw a sudden change in the attitude of the leading authorities of his Order. His general superior invited him to come to Rome with the evidently benevolent intention of introducing him to a certain number of ecclesiastical figures who were in a position to protect him. His friends gave him hope of at last publishing the two books delayed by the censors, *The Divine Milieu* and *The Phenomenon of Man,* of accepting a professorship that was offered him at the Collège de France and an invitation to give a series of lectures in the United States. Was this the end of the misunderstandings from which he had so long suffered? He left, deliberately optimistic, but ready for anything. I remember his parting remark: "I am glad to be seeing the head authority; I shall tell him everything that is in my mind." Then with a gleam of malice in his eyes, "You heard me; I said *in* my mind and not *on* my mind, for I don't have anything on my mind."

In Rome, he was won over by the simplicity and affability of the Reverend Father Janssens; he obediently made a certain number of visits and received a seemingly favorable welcome. But apparently neither he nor his general superior had correctly judged the force of the resistances to be overcome. His affairs, which had seemed well under way, took longer than he had foreseen. After a few weeks he left Rome, armed with vague promises in which he was beginning to discern the premonitory signs of a refusal. The answer was long in coming. Three times his letters to his American correspondents begin with the same words: "Still nothing from Rome!" The decision was finally imparted to him: defeat all along the line. Neither publication nor teaching were authorized, and soon he would be asked to leave Paris where, indeed, the restrictions imposed on the expression of his thought were making his situation untenable. For never had his moral authority been so great: the halo of persecution added still further to his prestige, and he recalled the painfully glorious precedent of Galileo.

He himself was sincerely grieved. What he had predicted and feared was being confirmed: "More important than the discovery of Galileo," he wrote, "we are gradually discovering a movement of Humanity as a whole, growing in organization and self-awareness. . . . Every day I test the power of this observation on the minds of men."

Teilhard wanted to leave France as quietly as possible: he decided to go to South Africa and, by this roundabout route, back to America, his land of refuge and the site of his last exile. Objectively his situation was much more difficult than in 1926. But in the past twenty years Teilhard had made a long journey. He felt no temptation to rebellion: peace had become a way of life. A peace now serene and now sorrowful, which he protected by this moving prayer: "Lord, give me the grace to end well!"

I have preferred to emphasize Father Teilhard's fidelity to his religious life because in reading this lovely book I myself have been especially aware of this aspect. There are others just as deserving of the reader's attention: I should like to underscore this one.

The Father's two correspondents, although they are just as open to the things of the spirit, just as aware of the originality of the thinker and the quality of the religious man, do not share his Christian faith. Because of this, the tone of the letters published here differs perceptibly from that of letters that have previously appeared. The religious vocabulary, the choice of subjects, and the light in which the great spiritual and human problems to which the Father devoted his life are present but are adjusted to the conditions of a dialogue that is always marked by candor, affection, and respect.

The reader will discover here certain well-known traits of Pierre Teilhard de Chardin's personality: the influence he exerted in circles far removed from Catholicism, his facility in speaking the language of "children of the century," his eagerness to compare his thought with that of nonbelievers of good will who were hungry for sincerity and thirsty for human communion.

Teilhard suffered too much from the narrow-mindedness and prejudices of certain Catholic circles not to feel a kind of relief in finding interlocutors who were strangers to the conformism of "right-thinking" Christians. "Once again I felt to what degree my sympathies and my nature, which are incapable of surviving without Christianity, are nevertheless one with this part of the World which is not yet Christianized." Teilhard also believed that feminine intuition and sensibility provided a precious complement to the too exclusively rational understanding of man, a complement that was, for him at least, indispensable. Thus he looked to his correspondents for light and help in choosing his path more precisely.

At the same time he was too keenly aware of the blessing of faith not to desire, insofar as possible, to offer to share it. So we find in this correspondence a kind of spiritual guidance which employs a different vocabulary from that of classic spiritual literature and which every person of good will can turn to account. "The difficulties and improbabilities that you are struggling against are the great, the fundamental, the eternal barriers that the spirit must cross in order to reach God. I personally believe the solution to lie in the eminent value of *spirit* and in the ultimate connection of all the substances of the World. . . . The more enormous the Universe is, the more precious is the *spirit* that required such a deployment of varied energies in order to be born; and the more numerous we are, the more magnificent is the synthesis which is being prepared for our reunion." And again: "We say that God must be conceived *in the direction* of a *super-person* (that is, an extension of the good qualities — and not of the individual limitations — of the human being). He must be as vast as the Universe and as warm as a human heart, and incomparably more besides. This is all we can say."

The Teilhardian formulas are more than a somewhat ingenious transposition of a received and transmitted doctrine; they express a personal experience. The Father experienced sincerely in his own heart the reluctance of men of our time before the exigencies of the Gospel, and it was in his own conscience that he also experienced the victory of faith and the triumph of Jesus Christ. This accounts for the astonishing "multivalency" of certain passages in which it is impossible to distinguish counsel from confession. In these passages the believer can decipher in filigree the traditional doctrine of the Church (on the mystic Body, on Grace) while the nonbeliever spontaneously recognizes the history of his own inner life, the voice of the unknown

God who speaks to him in the privacy of his heart. The correspondence abounds in passages of this kind. Here, for example, is the description of Christian renunciation: "The death of egoism is to understand that one is an element in a Universe that personalizes itself (if I may) by uniting itself with God (I do not say, by becoming God). So it is no longer oneself that one loves in oneself." Here is an evocation of the divine omnipresence in the apparent disorder of the Universe: "May Life become for you, not merely some favorable blind fatality, but a kind of living Presence or Benevolence in which it will be possible for you not only to trust but to confide."

Certain penetrating psychological observations expose illusions that are not the prerogative of devout minds. Is it not one of the most frequent temptations of our generation, which wants to be realistic, to confuse the real value of a life with its visible results? "The point is not to do remarkable things, but to do ordinary things with the conviction of their immense value." Or again: "What is an existence that is faithful to Life? Is it an existence that is *socially* successful, one with an outward continuity, recognized success, a tangible result, an acquired stability? Not necessarily. (Personally, I no longer concern myself with the outward success of my time on earth.)" Since he has entered the path of confession, he pursues his spiritual examination to the very end: "Why do you assume that an existence that does not succeed in taking root or bearing fruit in the form of a tangible work is less valuable than another? Why might not the World, which has need of stable families and settled people, need also those mobile and wandering creatures whose action takes the form of a series of seemingly unrelated trials or tests cutting across all kinds of areas? . . . It is a great thing not to have a place to lay your head if you carry faith in the World in your heart."

Above all, as might be suspected, Teilhard himself practiced and exhorted others to hope: "In itself, it is a magnificent human function," he wrote at the moment of the declaration of war, "to resist despair by faith in Existence. After this you will perhaps understand that, in the formidable human conflict into which we are entering, you can immerse yourself as in a better and new life. . . . Perhaps you do not belong to yourself. Have you thought of that?"

If Teilhard was demanding of those he loved, he was also realistic: he knew enough not to ask an impossible effort, to trust to the action of time: "Do not *brace* yourself against suffering. Try to close your eyes and surrender, as if to a great loving energy. This attitude is neither weak nor absurd. . . . It is still too soon, no doubt, for you to recover: try to 'sleep,' with that *active* sleep of confidence which is that of the seed in the fields in winter. . . . This is the true and great prayer of moments of great sickness."

The last letter is dated January 1952. Teilhard was seventy-one years old; he knew himself to be in danger. He ended with this admirable wish: "The movement of the Universe . . . reveals itself as necessarily belonging to the species of a Life, and even of a Love. Not the 'black pit,' but the burning center, whatever it is. May you and I grow in the Vision and the Presence of this Unique Necessity, through all the successes and failures of our lives!"

Surely the freshest and most dramatic contribution that this correspondence makes to the biography of Pierre Teilhard de Chardin has to do with the justification of his religious vocation in the Society of Jesus. Like many other friends (Boule, Rivet), his correspondents had trouble understanding the Father's persevering devotion to an Order that seemed not to recognize his value and that opposed the circulation of his thought. On this subject Teilhard expressed himself with total candor, admitting his uncertainties and his temptations to impatience, discouragement, or rebellion, but also his unshakable desire to remain faithful to the Church of Jesus Christ. "A revolutionary attitude would be agreeable, but it would be suicide." The Father believed steadfastly in what he called a "transformation" — today we would call it an *aggiornamento* — of the Church; he devoted himself to it with the whole measure of his strength and his ability. He was aware of his limitations, of the imperfection of his work; he did not doubt the rectitude of his intention. Knowing that he could not expect the support of the Roman Curia, he resisted provoking a rupture that would jeopardize the hoped-for reform. "I cannot make a break (which would be so agreeable in certain respects), since that would kill the thing that I wish not to destroy, but to liberate." His whole strategy if I may venture to use the word, consisted in keeping himself in a state of active expectation. "The more it [the human world] assumes this clarity and consistency in my eyes, the more I perceive that it can continue to exist only by its effort toward some divine principle. Would it be logical for me, by breaking with my Church, impatiently to force the growth of that Christian stem in which I am persuaded that the sap of the religion of tomorrow is forming? I am held fast in the Church by the very views which help me to see her insufficiencies. Is this not a bit dramatic or cosmic? Help me by having confidence in me."

Another time one of his American correspondents told him humorously that it was unseemly for a young swan to gambol among the ducks. Teilhard admitted the discomfort of the situation; but he meant to remain "among the ducks" to the very end. The scientific incompetence of the theologians who imposed silence on him seemed to him flagrant, as he admitted without equivocation. But he did not therefore reject the authority they exercised. It was to the historical Church composed of imperfect men that Christ delivered his message; these imperfect men represented for Teilhard "much more than what they were." He himself assumed in their eyes the aspect of an *enfant terrible,* or a lost child. No matter! By refusing to return to freedom, by remaining in the paternal house, "I am not," he wrote, "a prodigal son."

In 1955 Father Teilhard died, in apparent disgrace, within his Order. A dozen years have sufficed to make his life — thwarted, prevented, as he believed, from "bringing forth tangible fruit" — appear today as that of a precursor: the first draft of a work planned by the Spirit. As religious lives were once devoted to the care of lepers or the liberation of captives, he felt called to serve the liberation of man — a new type of man which he saw emerging from the womb of modern civilization in the vanguard of the evolution of the World, a man at once ambitious and delicate, now intoxicated by his power and now overwhelmed by it.

The life of a priest dedicated to the service of man! This vocation seemed singular at the time; today the whole Church has embraced it.

Here I should like to reproduce a few passages from Paul VI's speech at the end of the Second Vatican Council:

The religion of the God who became man has encountered the religion (for there is only one) of the man who became God. What has happened? Conflict, condemnation? This might have happened; but this has not occurred. The old story of the Good Samaritan has been the model for the spirituality of the Council: a boundless sympathy has pervaded it. . . .

The Church has proclaimed itself, so to speak, the servant of humanity. . . . The Catholic religion and human life thus reaffirm their alliance, their convergence in a single human reality: the Catholic religion is for humanity; in a certain sense it is the life of humanity. It is the life because of the explanation which our religion gives of man; the only explanation, in the last analysis, which is right and sublime. . . .

It gives this explanation precisely by virtue of its knowledge of God: to know man, true man, man as a whole, one must know God. . . .

But . . . if we recall that in the face of every man . . . we can and must recognize the face of Christ, the Son of man, and if in the face of Christ we can and must recognize the face of the heavenly Father . . . our humanism becomes Christianity, and our Christianity becomes theocentric, so that we can also declare that to know God, one must know man.

But then might not this Council, whose energies and preoccupations have been devoted principally to man, be destined to open once again to the modern world the paths of an ascension to freedom and true happiness? Might it not give, in the last analysis, the simple, new, and solemn doctrine to learn to love man in order to love God?

I knew Father Teilhard to be too indifferent to his personal success for me to be tempted to adopt a triumphant tone in speaking of him. Nor is this the place to pass judgment on his work, but only on the intention that guided his life. I cannot help thinking that he, before others, was able to discern the "signs of the time" and to discover one of the major tasks of the Christian community in the modern world: "to learn to love man in order to love God." Few thinkers of his generation have communicated as spontaneously with the depths of man, few Christians have recognized so clearly in man the face of Jesus Christ. In devoting himself to the service of the true grandeur of man, he sought only "the ever greater Christ."

When I evoke today the memory of the religious whose friend I was for many passionate and difficult years, the image that stands out in my mind is that of a priest who did honor to man, who made anyone who came in touch with him proud to be a man. To my eyes Teilhard was the living answer to Nietzsche and his sarcasm: he had "the air of being saved." This victorious radiance which emanated from his whole person proceeded from a hidden source: a grace, for which he attributed no merit to himself, had been given him. The power of his message, to quote the penetrating observation of Father de Lubac, lay less "in a more or less ingenious philosophy than in the extremely strong testimony of a man perfectly attuned to the ideas and preoccupations of his time," telling how he had found in his faith "the equilibrium of his inner life and through this, a peace and ripeness without end."

In an age when a rift seemed to be forming between the most vital elements of the modern world and the Church, when the men most passionately interested in the study or the advancement of man were turning away from the Catholic faith, the Father had the opposite experience. More than anyone he had shared the hopes, efforts, and ambitions of his contemporaries: to no domain of thought or action did he feel himself a stranger. But whereas a taste for terrestrial values distracted so many others from the religion of their childhood, his own faith was only confirmed by it. The modern world, as the Father knew with compelling certainty, had need of Jesus Christ. This was all his "gospel." What he called "the religion of tomorrow" — an expression that is ambiguous if you take it apart from its context — was really the most authentic Catholicism, the religion of Saint Paul and Saint John, and of his pious mother. A few days before his death, he declared this a last time: "Evidence of the identity of what I see with what I had been taught."

Hence that paradoxical blend of audacity and fidelity. As a

biologist, he frequently applied the laws of germination and evolution to the development of thought: "For ideas to prevail, many of their defenders must die in obscurity." As a believer, he knew that no spiritual progress takes place without the mediation of the Cross: "If, in my Gospel, there is a true ray of light, this ray will somehow shine in a heart richer, I hope, for having been guarded faithfully in me."

Such seems to me to be the vocation of Pierre Teilhard de Chardin. During those dark years in the history of the Church in the wake of Modernism, I see him like Isaiah's watcher, whose image he loved, discerning in the uncertain future the imperceptible glow of dawn: "Watcher, what sayst thou of the night?"

Anyone who really knew the Father would give the same testimony. I will cite only a single case: one of the recipients of the correspondence in the present volume has expressed the idea with perfect accuracy: "In rereading the letters of Pierre Teilhard de Chardin," she writes, "I have been struck by the image they offer us of an energetic and tenacious man fighting to save not only his own ideas, but the Church he loved; although he may have seen this Church as it would be tomorrow rather than as it was yesterday."

Is this not, precisely, the vision of a prophet?

—Translated from the French
by Helen Weaver

LETTERS I
1926-1952

Translated from the French by Helen Weaver

Straits of Bonifacio, April 24, 1926

I write these first lines to you from the Straits of Bonifacio, between the plains of southern Corsica and the rocky peaks of northern Sardinia. The sea is gray and choppy, and we have been tossed about violently since leaving Marseille. But we are heading toward the land of warmth and sunny skies. This year it seems to me that I am not leaving with the same youthful enthusiasm that possessed me when I passed these same coasts, first on my way to Egypt when I was twenty-four and again on my way to China three years ago. But after all I am still conscious of being possessed by the same persistent angel or devil who tells me that I will be myself only by trying to possess the Earth. . . .

The *Angkor* is a somewhat mediocre ship as far as comfort is concerned, but it seems to be making steady progress. No one, so far, whose acquaintance seems worth pursuing. In Marseille we picked up a detachment of Portuguese people some of whom are going to Timor, without suspecting their good fortune. I plan to work a little, do some thinking, write down some ideas in peace — which I have not been able to do for a year, because of my geological work.

April 27, 1926

The night before last we sailed through the Straits of Messina. Both banks sparkled with lights, and the ship glided through an atmosphere heavy with the smell of orange trees in bloom. It was (it had to be) very beautiful. But I find I have a curious inability to enjoy and to be excited by a whole category of things. I note that "nature" is almost dead for me. I used to be passionately fond of the outward apparel of the Earth. Now it seems to me that I love only the Life which is at the bottom of its heart.

On board, no one really interesting. I think that the people I would most like to talk to (the arrangement of the ship does not lend itself to sociability) are two Germans or Swiss, missionary doctors who are going to Abyssinia to carry the Gospel to some Negroes who, I am sure, killed the first white men who recently came to see them. But when you think about it, what can the Gospel accomplish all by itself? How can one preach goodness and love to men without at the same time offering them an interpretation of the World that justifies this goodness and this love? And unless this interpretation is strictly personal (and thus without much certainty) how can it fail to involve the carapace — always worn out, but always being renewed — of an orthodoxy?

Red Sea, May 3, 1926

After spending a whole day passing the white sands of the Isthmus of Suez, we have entered the Red Sea. In the evenings the sea often becomes sleek and oily, and its surface looks white and opaque, like milk. Other times, the great storms that break over the mountain of Africa form thick clouds which the setting sun paints glorious colors. All this is magnificent, because it provides a kind of new and constantly renewed expression for the aspirations and expectations of the spirit and the heart, so that it is something that you pass through and that passes through you.

Perhaps because of my first initiation and my first enchantment in Egypt, I have always had a predilection for these hot desert regions of Arabia, all perfumed with incense and coffee, and once again I felt to what degree my sympathies and my nature, which are incapable of surviving without Christianity, are nevertheless one with this part of the world which is not yet Christianized. I felt this with increased clarity, and I will not pretend that this observation does not have a distressing and somewhat tragic quality. What can I do, but vigorously pursue the course to which I find myself committed? I feel that if I were to hesitate, I would be lost — or at least I would lose all my force. I can no longer touch the Christ (the true, the great) in myself except in the world. Therefore the two must glorify one another mutually in me.

Indian Ocean, May, 1926

This landing at Djibouti was as abortive as the one at Port Said. We docked at nightfall under a fine warm rain and left again at dawn. So it was impossible to go and have the traditional coffee in the sun-drenched square, surrounded by Somalis with bronze torsos and pale Jews selling ostrich feathers. Above all I should like to have walked on one of the coral reefs which crowd the bay in order to gather from it — with the mind much more than with the hands — Life. I had to do without this. To make up for Djibouti, we had Aden, which I had not seen before. Picture a sandy bay wedged, as in a pincers, between two absolutely bare volcanos of reddish rock. The sand of the sea joins a pure white flat expanse of desert which bounds the high plateau of Yemen at the horizon. It is beautiful because of the light and the desolation. I was able to get off the boat for a few hours, time enough to observe the mountain's trachyte and to pick a handful of fragrant plants from a dry river bed. When I returned on board an Arab, balanced in his tiny canoe, was pulling up some enormous goldfish with a fishing line.

Day after tomorrow, Colombo.

Actually, I am eager to arrive as quickly as possible, so I can start work. However, the time passes quickly on board. Above all, I read (dear geologists) and write up the lecture on transformism which I gave several times this winter. I am not quite sure about the value of this project (which is almost finished), for I have written it in a rather informal manner. At least I am sure that I have put into it, more clearly than into other analogous works, certain ideas which I believe to be important. I will type it in Tientsin. Also, I will try to place it somewhere.

May 16, 1926 (before Singapore)

So far we have no news of what is happening in China. On the other hand, the radio brings us inadequate but disturbing reports on things in Europe. I do not know what to think or what to hope in all this chaos; and I am sorry to be absent at this particular moment.

The landing at Colombo was rather successful, although too brief (as usual) to allow time to go and see the wonders of the Ceylonese mountains and forest. In the company of a passenger who is conversant with the people and things in the ports of the Orient, I went to visit the shop of Ceylon's leading dealer in precious gems. He took some sapphires of admirable velvetiness out of his strongbox for our inspection. But it was the mine that I should most like to have seen! After that I made a tour of the Botanical Garden, which was filled with large brilliant butterflies, small striped squirrels, and Hindu women gardeners in gaudy dresses who were as pretty as flower beds (especially from a distance). At the museum I looked at the collection of chipped stone found on the island (crude quartz and microlithic tools of rock crystal). Unfortunately there is no indication of levels in this collection, which is already old; and I did not have with me the issue of *l'Anthropologie* (the latest, I believe) in which Sarrazin discusses these industries in great detail. I have finished the work I spoke of in my last letters. I hope that when I copy it over in Tientsin I will not find it too far short of what I wanted to say. But already this almost belongs to the realm of old ideas, of the *"déjà pensé."* I feel the need to begin again, to reorient myself — in the same direction, to be sure, but more clearly, more vigorously. I must return from this second voyage stronger in body and in soul. I owe this to God.

Saigon: two whole days in port. I used all this time to make an excursion to the borders of Annam, taking the little railroad which a few years from now will be the Trans-Indochinese line (from Saigon to Hanoi and Yunan-fou). I wanted to see the bush; and on this point I was entirely satisfied. On the trip that I took (six hours) the line cuts through dense forest for almost four hours: it is a real cutting, continuous, right through the trees. Sometimes you can see nothing but very dense thickets of bamboo and liana from which glossy white trunks emerge at great heights. Sometimes the underbrush is lighter (or lighted by fire), revealing a forest of full-grown trees as far as the eye can see. We are at the end of the dry season, and the rains are late, so the vegetation was very impoverished: many trees without leaves, most of the grass dead, a kind of winter in a stifling temperature. This poverty of foliage gave me an advantage in that the rock showed better: metamorphosed schist and granite running from north to south following the great fold axes so unmistakable throughout the face of Indochina and Malaysia. What impressed me even more than the luxuriance of the vegetable and animal life in these regions is the destructive and assimilative power of Man. Already the savages (the Mois) are fairly skilled in burning the bush. But before the Europeans with their roads and railroads the forest is literally melting. It is rubber, above all, which threatens to replace everything. Once I would have been furious and inconsolable at the sight of this devastation or conquest. Now I think I understand that we are witnessing the establishment of a new Zone of Life around the Earth, and that it would be absurd to regret the disappearance of an old envelope which *must* fall. (And this envelope includes the deer, the elephants, and the peacocks, but also these poor Mois who are so picturesque but who belong to a bygone age.) Temperamentally I am not disposed to think this way; it is through reflection and deliberation that I passionately welcome the life that is coming, without allowing myself to regret anything of the past. But it seems to me that this attitude succeeds and gives great strength. Certainly it is not true that the individuals composing the new layer are all — or even in the majority — more sympathetic than the savages. But at least the Life to come is in their mass; and then, at least we understand them a little. On this trip I am deeply impressed by the airtight compartments that separate human groups from each other. What is in the head and heart of a Malaysian or an Annamite?

S.S. Tangshan Maru, June 2, 1926

I am writing to you from a little Japanese boat that follows the Chinese coast between Shanghai and Tientsin. We arrived in Shanghai on the twenty-ninth, and as we got off the boat we learned that the railroads to the north were not yet operating. Since the trains were not running, almost all the agencies said that their steamers were full up well into the future. Luckily the *Tangshan Maru,* being less in demand with the Europeans, was there to take us.

From what I have written, you can already conclude that matters are not yet organized in China. It seems that for the moment the country is divided into five parts: Canton (followers of the late Sun Yat-sen), Shanghai, Peking (Ou-pei-fou, representing the former government), Mokden (Chang-tzo-lin, supported by Japan), finally the West, where Fun-yu-shien, aided by Moscow, rules. Within each of these compartments there is no disorder, and we have been repeatedly told by good sources that particularly in the West, Fun's troops are perfectly disciplined and travel reliable. Unfortunately it is less easy to go from one compartment to another. Around Peking the railroad service is poor; and when we left Shanghai the news (perhaps false) had arrived that General Fun was again descending upon the capital (which he had never left very far behind, since he still occupied the famous Nankou Pass by which one arrives at the first landing of the Mongol Plateau as you go west from Peking). In only a few days, when we get to Tientsin itself, we will be able to make definite plans for the summer trip. I have not lost hope that it will prove successful. On arriving in Shanghai I was surprised to see in the newspapers that the governor of

Shanghai had taken as his right-hand man my friend K. V. Ting, director (now honorary) of the Geological Department of Peking. I was not able to see him, but at least I sent him a word of congratulation. As M. Boule is fond of saying, one swallow does not make a spring. Ting really is a swallow, though. With several more like him, I believe that they would improve China remarkably. Naturally one hears many things for and more against what is happening in China right now. What struck me is the admission which I heard made by men hostile to Sun Yat-sen and Moscow that both in Canton and in the West, people were working and organizing.

For the spirit, as for the body, I will not be sorry to arrive soon at port. In the long run a voyage relaxes and dissolves, so to speak, the mind. I am eager to get back to books, fossils, and letters. And then I long also to find myself in the field again. After eighteen months of ruminating and meditating my past observations, I feel that the slightest new observation will be charged with an exquisite freshness. As a geologist, I really love this old land of China and all of gigantic Asia. Do not be afraid that I will lose the sense of Humanity. Yes, I will try to understand the Chinese soul, and not just the geology.

Tientsin, June 11, 1926

I will probably not be sending you this letter for four or five days, after my return from a little trip to Peking. But I want to start it now, so that the things I have to tell you will not pile up too much. As regards understanding of the Chinese and things Chinese, I am not as well situated as I should be to progress rapidly in this area. Here, in spite of the great freedom in which I live, I find myself necessarily in an isolating cage; people and events reach me only as filtered through the "missionary world." In the desert, or on trips, I hardly meet anyone but peasants or savages. It is still in Peking that I will best be able to find the little circle of personal friends who will reveal to me the China of today as it really is. Unfortunately, I can go to Peking only now and then; and, as I told you, my best guide, Dr. K. V. Ting, is right now an important political figure in the South, in Shanghai. Perhaps in Kansu where the Kuominchun ("army of the people") are in power I will have firsthand experience of the Russian influence on the Chinese. The more I hear about this Bolshevizing segment of China, the more I notice the praise concealed beneath the conventional criticism that is accorded it.

To get back to the Chinese in general, I continue to be puzzled by their incredible ability to "materialize" all things. Two days ago, someone showed me two little Buddhist idols (two marvels in chiseled wood, if one can apply that term to wood) which had belonged to a young Chinese of very high station. One is a happy Buddha — a plump little figure, represented in the attitude of a joyous dancer, who has nothing morally seductive about him. The other is a praying Buddha of a beauty that is all the more divine because it remains essentially human. Well, the owner of these two objects, when questioned as to the kind of sentiments he had for these symbols, did not express the slightest idea of the moral value of gaiety or of contemplation, nor of how to harmonize the two; he was content to say that he honored them "to protect his body" against the evil (purely physical) influences of the world. And yet works of art like these can only have been produced by souls profoundly sensitive to inner currents. Is this simply very old, stereotyped art? Or, under the ritualistic materialism, does the spiritual current still flow? I know nothing about it, but I wish I did.

I am extremely sensitive to the excess of complication and specialization that encumbers present-day religious confession. Owing to atavism and education, no doubt, but also to reason, I think, I seem to perceive in the parasitic network an inevitable biological phenomenon which requires and foretells a sloughing off. I admit all the defects, but I tolerate them even as I react against them, because for now they are inseparable from what seems to be the only axis along which human activity can legitimately progress. Believe me, when one has penetrated to this axis of the Christian attitude, the ritual, disciplinary and theological encrustations matter little more than musical or acoustical theories matter to the enjoyment of a beautiful piece of music. Truly, there is a Christian *note* which makes the whole World vibrate like an immense gong, in the divine Christ. This note is unique and universal and in it alone consists the Gospel. Only it is real (happily). And for this reason it is inevitable that, in trying to fix and hold its reality, men analyze it out of sight (as the physicist does with the most divine nuances of sound and color). This is what begets, under the very simple dogma, an unlimited complexity which is aggravated by theorists' presumption in substituting their constructs for reality. In any case, for you, as for everyone, there is only one road that can lead to God, and this is the fidelity to remain constantly true to yourself, to what you feel is highest in you. Do not worry about the rest. The road will open before you as you go.

Since my arrival here, I have been extremely busy making an inventory of an enormous find (5,000 kilograms of bones) brought back last year from a deposit that we located two years ago. The animal life seems to correspond to a rather old Pleistocene, but not to a Pliocene. There is a great deal of horse, of bos, gazelle, ibex, deer (munjack, sika, and *megaceros*, as well as some extinct species), wolf, badger, and in addition an antelope with spiral horns, some *machairodus*, a special fox, and a hyena and a rhinoceros which are neither the *Hyena spelaea* nor the *Rhinoceros tichorhinus*. The whole group is very fossilized. It is certainly older than the Sjara-osso-gol group, and there may not be a single species common to the two deposits; but the whole group seems to me very Quaternary. We should find some trace of Man in it! The day after tomorrow I am going to Peking, where I am to meet the whole American expedition. It will be a warm and joyous encounter. Andrews hopes to leave in July if the calm continues.

Peking, June 13

The difficulties and improbabilities against which you are struggling are the great, the fundamental, the eternal barriers which the spirit must cross in order to reach God. I personally believe the solution to lie in the eminent value of *spirit* and in the ultimate connection of all the substances of the World. The immensity of the material Cosmos need not overwhelm us if we perceive that ultimately matter, for all its admirable powers, realizes itself only in us; and the very multiplicity of human souls (not to mention other souls, perhaps) which is so frightening need not make us despair if we observe the immense possibility and need for union that stirs the thinking atoms that we are. The more enormous the Universe is, the more precious is the *spirit* that required such a deployment of varied energies in order to be born; and the more numerous we are, the more magnificent is the synthesis which is being prepared for our reunion. Trillions of vibrations make intoxicating nuances for our eyes. Trillions of souls, born of trillions and trillions of lower Units, received, joined, and animated by God, can make a single thought or feeling. As for this God, as you are right to think (and no real theologian would deny it, outside of the manuals), we cannot precisely distinguish his features. But since the human being, with his intelligence and his magnificent ability to love, is *the most perfect form* we know in the scale of elements in the world, we say that God must be conceived *in the direction* of a *super-person* (that is, an extension of the good qualities — and not of the individual limitations — of the human being). He must be as vast as the Universe and as warm as a human heart, and incomparably more besides. This is all we can say. A God who was "a Law" or an "abstract truth" would have less *being* than us! That is not possible. You mistrust the act which consists in believing because we need to believe. It seems to me that everything depends on the meaning given to the word *need*. If we mean an accessory, secondary, debatable need, you are right. But if it is a question of a need so fundamental and universal that it is part of the very essence of the life "which is in us without being us" (that is, received like a current which governs us), then I think that one can conclude from this need that *there is* an *Object* that satisfies it. Otherwise the World is stupid, destructive of itself, incapable of nourishing what is, to our knowledge, the most perfect thing it has brought forth, namely, an intelligent mind. It may be that for certain people faith is accompanied by some compelling belief, by evidence, by pure joy. I understand it more as a kind of calm *Weltanschauung,* in terms of which everything is illuminated and becomes livable, indefinitely, increasingly. This act requires both a passive sensitization of the mind in order to see and a positive act of the will in order to *try* to achieve the point of view. Practically, I think that every man who is true to his ideal arrives in a similar way at the same adoration of *That* which conducts and unifies the World. . . . Once having reached this summit, you will realize that nothing is isolated, nothing is either small or profane, since the humblest consciousness partially includes the destinies of the Universe and cannot improve itself without improving everything around it! The death of egoism is to understand that one is an element in a Universe that personalizes itself (if I may) by uniting itself with God (I do not say, by becoming God). So it is no longer oneself that one loves in oneself.

I leave you to go and visit the Americans. I shall walk there slowly, at sunset. I shall follow the little streets (*hutungs*) that zigzag between the tent-shaped houses shaded by large trees full of tame crows. I shall skirt the ancient imperial pavilion, the forbidden ex-city whose yellow and red walls are washed by wide moats filled with lotus and water lilies. And if the weather is clear I shall see, to the west, those western hills — the Si-chan — which are the gateway to Mongolia.

Tientsin, June 25, 1926

It seems decided, now, that we will leave Tientsin in three days, on the twenty-eighth. Our plan is to take the Peking-Hankow line at Peking and go down to Chengchow (a little south of the Hwang Ho), where we will take a train heading west, and to leave in convoy for Kansu (Lanchow). The difficult part (not dangerous, but subject to delays or stops) is going through Shensi. If we do not succeed, we shall still have the expedient of working there, although we did not plan to. There is no dearth of material to explore. All I ask is to reach a field of investigation, whatever it may be. If all goes well, our return to Tientsin is expected for November; it will be sooner if events disturb us.

My last letter was from Peking. I returned from there in the same train as Granger, Matthews, and Nelson, who came to the Museum here the next day. I took great pleasure and a certain pride in showing them the latest collection of fossils (the Pleistocene fossils I told you about). I believe they were seriously interested. We parted better friends than ever. Since then, I have been taken up by tiresome preparations: passports, arms permits, etc. These are endless procedures to which, to tell the truth, the Chinese authorities lend themselves with an ill grace: they are always afraid that traveling Europeans will make trouble for them. By the way, a conversation with Andrews showed me that relations between the Russians and the Third Asiatic Expedition are a bit dubious at the moment. It seems that the Russians (1) fear (wrongly, I think) that the Andrews mission may have economic repercussions, or even (2) take umbrage at the American scientific work. Andrews seems to think that the Russians would rather like to keep the "hunting rights" for themselves. In any case, geological emissaries have been sent from Urga to look for dinosaur eggs in the same deposit located by the Americans. How difficult it is to arrive at that disinterestedness that places love of Truth, in all its forms, above all individual or national interest! And yet we shall arrive at it, we must; or else it would be the end of Humanity, which I cannot accept.

Inwardly, I am fine. I have recovered that familiar and very precious state of mind which makes me see and grasp some vital and intoxicating element at the bottom (or more precisely, at the end) of everything that exists and everything that happens. This is that unique Note produced by the World that I mentioned in my last letter. Anyone who saw these lines without knowing me would think I am completely insane. And yet it has been over thirty years now that I have lived more or less consciously in this atmosphere, from which it seems to me that I draw all the joy, force, and precision of my activity. For if I am now in China and if I am to set off the day after tomorrow, I realize that it is solely to obey this mysterious Attraction of the World to serve and to make serve. I know very well that on this path no retreat is possible. But is it not written in the Gospel, "He who having put his hand to the plow looks back is not worthy of me"? Truly (perhaps because I am further away and more isolated from specific quarrels) I have confidence that my line of thought is essentially Christian, in spite of the fact that I am sometimes forced to define it to myself with a word that looks rather dangerous: hyper-Catholic.

July 8, 1926

This evening the rain keeps us in a village twenty-five kilometers east of Tangkwan, right below the great loop of the Hwang Ho River. Yesterday we left Shanchow (present terminus of the Franco-Belgian line known as Lung-hai) with our customary caravan of ten mules, which required six days of palavering to get ready! We hope to arrive in Lanchow at the beginning of August. So far the trip has gone rather well in spite of the delays and difficulties caused by the disorganization of the country. In Peking we arrived three hours late and left ten hours late due to the arrival of Marshal Ou-pei-fou, who had finally decided to meet his enemy Chang-tzo-lin, the king of Mukden, in Peking on the twenty-ninth of June. The incident made me very late for a luncheon at the French Legation where I met Mme. Herriot, but on the other hand, I was one of the only Europeans to witness the departure of Ou-pei-fou, whose train left in the evening from the same station as ours. Strange, infantile, and savage spectacle. Picture a hundred or so cars, headlights lit and interiors dark, armed soldiers on their runningboards, horns honking steadily, moving at top speed down the blocked and silent streets; station occupied by armed troops; military bands in cream-colored uniforms and immense braid-trimmed kepis; a group of stout high-ranking officers and weasel-faced Mandarins. It all smelled of conspiracy. As a matter of fact, it was a question of which of the two great leaders present could bring the most troops into Peking and not get assassinated. The conference does not seem to have had great results, especially since the Kuominchuns (Bolshevizers of the West) continue to threaten the East. What is certain is that here in Honan, as elsewhere, people are convinced that the "military" are the plague of China. There was much fighting in the country in the spring: the armies of Ou-pei-fou against the Kuominchun. At the present time the latter have been driven back as far as Sianfou. But there remain some deserters, antimilitary peasant groups, and one hears of nothing but executions. The soldiers are radically disorganizing the countryside, business, and also the railroads. In Shanchow, on the arrival of the train, there are scenes that are outrageous in their waste of resources and indifference to all regulation. It is a kind of vast chronic brigandage, without great violence, but profoundly harmful. It is impossible to build anything under these conditions. I have told you that the Kuominchun (people's army) seem not to act in this way; yet in their wake they raised the tax until 1930.

I am following the Hwang Ho River through an enormous loessic basin located between the bleak mountains of Chengh-sien and Honan. The rather smooth loess forms a terrace one hundred meters wide over the river: a sandy loess of the middle Pleistocene period lying, with an intervening layer of gravel, over the famous ancient Pleistocene beds with the large mussels (Quadrila), whose study is becoming so interesting. I have taken cuttings here which I believe no one has published. No fossilized mammals, unfortunately. The trip by mule does not have the charm of the crossing of the Mongol steppes. We are going through the oldest provinces of the Chinese empire, whose first capital was Laoyang (east of Shanchow) and whose second Sianfou. Everything is cultivated on the loess. Everywhere there are towns enclosed by crenelated walls, dilapidated pagodas surrounded by cypress trees and, in the middle of fields, high rectangular steles resting on tortoises. One should be able to savor this ancient past but the retrospective charm is dominated by the desolation and insecurity of the present. Honan is a hard country, with all the hardships of China: drought, floods, heat, dust, deforestation, dilapidation. Note that I am not a Sinophobe, on the contrary; but I see China as an immense edifice to be rebuilt. And to rebuild it, it would probably be necessary to turn it inside out.

We run no risks and the fatigue is healthy. Inwardly I feel calm and at peace, but without great excitement for things. I desire this trip, its effort and its results, tenaciously, with all the force and logic of my life; but I cannot say that I am enjoying it. It is rather curious.

Tangkwan, July 10, 1926

The rain has stopped and we arrived here yesterday in the night. Everything seems to indicate a smooth departure with an escort, from the immediate vicinity of Sianfou. The town of Sianfou is still occupied by the Kuominchun, but surrounded by Ou-pei-fou's troops. Tangkwan is a very picturesque town but unfortunately a very dirty one, especially after the rain. Directly to the south a magnificent jagged chain of mountains cuts off the horizon: the Houochan, a branch of the Tsinlings, which I will follow for a long time without, however, having to climb them.

Tangkwan, July 19, 1926

This letter, like the one that preceded it, is from Tangkwan. We have come back here. Wednesday we arrived at the walls (five kilometers away) of Sianfou, the besieged town, and there we realized that to go straight ahead, that is, to reach Kansu, was impossible. We had to retrace the 150 kilometers we had come. It is a serious setback, and a disappointment.

This business upsets all my plans for work in China. We are going to begin by spending about three weeks exploring the south of Shensi, a province which is peaceful but very ordinary. Then we will return to Tientsin — toward mid-August, no doubt. After that we will have to await the development of political events.

August 6, 1926

This time I am writing you from a little inn located somewhere in the southern third of Shensi. It is raining. As I told you, we have employed our caravan (paid one month in advance) to travel in the south and southwest of this province. There have been no sensational results. I have seen and learned much; I have gathered the elements of a study on the Chinese Quaternary in these regions; but I have encountered neither fossil-bearing layers, nor traces of human beings (even Neolithic!). M. Boule, who likes results that lend themselves to exhibition in showcases, is not going to be satisfied. If only Kalgan became accessible, we would go in the fall and work the fine strata of Sangkan Ho. I am afraid, alas! that in this area, too, the fronts are stabilizing. Unless combined Chinese forces intervene, I do not see how either of the two parties (Peking and the revolutionists or Kuominchun) will be able to defeat the other. Perhaps we will have some news on the subject in a week when we arrive at Tai-yuan-fou, the capital of Shensi. At that point the present and mediocre trip will end: Tai-yuan-fou is a railroad terminus. Once there, we will be within twenty-four hours of Tientsin.

Once the disappointment of Sianfou was over, the last three weeks have not been completely disagreeable, after all. Even so, I am returning to Tientsin somewhat in the state of a man leaving a restaurant without having eaten enough. I feel a kind of physical privation at not having been able to taste either the joy of the desert or the joy of handling fine fossils. I believe one should be able to place the substance of one's joy above things of this kind and I am trying to arrive at that point.

The landscape I have been over is rather monotonous. Imagine wide parallel valleys separated from each other by high mountains which are for the most part very bare: that is the setting. The valleys, marshy at the bottom, are bounded by high Quaternary terraces (loess, mostly) featuring unusual fissures which may be fifty meters deep and several kilometers long. Where erosion has not yet done its worst and where the moisture is sufficient, you travel through an ocean of corn, cotton, and sorghum. Certain sections are real forests of fruit-bearing trees (kakis and jujubes especially); but as a whole the area is rather bare. The road goes through an interminable series of villages, usually enclosed by walls. From far away they look attractive; from close to, you discover the dirt and dilapidation. And yet the people around here are rich, but they seem completely lacking in foresight and method. They are the peasant masses in the bottom of their rut. Good people, all the same; only it is certainly not they who will build the new China. At the entrances to the villages the rural pagodas are numerous and seem to be used rather often — for waiting for a son or keeping out of the rain. In them I have seen little besides the figures of grotesque or childish divinities. Evidently the interesting China is not to be found in the country; here there is only an inert mass which awaits leaven from another source. We found the beginning of a highway and even a few bicycles jogging along. These are symptoms of change.

Naturally, we did not keep to the cultivated plains except for the necessities of traveling. The mountains are much more interesting. With reason, L. laments the incredible negligence of the Chinese, who are destroying and wasting all their forests without seeming to suspect that they are helping to feed the floods and to destroy their fields. But while I regretted the disappearance of beautiful plants and green valleys, as a geologist I profited by the deforestation: the structure of the ranges stood out less clearly than in the desert, but with a fine vigor. Formations that are rather well known now, though, and rather monotonous: an immense series ranging from Precambrian to the Carboniferous, almost always formed of massive limestone in which the fossils are very difficult to find. Over these rocks fly large black butterflies with metallic-green reflections and long tails.

Physically I am very well. Mentally, as I told you, I lack that precious inner dilation of excitement and success; but I have enough "deep relish" for life to continue the effort. You know me well enough to know the kind of not-exactly-passive adoration I profess for the internal and external forces of the World. Even in failure or indifferent success I try to live by this faith, and to find in it a compensation for the rest.

Like every man, and perhaps more than most, because I am possessed by a certain demon or angel of the All and the Universal, I have need of a rich and lasting contact with the individual concrete.

I sometimes live in the frustrating state of a deaf man straining in his effort to hear a music which he knows to be all around him. We live within an immense and magnificent drama of which we perceive only stifled rumors. Who will give us the perception of roundness, intensity, and harmony which Man could attain this very moment if he knew how, or dared, to live? Do you know that the *Nuit dur de Transsibirien* that you sent me is strangely suggestive and pathetic? But if you think it over you realize that the magic and mystery that surround that remote vision belong in reality neither to Asia, nor to the Mongols, but to the evocation of human force which desires at all costs to be born through us. . . . You know my "faith": I think that Christianity will recover that force of contagion and conquest which is the only method of propagation worthy of the Truth only when men have perceived more distinctly the World through Christ, or better, Christ at the end of the World. It is the conjunction of the two realities that will save us, whereas their present opposition is our undoing. If you only knew how I should like to have been for ten minutes in the Chicago Stadium to shout to the crowd what it is to "communicate" and to "sympathize." It seems to me that a whole lifetime of effort would be nothing if only I could reveal for one instant what I see.

My trip since Tai-yuan-fou has ended peacefully, the only difficulties being caused by a railway system that is completely disorganized. Along the way I made one or two geological excursions in the course of which I collected a bit of Neolithic (not recorded in the region) and an interesting rock. Eventually my cases of findings, which are rather minimal, will have a certain value. I have some hope that when I compare my cuttings and specimens (even Paleozoic) with those of the Geological Survey, I may confirm my feeling that I have something new, even for the structure of the old mountains. You know that the Kuomin-

chun (supported by Moscow) have been driven back west of Kalgan; this will enable me, I hope, to go and work the lower Quaternary of Sangkan Ho (two days west of Peking) in September:
and in this respect the victory of Peking would be useful to me.
For the good of China, however, I wonder whether the Kuominchun would not be preferable to the soldier-bandits of Ou-pei-
fou and Chang-tzo-lin. The final word has not been said. I am
always in search of opportunities to approach active Chinese circles but this is not easy. As I wrote you, the country is sluggish:
an ocean of sorghum and cotton, scattered with decrepit pagodas
and muddy steles. It is the end of one order and the indifferent
waiting for another. As I was approaching Tai-yuan-fou, I came
upon a landscape profoundly symbolic of this end and this waiting: in the center, a road — the great Mandarinal road from the
west — in the condition of an immense rut filled with water; to
the left, a ruined pagoda; to the right, a tall secular tree, verdant
toward the bottom, dead in its high branches; all this under a
pure and gilded sky. I wished I were a watercolorist, or could
have meditated before this for a long time. I should add that a
little way away a highway had just been opened.

Tientsin, September 15, 1926

I enjoyed with you that plunge into "the Elements," an immersion for which I periodically experience an intense need. The
mass of humanity is also a magnificent element. But ordinarily
we perceive, of necessity, only the atoms, the individuals, and as
a result its grandeur escapes us. I find that the sea, the mountains, the Milky Way, reveal and enhance Humanity as an immense cosmic energy; and it seems to me that this grandeur, far
from overpowering the individual, imparts to him an inexhaust-
ible charm and mystery.

I feel a distaste for hunting, first because of a kind of Buddhist respect for the unity and sacredness of all life, and also
because the pursuit of a hare or chamois strikes me as a kind of
"escape of energy," that is, the expenditure of our effort in

an illusory end, one devoid of profit. Of course, the exercise in itself is a stimulant, an inducement to pursue other, more substantial, prey; and indeed we all know remarkable men who are ardent hunters. All the same, the pursuit of things unknown strikes me as more worthy of us than the pursuit of things to eat. Getting back to the respect for Life, we find ourselves, of course, in a natural system in which the mutual destruction of living things seems to be a condition of equilibrium and survival. But what is true of the animal world may perhaps diminish progressively with the establishment of the human sphere: a decline in useless destruction and, as Vernadsky predicts, the discovery of nourishment drawn from the inorganic. Horrible prospect, which warns me of the danger of overintellectualizing on the subject of life! I think you have submissively accepted the fatal prophecy of your dramatic shepherd: "And there is nothing, nothing." If this were true our human life *would have to* come to an end immediately, and this is impossible to accept: that the immense resources of goodness, light, and love enlisted in the world are condemned to disappear by the very fact of their being perceived. What is true is that for a thinking person it is "all or nothing." If it is not "nothing," as I just said, it must be "all": which is to say that our hopes are insatiable and require a divine end.

What can I say of my activities of these last two weeks? Nothing very important. I have been occupied with the classification of my findings, and the writing of a rather long report with numerous cuttings on the Pleistocene of the Shensi, which I took to Peking three days ago. I took advantage of the opportunity to submit my Paleozoic fossils to my friend Grabau. They have merit: there is a pygidium of a large Ordovician trilobite which is something entirely new for China; and small organisms in the shape of horns or cones which are also new to China and which may represent a type of primitive cephalopod, having therefore a general paleontological value (they come from the lowest Cambrian). But this last point seems doubtful to me; I am more inclined to believe them pteropods. Cuttings are to be made. This consoles me for a profound photographic vexation. Throughout this ill-fated excursion, one button of my Verascope (a borrowed camera, quite different from the one I had in 1923–1924) stayed at exposure, with the result that all my negatives are fogged and ruined. The loss is not serious, but annoying: I do not think I would have published any of the shots I took, but they were souvenirs. In such cases I try to apply my philosophy of serenity by abandoning myself to the forces of this World, which I believe to be animated (or at least capable of being animated) even in their apparently most insignificant details. But it is not easy to put a philosophy into practice.

We are still contemplating going to the famous deposit of Kalgan. But we must continue to wait. Although cleared of soldiers, the region remains in such a state of disorganization that means of transportation seem still to be lacking. On the whole, China seems to be going from bad to worse. The North is no sooner calm than the South is upside down, from Canton to Yangtze. My friend Wang, director of the Geological Survey, seemed rather anxious and foresaw great changes. This is only the beginning, he told me. As far as geology is concerned, it is certain that travel in the country becomes more difficult from one day to the next, even for the Chinese.

Tientsin, October 12, 1926
(on returning from Sangkan Ho)

In spite of the part of my life that is turned toward God — or rather, precisely because of this part, which stimulates my inner forces instead of absorbing them — I have need of an "outlet." As I have, unfortunately, no aptitude for either music or poetry, nor even (which I regret most of all) the talent or art of the novelist, I have up to now tried to express myself in all kinds of philosophico-literary essays of which I have had occasion to show you only an infinitesimal part. Unfortunately, these essays are almost all destined to perish in my desk drawers, or at any rate, to be read only by a limited group of friends. It seems to me that I have arrived at the point in my life when the best outlet would be speech. To awaken a spirit, a flow of passions in a group of people: this is what I would like to do. Not, I think, for the simplest enjoyment of acting and influencing, but because I seem to have, deep inside myself, something that needs to emerge and to be disseminated: a certain enthusiastic vision of the immensity and promise of the World, a certain relish, a certain intoxication with real concrete "being" as it is revealed to us in the Universe. In the end, if I have come to China, if I am burying myself in my masses of fossils, if I am playing the part of the "Knight Errant," it is in the hope of better feeding this inner flame at all the great sources of inspiration of the Earth, and of acquiring, through a bit of notoriety or foreignness, the power to make myself heard, if only for one brief moment, before I die. However, public action and speech is, in the majority of lives, exceptional. So one must return to the written word. To write about China is beyond my capacities. Of China I have seen the hard life, the desolation, the immense layer of dust over people and things. I possess neither the knowledge of the language and the past that would open the hidden treasure for me rationally, nor the magical intuition that would enable me to perceive the secret beauty instinctively and more surely than any science. One thing only would inspire me: to discover the new spirit that is struggling to emerge from the ruins of the old crenelated towns and the old pagodas; to recognize and reveal that specific and essential element which the East must bring to the West so the Earth will be complete. But, as I told you, even for this I am badly handicapped by my ignorance of the language and also by a kind of existence which does not allow me to immerse myself freely in the Chinese mass any more than in the Parisian mass. The only book I want to and need to write would not be the book of China, but "the book of the Earth." In short, I would like to speak as I think, without concern for what is accepted, with the sole idea of translating as faithfully as possible what I hear murmuring in me like a voice or a song which are not of me, but of the World in me. I would like to express the thoughts of a man who, having finally penetrated the partitions and ceilings of little countries, little coteries, little sects, rises above all these categories and finds himself a child and citizen of the Earth. "Nothing but the Earth," Paul Morand said in a recent publication, and these four words are worth more than the whole book. There is a whole gamut of impressions and passions which belong to what I would like to say: there is first of all the deep joy, which we owe to our new perspectives on Life, of feeling our being expand to the measure of all the past, all the future, all space: our rootedness in Matter which wraps us round, weaves us, binds us together, and is spiritualized in us. It is the Note of China, the Note of the All, joyous and magnificent. Then there is the anger against the ridiculous disproportion which is everywhere manifested between these perspectives of unity or common pursuit and the egoistical preoccupations of almost all present social institutions. I am too soft, perhaps, or too much the pure theorist to call for an immediate destruction of what exists. But what I think I understand very clearly is that the only natural condition of the human stratum of this earth is a joining, a continuity that can be established only by tearing down all kinds of old walls. This is the gesture of Man waking, stretching, and taking possession of himself. But after this exaltation and this expansion, I foresee other links in the chain of human impressions: I mean the awareness of our imprisonment and the vertigo of our solitude. Have you ever thought how humiliating and distressing it was to be placed upon a sphere? For friendship it is a boon never to be able to be further apart than the antipodes. But suppose that you are leaving together to go on and on; it is impossible. To go beyond a certain point is to return to where you began. When I am here, the West fascinates me: but once west of Turkistan, I would dream of the East. You would not believe how conscious I have been this year of this limitation of our spatial excursions or how physically I have felt that the geographic mystery of our Earth was melting like snow in the summer sun. Already, even in Asia, only shreds of the unknown remain. Thus, at the same time that the human stratum is being united in exaltation and rebellion, by the same impulse we are moving toward another realization, which is a sense of the meagerness of the domain which we thought vast. I think there will be a moment when the Earth will be for men as if exhausted, uninteresting, inadequate; and at the same moment men, less preoccupied with looking at the ground under their feet or with quarreling among themselves, will look around them and will be as frightened at feeling themselves *alone* on the Earth as a child who wakes up in a dark room in the middle of the night. Feelings of glorious unity and of profound lassitude, dreams of conquest and of flight, aggressive confidence and anguish: how is it that this vast psychological domain is still virtually closed to men, who think, desire, or love like Frenchmen, Americans, or Chinese, and *never* like *men,* that is, like inhabitants of the Earth. I know that I shall be thought mad if I write these things. But why? Is it not the sensible and the reasonable who are blind? Truly, we lead a circumscribed existence in a milieu that requires unlimited respiration. This, in some form or other, is what I should like to put into a book of the Earth. What do you think? I would want it to be a work of *art* as well as of thought.

I am back from Sangkan Ho with seven crates of fossils, most of them good, but not sensational: *Rhinoceros sp.,* a large horse, spiral-form antelope horns, deer antlers of the *megaceros* type. The layers are geologically very interesting: they form a great homogeneous whole (lake bottom?) whose age seems more and more certainly to be early Pleistocene. It would be the very place to find Chellean Man. Unfortunately the deposits, which are completely muddy or torrential, could not provide any center, and there are no really good stones in the vicinity to have served the Paleolithics. If something human is found there some day it will be a femur or a jawbone, and it would be a magnificent discovery, because the level can be very well dated. At this moment I do not see any spot more promising than Sangkan Ho for encountering very early Man in China.

The trip went well, except for the usual difficulties of travel. We only stayed two weeks for the following reasons: the necessity of returning a borrowed car, the onset of frost, and the troublesome proximity of a band of brigands who plundered two villages near our own. I saw the women and children of our village escape to the ravines nearby; the few animals not yet carried off by the soldiers were concealed; the men banded together to make plans. One sensed a habitual, often repeated maneuver, and it was infinitely sad. The military plague in China (the bandits are former soldiers, and vice versa, and there is, in practice, neither commissariat nor regular pay) exceeds anything one can imagine, and the intensive recruitments of this war year are drawing off a very bad element. The peasants of Sangkan Ho, after being impressed by two armies at war, are now held by garrisons "of peace"; and when the latter remain within their walls, it is the bandits who come out of the mountains. Poor people, resigned and passive unless they engage in counter-brigandage. The Kuominchun have left a good impression, but they are terribly xenophobic. I am beginning to believe that China will be reorganized only through the success of the Cantonese in the South and the Kuominchun in the West; but it will be a hard blow for the American-European installations. Perhaps this *tabula rasa* is necessary; the strength of the Chinese revolutionaries consists in having a kind of faith and ideal. Opposing them they find only leaders and armies who are crudely egoistical, vulgar appetites.

We stayed pleasantly in a little Chinese house. A land completely earth-colored in this season when the poor fields of sorghum and millet have been harvested, but a light incredibly golden and transparent, in which the jagged crests of the mountains and the vast surfaces of erosion took on harmonies of design and nuances of color of which the eye never managed to tire.

And now I am at peace. On the twenty-first I am going to Peking to speak at a meeting being held in honor of the Prince of Sweden, who is an enthusiastic archeologist.

Tientsin, October 30, 1926

I agree completely and have for some time with the principle, "Spirit through Matter." Some day I shall have to show you a semifictional piece I have written on "the Spiritual Power of Matter," with a kind of hymn to "Holy Matter." The principle seems to me not just true, but so essential that I do not understand how a man who has not understood it can live fully and consciously without falling (or without being unable to explain why he does not fall) into either the Charybdis of pleasure and gross egoism, or the Scylla of a false and debilitating asceticism. The delicate part is to adapt the general principle to each individual life. You see, I think that life places each of us at a specific point on the material slope which leads to the spirit, and each of us must embrace and attack this matter from the point where he finds himself, neither to one side, higher, nor lower.

It gives me pleasure that you are rediscovering the Son after the Father in the New Testament. However, I will say this: I do not like that evangelism which limits itself to a glorification of the purely human or moral qualities of Jesus. If Jesus were no more than "a father, a mother, a brother, a sister" to us, I would not have need of Him; and, in a sense, the past does not interest me. What I "ask" of Christ is that He be a Force that is immense, present, universal, as real (more real) than Matter, which I can *adore;* in short, I ask Him to be for me the Universe: complete, concentrated, and capable of being adored. This is why, while acknowledging the irreplaceable value of the first three Gospels in presenting the real, historical *beginnings* of Christ (with a practical code of moral comparison with Him), I prefer Saint John and Saint Paul, who really present in the *resurrected* Christ a being as vast as the World of all time. Have you read, for example, the beginning of the Epistle to the Colossians (Chapter I, verses 12–23), and tried to give it the full, organic meaning it requires? Here Christ appears as a true soul of the World. It is only thus that I love Him.

Since my last letter I have made the little trip to Peking which I told you about. The meeting presented by the Peking Societies of Geology and Natural History to honor the Crown Prince of Sweden was very brilliant, and it was quite an honor for me to have to give (in English!) one of the three speeches. I spoke after a Chinese and before a Swede, an internationalism that I triumphantly savored. The same internationalism reigned at the banquet. The prince is very charming and seems quite a scholar. He is certainly one of those men whom every democracy should maintain and multiply, even if they are pleased to change their names. Almost all my time in Peking was spent with my geologist friends, Chinese and Americans. Did I tell you that some little conical organisms that I collected at the end of July in the lowest Cambrian of Shensi are probably ultra-primitive cephalopods? The walls are difficult to distinguish, but they now seem certain.

You would like Peking at this season: there is a little too much dust, the leaves have fallen and the great water lilies are withering around the yellow and red walls of the Imperial Palace, but the light is admirably pure, and it is an unending spectacle, as much for the spirit as for the eyes, to trace, beyond the crenelated walls of the old capital, the jagged violet line of the western mountains, the gilded sky which bends toward Turkistan and Europe.

Here, in Tientsin, I am working in peace; and for the moment, I have plenty to keep me busy with preliminary study of the fossils of Sangkan Ho (the definitive study cannot be done until I reach Paris). Incidentally, I have discovered among my findings of three weeks ago some pieces of the foot of an enormous rhinoceros — at least half again as big as a good-sized *tichorhinus!* If it is not an *elasmotherium,* it is an absolutely new form. What a shame not to have a tooth!

I have made a clear copy and had typed a kind of dissertation that I wrote on the ship. In this paper I clarify the ideas on evolution that I expounded four or five times in lectures last winter. I will send you a copy of it. I am not absolutely without hope that I may have it published in Louvain. I would like this publicity, for I have the feeling that I say sincere and incontestable things. I am more and more struck by the emptiness or rigidity of what is being written in France. Writers say the same things over and over again or, if they add some new nutritive element, it is in a tiny dose: a grain of wheat in a ton of sawdust. They are not *truthful,* and this irritates me. Men love only those who heal or liberate them: the Church too often forgets to imitate Jesus Christ on this last point.

Tientsin, November 14, 1926

What to tell you of my Chinese existence? Since my last letter I have not moved a kilometer beyond the university, whose large airy spaces satisfy me. Have I told you that my window looks out onto ponds or marshes where, in 1925, I still saw cormorants fishing? Now the nearest ponds are partly filled in, but I still have a wide vista of fields and fresh water which enchants me every evening with the sweetness and purity of the hues it takes on in the setting sun. I spend the daylight hours at the Licent Museum, where I am preparing under the microscope a whole family of little animals (Siphnes, Lagomys, hedgehogs) whom I find admirable. How I wish I could return to the deposit! When night comes I write letters, as I am doing now. Also I work on a project that is going to amaze you: I am starting to put down in as simple a form as possible, *with the idea of seriously attempting its publication,* my religious point of view, not in its theoretical foundations, but in its practical applications. I call this *The Divine Milieu,* and I am trying to show how Christianity can and must fill human life with God without dehumanizing it. I have said that you may be disappointed to learn that I am writing a book "of piety" instead of the Book of the Earth; but this does not mean that I am abandoning the latter. I am beginning with the other because it has long been ready in my mind, and because it suddenly occurred to me that the tranquillity of Tientsin was the opportunity I have been awaiting to put into words what I have so long been saying. This in no way resembles a sermon, and it is the sincerest expression of my Christian thought. As I told you in October, I feel that I have arrived at the moment when I must try to communicate what I have seen over ten years of calm inner delight.

In the realm of outward event I find very little to note besides a visit to the museum last Wednesday (the twelfth) by the Prince of Sweden. Unfortunately the visit coincided with a frightful snowstorm which made the crossing of the yards of the university, which are still full of rubbish, extremely unceremonial. I am now on good terms with some members of the Swedish colony of Peking, which is not unpleasant. I believe that if the university were in Peking instead of Tientsin I would lead almost as hectic a life as I do in Paris. As I was saying, the arrival of the Prince of Sweden coincided with that of the cold. On that very night I came home around midnight from a boisterous dinner of veterans. It was mild and peaceful. Suddenly I was amazed to hear a flock of wild geese go by, honking. An hour later winter was upon us. Every year it begins abruptly like this, when the Siberian regime arrives to replace the other, and settles down over Northern China.

Politically China appears more and more unsettled. For the moment the storm is confined to the area of Nanking, where the Cantonese seem to be about to arrive. But it is probable that the West will begin to move again. The Kuominchun have raised the blockade of Sianfou (the point where I was stopped in July), and they threaten to reappear in coastal China along the valley of the Hwang Ho. I am growing more certain that it is the "Reds" who are going to reorganize China. If only they could let me work in the spring!

Peking, November 28, 1926

I am writing you from Peking. I came here the day before yesterday to meet M. Lacroix. Now it appears that he is traveling the length of Japan and will not be here until the eighth of December! I have temporarily decided to wait for him here, and not to return to Tientsin, and in his absence I am making connections with certain members of Congress, which partly makes up for the mistake I made, I fear, in not going to Tokyo. Yesterday I spent the day in the company of Chinese, Americans, Australians, and New Zealanders, which allowed me to savor that rich delight of being a "citizen of the Earth." Yes, I believe we are approaching the moment when new affinities — the true panhuman affinities — will break down nationalistic boundaries, in politics as in religion. And I imagine that, in accordance with a general law of matter, this enormous quantitative modification will produce new qualities on our Earth.

In the Book of the Earth I mean to devote a paragraph to that "power to love" which is now scattered and diffused throughout the human dust. People are preoccupied with reserves of mechanical energy on the Earth. When will they realize that billions of horsepower and kilowatts are nothing, *physically,* compared with the voltages and possibilities for transformation stored in our minds and hearts? When will they stop relegating to narrow-minded casuists, rigid moralists, or Freudian analysts — when, in short, will they regard as other than the work of mystical dreamers — the task of saving and liberating what is the essential resource of the world? What accounts for the immortal power of Christianity and is the underlying source of Saint Paul's success is that the Church channels toward a precise end, or at least along a precise axis, those hopes for universal union which are, in terms of cold psychological analysis, our sole definitive reason for performing the smallest action.

To return to my outward activities, the days spent in Tientsin passed peacefully, following the same rhythm and plan. More interesting finds among my Kalgan collection: more fragments of the large rhinoceros, a huge enigmatic radius, the jawbone of a curious ruminant similar to the musk ox, etc. Since this work involves constant comparison with or reference to the Licent material, which I cannot consider transporting to Paris *en masse,* it does not duplicate what I might do in Paris. In another area, I have finished the first of three parts of *The Divine Milieu.* Here in Peking, my schedule is determined by the visits of various interesting geologists and by meetings with Pekinese friends. It is, accordingly, a little confused. Thursday I am to see Bailey Willis, who is one of the current leaders in the science of the Earth. Tuesday I am having lunch at the Peking Union Medical College (Rockefeller Foundation) with a Professor Parker of Harvard. I no longer entertain Americans.

I am taking advantage of my prolonged visit here — and also, occasionally, of the cars furnished to the Pan-Pacifics — to see more of the city than I have done before. Thus, yesterday I went to the Summer Palace. Somewhat childish in certain respects, bizarre too, crumbling and dusty, alas! like all things Chinese, it is, on the whole, a splendid creation. Very much like the Palace of Peking, whose yellows, reds, marbles, and monumental doors emerge from and contrast so singularly with the delicate dustiness of individual constructions or ornaments, the Summer Palace charmed me, despite the gray of winter, with the total effect of its colors and lines. I am beginning to have, in the presence of ancient China, the curious impression of a productive power which crumbled into bits as it created. Was this a weakness in the creative spirit, a weakness in the materials available, or a weakness in the will which could neither complete nor conserve? I do not know the country or its history well enough to try to decide. The real answer will be given a century from now by young China.

Peking, December 16, 1926

I am writing you a little late, and still from Peking. The two things have the same cause, namely, M. Lacroix's trip to China. M. Lacroix is a man whom I like and admire very much, besides being one of the strongest supporters of my scientific mission in China. So I do all I can to be with him and welcome him here, which in turn enables me to benefit from the facilities placed at his disposal for seeing all the beauties or curiosities of Peking and its environs. The most important item on the agenda was an excursion to Kalgan, which we succeeded in making without too much difficulty in three days. In spite of the personal support of the Director of the Geological Survey, who accompanied us, the train ride was arduous: fourteen hours in cars with broken windows, arriving at two o'clock in the morning. Fortunately we survived with a few head colds (I escaped even that), and we conquered the tedium by laughing a good deal. In Kalgan, thanks to a passport obtained through the American consul, we were able to go by car on the Urga road to the basaltic edge of the Mongolian High Plateau, which gave M. Lacroix an excellent idea of the principal eruptive ranges of Northern China. The "local color" was violent: never had I seen Kalgan so intensely Asiatic and Siberian as it was in this glacial cold and this state of siege. No Europeans, except for a few Russians or Americans. Everywhere, soldiers or Mongols wearing enormous fur hats, galloping on wild little horses at breakneck speed. On our way up to look at the basalts we passed the automobiles that cover the Kalgan-Urga road in four days: two little cars that would normally hold six persons, each containing some fifteen Mongols, shaggy with furs and flushed with the cold, all this in a cloud of dust. The whole effect was extraordinarily savage and intense, with a savagery and an intensity that were human. I was not displeased that M. Lacroix observed for himself the difficulties of traveling and geological work in China. After the strain of Kalgan, we relaxed with easy little outings to palaces, pagodas, etc., and endured numerous dinners. I am trying to increase my contacts with the people of Peking, insofar as this fatal plurality of languages permits, and I miss no occasion to introduce my "humanitarian" ideas. I almost always notice that they sink in immediately, which is to say that they preexist in my interlocutor. As for myself, I am amazed at the invasion I have undergone for the past two years at the hands of these humane preoccupations or aspirations. The study and love of the Earth and of Life, sustained by the precision and power of Christian perspectives, have introduced me to a view of the "human terrestrial stratum" and an awareness of its biological autonomy, its order of grandeur, and its value, which tend increasingly to absorb my preoccupations. It is in the discovery, analysis, and presentation of this immense and mysterious entity that I shall, no doubt, be increasingly engaged. I hope that the inner path will become clearer to me with each step.

As for China, everything I see and hear points toward an acceleration of the crisis. The party of the North (Chang-tzo-lin), which seemed to be concentrating and consolidating, now seems to be dividing. The Cantonese also have their difficulties (caused by jealousies between leaders), but they are moving like water over damp soil that is ready to receive them. An official of the Peking government said recently, in conversation, that the present drama had to do with the fact that China is simultaneously undergoing three revolutions which other states have known only successively: an intellectual revolution, a political revolution, and a social revolution. This interpretation is probably very accurate.

While waiting for the new China, whose elements I like to recognize in a few good Chinese friends, to discover herself, it is a curious pilgrimage to visit the abandoned palaces and temples, as I have been doing for two weeks. I am more and more struck by the element of childishness and the absence of solid materiality which characterize the finest Chinese creations. Except for jade, bronze, and porcelain, everything crumbles, and the most magnificent lines fall into dust. Moreover, when one looks at the most magnificent bronzes, one is always shocked by an anatomical strangeness or an infantilism. There is nothing that has the total majesty of Egypt or Assyria. The most terrible lions show a ridiculous number of teeth and wear little bells around their necks.

Tientsin, December 25, 1926

. . . Either because of my findings themselves (the fauna of Sangkan Ho is one of the finest fossil faunas of China at the present time), or because of the fact that this work is part of the vast scientific and humanistic work which is now being done around the Pacific, I am sure that my year has been better employed here than in France. My roots are in Paris, and I will not pull them up. But if you only knew what a marvelous field of action there is here right now, and what a wide space to breathe in, despite the political unrest! In four or five months I shall feel the imperious need to come and immerse myself again in the incomparable milieu of that warm and wonderful Paris. But I cannot regret, even scientifically, having responded to the call of events and risked the journey of this year 1926.

M. Lacroix is in Tientsin, waiting for his boat for Shanghai. When he is gone, I will return to a peace that I desire. Spring will come very quickly now, and I will have to think again about going into the country. Mentally I need a few weeks of peace. Physically I am absolutely fine.

Tientsin, January 22, 1927

If you ever read my "pious book," you will see that there is a paragraph devoted to Holy Matter, a matter that has nothing emaciated or Franciscan about it. You see, if you continue to be true to yourself, I think you will come to realize that Spirit is not the fleshless thing, the insubstantial specter, that is sometimes presented to us. True spirit must be formed of all the vitality and all the consistency of the body: it is an extension in the same direction. The spiritual life of all the great saints has been a richer and more intense life, not a restricted life. We live, in this respect, in a dim ambiguity. And it is my fundamental difficulty not to be able to voice as I would, by word and by example, my certitude that the Kingdom of God can only be established by a much more complete immersion of the Christian forces in the most powerful currents of the Earth. Ah, the great symbol of Baptism, in which ordinarily men see no more than the drop of water that cleanses, and miss the river that sweeps away! In everything that I have happened to read on the World, I seem never to have found an accent, a cry, that has not already escaped me. I repeat: Spirit is the most violent, the most incendiary of Matters.

Outwardly, a trying piece of news: I have just learned that, despite the efforts of Monsignor B., Rome does not want me to return to my professorship. They do not seem to have taken a dislike to me, far from it; but they want to save Religion. So I am beginning to think about reinforcing my roots in Paris. I foresee stays at the laboratory interrupted by trips enabling me to pursue my scientific efforts without losing opportunities for a steadier position in a few years. At bottom, I remain quite calm. The less the people who inconvenience me (by doing their job, I realize) interest me, the greater is my passionate confidence in the Force — much greater than they — which they represent in my eyes. I would take enormous delight in breaking all ties; but that would be a vital absurdity, and I do not believe that solution can even be considered right now. Naturally, I still expect to be taken back in November.

We are in the middle of the cold season here. A dry cold, from fifteen to twenty below, following a snowfall. I work at the Licent Museum or at my desk: various geological notes, and the "pious book" of which I am about to begin the third and final part, which is already very much prepared. The "Noosphere" looms ever larger on my horizon, and I am beginning to believe that its manifestation represents the properly human or profane aspect of the species of little spiritual "mission" to which I feel I am destined, and from which I feel no power in the world can dissuade me. Still plenty of socializing and projects with my Peking friends. The work and the possibilities for work multiply before one's eyes. If only one had a little peace! (Actually, I am perhaps illogical in desiring this peace, when the present agitation is undoubtedly productive: the formation of a mountain is of greater value to a geologist than the opportunity to study those that already exist.) Sven Hedin is to leave Peking in April for Tien-chan, with a veritable army. If only I could go with him!

Peking, February 14, 1927

The day before yesterday at a dinner I found myself sitting next to a quietly desperate woman who told me that one day she had awakened to the view that the World was empty. And so while in the setting and under the guise of a mundane conversation, we thus touched on what is most dramatic in human relations — namely the problem of faith in Life discussed *in vivo*, between persons who speak without concealing anything — with a kind of start, I swore to myself once again that I would have so much faith in the divine virtue that impinges on us through all things, that I would end by setting fire to what is around me and first of all to what is closest to me. Let us not doubt it, and let us awaken to that light: the world is full of God. For if it were empty, the world would long ago have died of disgust.

I am writing you from Peking. The meeting of the Geological Society is proceeding with its customary cordiality; I would even say that from one year to the next there is a perceptible increase in the warmth and mutual sympathy of the members. If only you had seen the banquet the day before yesterday: Chinese, Americans, Swedes, Germans, Frenchmen (myself and a guest of mine). What warm and intelligent internationalism! And what a practical demonstration of the reality of those new forces which can emerge from a synthesis of nations! The meeting was reinforced by the presence of Sven Hedin, who is about to leave for Turkistan again. He is a strange man; insolently young beneath his sixty years, truculent in his Nordic coldness, brimming over with kindness despite an incontestable vanity, ready for any sacrifice for the sake of "knowledge" despite his egoism. We are to dine together this evening. He would take me with him at the drop of a hat. But how to come back in three weeks with all the ties that bind me?

I wish I knew that you were not too alarmed by my dismissal from the Catholic Institute. In your heart, I know, like Boule and like many other friends, you will find me weak, and perhaps you will think less of me, because I shall not make the gesture (which would be such a relief for me) of dropping those who prevent me from telling what I see. Understand me: in this whole business only one thing concerns me, only one thing guides me: to try to be as true as possible to Life. As I have told you, before my eyes the World — particularly the human world — grows, I would almost venture to say, from week to week. Now, the more it assumes this clarity and consistency in my eyes, the more I perceive that it can continue to exist only by its effort toward some divine principle. Would it be logical for me, by breaking with my Church, impatiently to force the growth of that Christian stem in which I am persuaded that the sap of the religion of tomorrow is forming? I am held fast in the Church by the very views which help me to see her insufficiencies. Is this not a bit dramatic or cosmic? Help me by having confidence in me. I still do not know what my life will be. I would like to make the role of Paris as large as possible. But I suspect that I will also have to make the role of work here rather large (to save Paris). I have decided to go forward with a shameless optimism. If there is a God, as I believe, he will make the obstacles serve my progress; and in the end I will find myself more able than ever to make the light shine which some would like to see extinguished. . . . In this connection, I have made (or more precisely made again, with greater clarity) a personal discovery. It is that, fundamentally, what I desire so greatly to propagate is not exactly a theory, a system, a *Weltanschauung,* but a certain taste, a certain perception of the beauty, the pathos, and the unity of *being.* This may even account for the incomprehension I encounter. I try to translate the species of calm intoxication produced in me by an awareness of the profound substance of things into theories (how I wish I could translate it into music!), but these theories really matter to me only by their vibrations in a province of the soul which is not that of intellectualism. Those who do not hear the fundamental harmony of the Universe which I try to transcribe (fortunately, many do) look in what I write for some kind of narrowly logical system, and are confused or angry. Fundamentally, it is not possible to transmit directly by words the perception of a quality, a taste. Once again, it would be more to my purpose to be a shadow of Wagner than a shadow of Darwin. Taking myself as I am, I see no better course than to strive by all means to reveal Humanity to Men.

In any case, I expect to return to Paris in the fall. Between now and then I will undoubtedly make a trip to the northeast of Peking (April–August). M. Boule is not giving me money this year; but I am only half sorry about this. It leaves me free to undertake a broad geological research whose importance, oddly enough, exaggerated anxieties of a "Gallery curator" completely prevent my dear old teacher from perceiving. In reality I continue here *ex aequo* with the Americans and the Swedes; and I am now, by mutual agreement, in charge of "supervision" of Paleontological Studies (Vertebrates) at the Chinese Survey. I can do without the 10,000 francs from the I.P.H. — now nationalism is killing minds, now, after systematically elevating them for centuries! It is because something else is being born.

Tientsin, February 27, 1927

And now what to tell you on the subject of Boule? As a matter of fact I had a letter to him on my desk that might have brought out his bad *auvergnat* side. I tore it up, and I have written another in which I have said the same things in a different tone of voice. Briefly, I remind him that I came to China this year because this seemed the only way for me to remain in paleontology and in the laboratory (short of breaking with my Order, which I would have regarded as a moral blunder). I point out that I work for Licent only very secondarily: my center is in *Peking*, where I am looked upon essentially as "Boule's student" and the representative of the museum. Finally, I assure him that I am not the least bit annoyed that he has cut off my salary this year. I still have enough to travel this spring, and I prefer not to have new financial responsibilities, given the political situation. If I find fossils there will always be time to send me funds afterwards. I have written to Lacroix asking him not to be too insistent with the faculty meeting. I have said all this as nicely as possible. This done, I have sent a note to Lacroix and a long letter to my friend Lemoine (Professor of Geology at the museum) letting him know discreetly that Professor Licent had taken away *none* of the fifty crates brought back by me in 1924 but only a load sent by him for study in 1922. (In this affair Licent has been just as *auvergnat* as Boule, but correct.) To Lemoine, who is influential and a smooth talker, I have openly and without modesty given a summary of my work here for the past eight months. After all, these things must be known. I fail to understand why Boule is so fascinated by his showcases or his little personal advantage that he does not wish to interest himself in the findings of which my letters are full (and which bear directly on that Pliocene he loves so much). This pains me, for him more than for myself. But it does not bother me in the least. I would say rather that it is for me a kind of goad which points and keeps me more fiercely than ever in that single direction: to penetrate everything that is not, or everyone who does not love, only the Truth. "Truth"! Does not the Gospel say, *Veritas liberabit vos?* I want to do everything I can to surround my old master, to whom I owe so much, with affection and respect. But I will never put the museum before the general interests of human research.

I wrote you last, if I am not mistaken, on my return from the

---

meeting of the Geological Society. Since then my time has still been rather taken up. To begin with, for two days I have had four young members of the Sven Hedin expedition to whom I was supposed to give as much information as possible on research on the Paleolithic and vertebrate fossils. Next, I spent three days at the mining center of "Kailan" three hours north of Tientsin by train. Kailan is probably the second largest coal mine in the world for production, and since its isolation obliges it to be self-sufficient, it forms a veritable little state that even manufactures its own trucks and its own central heating. The governor of this city, an excellent Belgian, received me in an extremely cordial and princely manner. I lived in an atmosphere of cigars and champagne! The real purpose of my visit was to look in the quarries of the region for cracks with fossil-bearing filling such as exist south of Peking. The cracks were numerous, but almost all sterile. Even so I eventually found one that contained some hedgehogs, rodents, etc. This first find will perhaps develop further. For lack of enough bones, I collected a series of interesting Ordovician cephalopods: *Actinoceras, Endoceras,* etc. These fossils are found in excessively hard gray-blue limestone in which their sections appear sculpted by the superficial disintegration of the rock. In the kingdom of Kailan their collection is exceedingly simple. I was escorted by three or four Chinese armed with chisels and hammers. I would draw chalk circles around the desirable sections, and move majestically on. Then a coolie would start to work, and in the evening I would be brought the specimens, quarried from the living rock. I wish I had extractors like these when I travel! Among the Chinese who accompanied me in this way there was one marvelous one who has long been the "boy" of a prospector of the mine. I would love to take him away with me some day.

Nothing new with my personal affairs. The man with whom I can discuss them (by correspondence) will not return to Lyon (from Syria) until the beginning of March. My letters are waiting for him, but I will have no answer before a month. The more I think about it, anyway, the more necessary my return in the fall seems. I have too much work to finish and too many shadows to dispel (in Paris and in Rome).

Very little has happened since my last letter. I have led a perfectly peaceful life between my typewriter (I am typing my "pious" book), and a binocular microscope or a *camera lucida* at the museum. I will not say that this life absolutely satisfies me, or that the absence of the social factor does not seem excessive. But after all, it is only a temporary period. I will probably go to Peking shortly; and the presence there of one of my friends, Dr. Ting, who seems to be returning to geology after being a big political man in Shanghai for a year, promises renewed entry into the young China milieu. If I succeed in catching this Dr. Ting in private conversation, I imagine we will embark together on vast utopias embracing the pan-Pacific world and the entire globe. Speaking of Peking, I will tell you that I am receiving increasingly urgent and definite offers to take charge of vertebrates at the Geological Survey down there, allowing for all the necessary part of my time spent in Paris. I do not yet know how all this will end, since I cannot have news from Rome before the beginning of April. But Boule is really too simple in imagining that a change in my schedule is going to "lose me for science," or even further, to prevent me from engaging in *free* science. I feel a sacred aversion to ecclesiasticism, and anything that happens to me can only serve to reinforce these sentiments. You know, I understand very well the preference of certain persons for rebellion and rebels. And I will say again that nothing would be easier or more appealing to me than this attitude. Unfortunately (and perhaps you will say that here precisely lies my weakness or my tameness) I do not feel I have the right, just now, to adopt it. First of all, because I am not being asked to make any theoretical renunciation of what I believe to be true (they are content to impose restrictions which will not, if God is with me, prevent me from going where I will). Next, because I feel too much a part of a mass of people who cannot go as fast as I, to dare to jeopardize the movement of life by making a break for my personal satisfaction. To tell the truth, all this is not as absolutely clear in my mind as it is on paper. I let things take their course with the firm hope that I shall not arrive at an impasse.

I have experienced for a long time and I still experience, as a first reaction, your antipathy for Man. I have tried to analyze it, and it seems to me that it has to do with the fact that another Man is, for each of us, another World, a rival World to our own, that is, the one centered around us. Animals seem to belong to *our* World, because they are subordinate to us in some way; so they do not bother us. We assume that they have no *Weltanschauung*, or else we lend them ours. Another Man is another *Weltanschauung;* this is what bothers us, or even gives us a constantly renewed hatred for him. It seems to me that this repulsion between men is something that must be overcome in order to arrive at a higher human state. To attain this result I have found no other method than to look at Man either impersonally, in the Noosphere, as a drop of water in the sea, or as an atom in Matter (why do you not love the Noosphere if you love the sea and the sky?), or else personally, in Him in whom, for the Christian faith, all are and shall be physically *one* (but here again, as in mutual affection, plurality, *the other,* disappears as a rival, and survives only as the increase that it brings).

It is really *the other,* the rival, whom we fear and hate in Man; and this aversion ceases as soon as we find a way to bring this other back into our unity.

I need to make a trip to Peking since I cannot make one to Paris, which would be infinitely superior for restoring my tone. To tell the truth, at certain moments it seems to me that I no longer feel anything, but that I have passed into a state of pure force, that I am turned toward something great in which I lose myself without yet being able to make out either the face or the name.

Peking, March 24, 1927

Here I am in Peking again. I have come for the annual meeting of the Society of Natural History, a recent offshoot of the Geological Society. Nothing new since my last letter. Still no word from Rome or Lyon that might help me to make my plans for the future. I am reduced to idle conjecture, and to following the course of events in China, which is more and more troubled. Politically, what is happening in Shanghai and Nanking seems to be the climax of the crisis, and possible indication of an understanding between the North and the South at the expense of the foreigners (without violence, but by a process of elimination). Deeper than politics is the growing movement of antipathy toward everything that is not Chinese. Even here in Peking we just had a demonstration against Sven Hedin by some student organizations — a very ill-conceived act, considering the fact that Sven Hedin took some Chinese geologists with him by agreement with the Geological Survey. But the "young Chinese" do not look that closely, and do not wish to tolerate any expeditions that are not *led* by Chinese. Andrews will have difficulty doing anything this year. What the Chinese do have a right to protest are the forays made in their country by foreign investigators. In this they talk exactly like Boule on the subject of French deposits. Nevertheless they should understand (as the most intelligent among them do) that they still need to be helped and educated. All this convinces me that the stage of the "Museum missions" in China is gone forever, and that we have arrived at the age of "collaboration." This collaboration is being asked of me more and more formally. The other evening I had dinner with the Director (Wong) and the former Director (Ting) of the Survey. Once again they urged me to take charge of the Department of Vertebrate Paleontology without jeopardizing possible stays in Paris. I had not seen Ting since 1924 (on my return to China, he was in Shanghai), and I almost embraced him when I saw him again. We understand one another admirably, he and I. His is a remarkably open mind — geologist, historian, philosopher; he is deeply Chinese, without being at all xenophobic. For me he represents, in his ideas, the axis along which China must reorganize and advance, and in his very person he may well make a considerable contribution to domestication and orientation of the new forces. So far, the North of China is perfectly calm. I still hope to make a small trip at the end of April.

As I have told you quite often already, I feel completely at home in Peking, where I lead the social life that all Christians should lead, and breathe a good humane air which is cleared of a great many prejudices. Even so, the atmosphere does not equal that of Paris; and although the Far East may be a favorable place to widen one's personal experience and enrich one's own ideas, it will never be a soil that I can work or a milieu that I can re-create in speaking or in writing. I am born to speak in French to Europeans. So you need not fear that I will let myself be diverted from my objective, which is some day to reappear definitively in France, better armed to make myself heard. I remain, at heart, of an invincible optimism.

A week ago I found, in the bottom of an old crate in the Licent Museum, a human incisor, very fossilized, taken by my colleague with some gazelle's teeth from the Paleolithic strata of Ordos. This tooth will tell us nothing either about the existence of Man (since we already have tools) nor about his anthropological characteristics, but it is the first fragment of Paleolithic Man in China, which is always interesting. It will be described in Peking.

April 6, 1927

On my return from Peking last week I found a letter from Rome. It seems that the authorities are not yet desirous of having me reenter the domain of ideas by way of teaching, but that they see no difficulty in my returning for a few months to Paris for my scientific work. The idea that I might eventually be relocated permanently in Paris (restricted to pure science) is not dismissed. Under the circumstances I am contemplating returning to France at the end of the summer and staying long enough to write up a report on my Pliocene fauna. Afterwards I would return to China. If the country has not become completely xenophobic, I will have a very interesting position with the Geological Survey, in a Chinese-American-Swedish milieu which I like very much. This would enable me to combine Paris and Peking in a way that would place at my disposal the double and complementary riches of East and West, not to mention that my quality of perpetual "traveler" both here and there would, I hope, allay much suspicion. I am, therefore, moving in the direction of this arrangement of my life. Moreover, I remain absolutely determined to do all I can to "swallow" the obstacle, that is, to spread as many of my ideas as I can by utilizing the very restrictive conditions that certain elements are trying to impose on me. I have not concealed this from my "authorities," and I have told them that I was counting on them to help me! Actually, it is useless to discuss theoretically what I will or will not be permitted to do. As in so many cases, I hope that the problem will resolve itself very simply by movement. One thing is certain, that they will have trouble confining me to pure science. For me, geology is like a root that pushes me with its sap toward the human questions: unification, prospection, and organization (especially psychological) of the human stratum. I cannot live outside of this realm.

Although you mischievously claim that in these tastes I am like the men of the eighteenth century (such a nice century, if it hadn't been such an unimaginative one!), I think I am rather different, in my perspectives and preoccupations, from my respectable great uncle! I neither believe in nor sympathize with *logical* systems or frameworks. But I am very sensitive to the existence and value of living organisms, and it is from this point of view that I try to interpret Humanity. For us it is a question of becoming collectively more sensitive, more receptive, more free: a question of life or death, which we shall be more and more obliged to face.

Meanwhile, China is more and more in a state of crisis. If Chang-tzo-lin does not succeed in stopping the Cantonese in their march toward the Yellow River, we will be Red — here and Peking — in twenty-four hours. Chang-tzo-lin has no sympathy in China and the terrain that he still occupies is heavily undermined, that is, favorable to the South, or even ripe for rebellion. The American and English consuls are already beginning to recall their nationals to Tientsin! Here we fear nothing, except superficial inconveniences (like partial evacuation); and these are still only pessimistic prognoses. The European troops are strong. Besides, the Southern movement will surely reach us in reduced form. Fong-hin-shiang would be our future master: he does not have the reputation of being brutal. In the end, nobody knows what will be left of the European establishments (notably the missions) in China in a year, short of very considerable foreign intervention (and even in this case, we will probably be under a regime similar to the Turkish regime). I cannot yet foresee that the North will allow itself to be Sovietized. From my insignificant point of view this squall is rather ill-timed, since it threatens to buffet the young and promising tree of the Geological Survey in Peking. I imagine that my friends will remain in charge (they are irreplaceable, and besides very nationalist); but will they be able to resume, before several years, that friendly collaboration with the "whites" which is the charm of Pekinese scientific life just now? That is the question. They have to reckon with a group of ignorant young xenophobes who are very vocal (as Sven Hedin can testify). Six months from now, I guess, all this will begin to be clear.

Whatever happens, I am not sorry to be an eyewitness to this great human movement of truly geological magnitude. It is the modern individualization of Asia that is taking place. A surprising aspect of this phenomenon is the infinitesimal part that seems to be played in the event by the so-called good powers. In reality I imagine that this is an appearance. Under the inevitable surface foam the forces that are bubbling up are fine and noble. But what a pity constantly to see the good identified with memories of the past or of the established order!

As regards China, I am beginning to be puzzled about her real possibilities. Up to now I have held — and I am still inclined to believe — that our inability to come to an understanding with this country is due to the fact that we regard it with eyes and minds that are narrow and Mediterranean. In the light of the convergent evidence that I have gathered here from the most diverse men, I see an increasing possibility for another hypothesis, namely, that the Chinese are arrested primitives, victims of retarded development whose anthropological substance is inferior to ours. "They have quick minds," one hears, "but no constructive ability, no tenacity to sustain an effort, no will power, no great passion. And there emanates from their mass an invincible force of leveling and 'dissolution.' Everything that tends to stand out among them is immediately reduced to zero. Everything that lives for a long time among them is psychologically diminished, weakened." I have a good half-dozen friends who do not seem to me to correspond to this portrait. But are they exceptional, terminal individuals, or do they represent a germ and a blueprint for the future? Scientifically, I believe that the problem is still unsolved and that it is the outcome of the present crisis which will begin to determine the solution. Neither the Christian attitude of love for all mankind, nor humane hopes for an organized society must cause us to forget that the "human stratum" may not be homogeneous. If it were not, it would be necessary to find for the Chinese, as for the Negroes, their special function, which may not (by *biological* impossibility) be that of the whites. I do not like these prospects. But they may some day become necessary. Is not the real way to conquer the world to utilize its faults, and not to deny them, *if* they are irremediable? Think it over and you will see that it is not "opium" that I am offering you.

Your visit to Breuil amused me very much. The fact is that this old archeologist has fitted out a delightful cave for himself; and, by the way, I think that an artistic and personal setting must be one of the rarest pleasures and stimulants of life. Unfortunately it is the one that a "communistic" life like mine renders most impossible to achieve. But after all, is not this privation compensated by a kind of liberation? I would rather inhabit "the World" than a home.

Tientsin, April 20, 1927

I am more uncertain than ever about what I shall be able to do this summer before my return to France. Yesterday we were in the midst of preparing for a trip to the west of Mukden (a region of mediocre interest), when a missionary told us that there, too, the Chinese masses had suddenly begun to rise. I still hope that this is a false report. But if it is confirmed, the possibilities for field work tend rapidly to approach zero. Meanwhile, I am beginning to feel an intense need to return somewhere, to look for anything at all. The fine weather is almost here, and it would be really annoying to be here, on site, without being able to use a year. I am sick and tired of poring indefinitely over specimens collected last year. The "new" is not far away, and it is the "new" for which I long.

Things are happening so fast here that it is almost pointless to describe a situation that will no longer be true by the time you read these lines. Briefly, it is this. Since my last letter, the halting of the Southerners north of the Yangtze, together with the dissension that seems to be breaking out in their ranks between the civilian-extremist faction and the military-moderate party, has averted the risk of a sudden and brutal revolution in Northern China. Chang-tzo-lin is dealing harshly with the Kuomintang propagandists of Peking and Tientsin, and his handful of brigands, however unpopular, is still secure and feared. He is evidently being supported by the Japanese and the whites. Under the circumstances the crisis will probably assume a slow pace; but it has not been stopped. The whole country is undermined in its deepest strata, and the English forces will not prevent the birth or individualization of a new China and a new Asia which is taking place. As I may already have said, one may well wonder what is going to emerge from this difficult labor: an abortion or a real man. But something is coming. I still see a good number of Europeans who imagine that after a vigorous foreign intervention, things will return to the calm and freedom that followed the Boxer Rebellion. This hope seems to me a childish illusion such as could only be entertained by diplomats, soldiers, or businessmen, for whom spiritual forces do not exist. Nothing stops ideas; outward restraint only lends them force. It seems unbelievable that intelligent people have not yet accepted this fact, which fills the history of the World! Meanwhile, China is probably becoming the most difficult country on earth to travel in. The West is openly deteriorated. In Ordos, the missionaries are abandoning two thirds of their Christendoms and banding together in a general residence for protection. Even here the consuls are recalling many people from the interior; but I confess that I do not understand the move, unless armed intervention is secretly being prepared. To finish with the subject of China, I should tell you that I sent a moderately pro-China and humanitarian article to an (intelligent) new Catholic journal in Calcutta, *The Week* (first issue). It was received with the highest praise! Unfortunately I do not have a copy to send to you (they have not sent me a single one!). It was a satisfaction to be able to say in India a little bit more than would have passed in Paris. After long being absorbed by the physical zones of the Earth, I am beginning to feel increasingly familiarized, by that very Matter, with the taste and preoccupations of the "human stratum"; and in this new domain I perceive that theoretical research is being inexorably transformed into a need to influence and manipulate which leads logically to social conflicts and struggles. I observe this shift in direction in myself with curiosity, without having the slightest idea where it is taking me. But I am fully aware of the savage beast that sleeps within the instinct to preserve "established orders."

The latest issue of *l'Anthropologie,* which arrived here the day before yesterday, plunged me once again into the Museum–I.P.H. milieu and made me realize forcibly that I have an intellectual and physical need to return to it sometime. China alone would be just as stifling, after a certain point, as Paris alone.

As I have already said, the fine weather is arriving. But the Chinese spring is not a real spring: it is a series of gusts of increasing heat, laced with violent dust squalls. Besides, around Tientsin, there is nothing to turn green except some scraggly willows. Even so, after the cold, one enjoys these meager and austere favors.

Tientsin, April 30, 1927

I am a bit late in writing you because of a little trip to Peking from which I did not return until the day before yesterday. At present the state of China seems much calmer. Apparently nothing (fortunately!) is to stop the transformation in progress. But it seems that they have managed almost to brake a machine that was accelerating wildly. The raid on the Russian embassy in Peking seems to have contributed as forcefully to the restoration of calm as the dissension among the Southerners and their halt north of the Yangtze. The fact is that in the course of this raid some documents were found that are singularly compromising to Moscow, not only from the diplomatic point of view, which would not impress me very much, but from the human point of view. There was a whole plan of agitation, not excluding bloodshed, which is absolutely lacking in idealism or nobility. The more I try to understand and to understand myself, the more I long — as much as any communist, I suppose — for a human renovation; but also the more convinced I am that the future belongs to those who, across all nationalist and bourgeois conventions, boldly give the example of a greater faith in the forces of good and intelligence hidden in Man and a greater love for everything that rises or tries to rise. We have need of a group of new Saint Francises — broader, more aggressive, and more modern than he was in their way of loving the World, but just as logical and nonconformist as he was in the practice of their ideal. We must leave the dead with their dead money, their dead nationalism, their dead ideas, and create, by living it, an atmosphere of new hopes, ambitions, and sympathies. "Spirit" is a much greater destroyer than violence, and it builds with the same gesture with which it tears down. Oh, how I would love to be able to live, like a madman or a lama, the Humanity that I discover.

In those last days in Peking I once again felt intensely the presence of that new spirit. On the occasion of Dr. Andersson's departure for a year in Europe, we attended an informal dinner given by Ting, of whom I have often spoken to you — he is the most remarkable neo-Chinese I know. There were three other Chinese (the Director of the Geological Survey, a professor at the National University and finally, a representative of the old Pekinese aristocracy), as well as Sven Hedin, Granger (the "splendid fellow" of the Osborne expedition), Dr. Grabau, Dr. Black (of the Rockefeller Institute), and another geologist, Barbour. I believe that never in all my life — family life included — have I spent hours so rich and cordial as that evening. As so many other times in Peking, the occasion was pervaded by a dimly sensed triumph at the overcoming of racial, national, and religious barriers. But combined with this there was that special intimacy of eves of departure or times of trouble: Andersson was going away for some time; Hedin was about to set off for Turkistan; Granger was unhappy, at heart, because his mission is temporarily impossible. Well, in this almost pathetic atmosphere, in a China full of incomprehension, everyone freely opened his heart; and before the profusion of apple blossoms that covered the table in a symbol of spring and transience, we spoke of mutual aid, glorious collaboration, and the future. And I thought of the parable of the mustard seed. As you know, I believe that nothing human will be built without the support of a Divine Center, distinct from Man; but I also believe that for this Divine Center there were not, that day, many temples more agreeable than that room in the North Hotel, Hata-men Street, in Peking.

Two days after this dinner a small group of us went to see the excavations presently being made in Chou-kou-tien. I am a bit skeptical about the presence of a Man or an anthropoid in this region, but Zdansky continues to be so affirmative that I feel myself wavering a little. One would have to see the casting of his pieces. While awaiting the discovery of the "Peking Lady," as the alleged prehistoric creature is known here among friends, the excavations are amassing numerous fossils: rodents, bats, and larger animals. We ourselves found a fine macaco jawbone. The day was pleasant, but in the afternoon a violent "yellow wind" arose, and it was in the middle of an unbelievable dust storm that our car returned to Peking.

I now hope to leave in a few days for the region southeast of Mukden. The country is calm and we were given our passports without difficulties. In itself the objective is not exciting, and we shall not go very far from civilized regions; but one always gains something by going into the field.

P.S. When I wrote you that "I no longer feel anything," as if "I had passed into the state of force," I was trying to express a state which is not exactly an absence but no doubt an extreme, a climax of sensibility.

I left Tientsin twelve days ago and I am writing you on the eve of our departure, in a caravan, for the region of Dalai-nor. We are in a large Belgian mission center, full of devoted friends; it is the same spot that I left in 1924 to enter the eastern Gobi. I had a curious sensation on finding myself here after three years: the same but not the same.

To get here we took the Mukden railroad almost to the bottom of the Gulf of Petchili and from there, cars. After tomorrow we will be using mules. It is an extremely dismal landscape: rocky or glaciated, ravaged by innumerable severe floods, with no vegetation other than clumps of poplars and willows in the low places, and a soil that is uniformly gray. The vegetation is barely in bloom and the weather is still heavy with squalls. But we are moving toward the fine weather, and also toward a country that is said to be rich in fine mountains and even in impressive remains of forests. The land is calm and the little bandits respectful. If all continues to go well, I think we will indeed be getting back to Tientsin by the end of July. The exorbitant price of the mules is enough to oblige us to do so. I have begun to gather an impressive number of geological notes. The day before yesterday we visited a "petrified forest" which has been known for a long time, but which is badly situated geologically (it is Upper Jurassic). In addition to the silicified trunks (stumps) for which the spot is celebrated, I observed a very fine flora of ferns and conifers. In a few days we will go through a stretch of shale with fish of approximately the same age.

Personally I am fine. I have been sufficiently absorbed in study of the terrain not to have time to think about personal or serious things. But as I was telling you, this contact with the real does me good. And then, amid the complexity and immobility of the rocks there rise suddenly toward me "gusts of being," sudden and brief fits of awareness of the laborious unification of things, and it is no longer myself thinking, but the Earth acting. It is infinitely better.

I am writing you from a little Belgian mission lost in the Wei-tchang mountain near the southern extremity of the Grand Khingan (a mountain on the eastern border of the High Mongolian Plateau). We have almost reached the central point from which we plan to radiate for three weeks or so into the marginal zone of the Gobi. Here there are vestiges of what was once a great forest, in which Licent hopes to kill lynx, panthers, grouse, etc.; and I can always find work to do in this chaotic and complex country. For the past three weeks I have had my hands full keeping up to date the geological log of our itinerary, which has led us, at the rate of forty kilometers a day, through stretches of rock separated by breaks from which streams of various lavas have emerged. The region is very picturesque and must have been even more so fifty years ago, before the Chinese tenant farmers stupidly cleared it of trees. Imagine a plateau fifteen to seventeen hundred meters high and divided by a labyrinth of valleys into a series of rocky hills, most of which look toward the northeast. It is across these obstacles that our caravan has been finding its way since my last letter. It is not a thrilling trip, for it lacks the vast horizons of the West, but an interesting one nevertheless. My cargo of rock specimens is growing with a rapidity that is almost alarming. For example, aside from a group of Cretaceous fish and a few plants, I have nothing in the way of fossils, nor do I foresee finding any. The chief results of the excursion will take the form of a map. The country is calm because the bad elements have enlisted in the armies of Chang-tzo-lin. We have encountered small groups of bandits (in three passes out of five). But these are "little" bandits who are content to rob or tax humble solitary travelers. They let us pass very civilly. Physically I am very well. So the trip has a good chance of ending without incident. The only question would be how Chang-tzo-lin is holding out against the Southerners. The latest rumors we have heard seem to indicate that the situation is not victorious in that respect. Our plans are, therefore, to radiate from this center for about three weeks, after which we will work our way back down to Jehol and Peking. I still plan to be in Tientsin by the beginning of August.

As you see, all is going well for me on the whole. I am sufficiently happy in an isolated and independent life which prevents me from feeling the discordances that exist between me and my milieu. But I also understand clearly that I must not become too satisfied and that, whatever the reactions to this new contact may be, I need to immerse myself again in the European milieu. I vitally need to be in Paris for a while to understand myself and to get back into life again.

Tong-kia-yinze, July 4, 1927

I am writing you only a few kilometers from the Belgian mission. For three weeks we have been constantly radiating in the region, first camping in the forests and pasturages of Wei-tchang, then making a trip to Ting-pang (three days from here), a remote little town on the edge of the Gobi, eighty kilometers southeast of the large lake Dalai-nor.

You would have loved Wei-tchang. Picture an immense basaltic plateau, averaging eighteen hundred meters in height, covered with vast meadows, without a living soul, and here and there in the ravines or on the ridges, bits of forest land: fir, larch, birch. Especially since the wars of last year, the country is entirely deserted and considered dangerous. But we had a considerable escort of Christians (all the peasants are armed and mounted in this region) and so were able to enjoy the landscape with easy minds. Except for two periods of rather intense cold (down to two degrees above zero), the weather was magnificent. While our men hunted deer and grouse and Licent gathered plants, I made some interesting geological discoveries; but this work did not prevent me from keenly enjoying this luxuriant solitude which was, in certain respects, so similar to that of my lofty Auvergne. In this rugged country the flowering season is sudden and opulent, as I imagine it is in Siberia. Everywhere there were carpets of yellow and red lilies, dwarf or tall iris, tall scarlet primroses, large white peonies, rhubarb with cream-colored tufts, silver, violet, or turquoise blue flowers. In the moist lowlands, orchids (lady's slippers) flaunted calyxes as fat as walnuts. It was enchanting in its life, spaciousness, and solitude.

The landscape of Ting-pang is absolutely different. There there is no more tabular basalt, but a series of high jagged ridges at first covered with verdure and then gradually disappearing under a shroud of white sand from which the peaks of dark rock emerge like mountains from snow. This is the beginning of the great western dunes which took us three days to cross at their narrowest point in 1924. Ting-pang is a picturesque little town nestled between dunes and mountains. Unfortunately it is also the home of a garrison of such dubious character that we thought it best to break camp on the morning after our arrival for fear our arms and mules would be confiscated. However curtailed it has been, this trip has taught me many things, and has enabled me to fix clearly the geological shape of this almost unknown region, which is virtually inaccessible to Europeans. I am bringing back a load of rocks, for M. Lacroix especially. No fossils around here, but a profusion of volcanic rock.

Now we are planning our return. We are waiting for the latest news to see whether we can go back by way of Jehol and Peking. I hope to be in Tientsin by the beginning of August.

Jehol, July 24, 1927

Just a word to let you know that all continues to go well, and that in twelve days I expect to arrive in Tientsin. We are now in Jehol, a small town, but famous for its lamaic temples, north of the Great Wall and Peking. It is very warm and humid in spite of the mountainous country: this temperature is a disagreeable change for us after the coolness of Wei-tchang.

Nothing new during the last weeks of travel. I merely continued to improve my knowledge of the structure of the region. As we leave here to go toward the sea, the area is better known; and I do not think I will find anything new. So I am eager to get as fast as possible to Tientsin, where a tiresome job of packing awaits me.

The country — that is, China — seems to be in a period of lull. But it is still far from the calm that would permit normal work. If it were not for friends in Europe as well as "causes" to defend, I believe I would prefer not to return to France. But there are the friends, and there are the causes. It is absolutely necessary that I return in order to try and reconstruct a solid base for the work ahead. I believe that God will help me to do it.

Tientsin, August 6, 1927

I got back to Tientsin two days ago, after a favorable end of the trip. Circumstances were very much with us from Jehol. The mountain was swarming with bandits and for a time it would have been impossible for us to continue our journey. By good fortune, in the worst place, we came upon a convoy escorted by one hundred soldiers (!) and were able to travel in its wake. In spite of everything, I was able to complete my geological profile in a satisfactory manner, but I lost my fountain pen, and now I am writing painfully with a bad quill pen.

For reasons of scientific positivism, or inability to overcome a tide of universal prejudice, I was able to "question" the human value of the Chinese and to judge the Russian action in China severely (this severity was born largely of disappointment). But never has my faith in Humanity as a whole diminished for a single minute. It is even with curiosity that I observe the extent to which, after the simplification and consolidation which these months of traveling have produced in my head, faith and hope in the terrestrial World have come to dominate my inner life like great mountains. I find myself *fiercely* determined to defend Humanity and Matter on all occasions and against all opponents. The solution is there. Probably for reasons of environment and heredity, perhaps with an excess of theory, but very sincerely in any case, I believe that faith in Humanity can find its final expression and its ultimate assurance only in a consciousness superior to ours, in which the individual consciences (the flower of Humanity) will lose themselves without ceasing to be themselves.

I am surrounded by heat, humidity, and — what is worse — packing cases. I should like to be able to take the boat on the twenty-seventh of August, but I do not know whether I will be ready in time. It seems to me that I leave for Europe as one moving toward a great cloud: so many uncertain and shifting things. But God also inhabits the clouds, and it is his trace that I come to seek.

Shanghai, August 27, 1927

I am sailing in a few hours on the *Chenonceaux,* which will bring me to Marseilles at the beginning of October.

Marseilles, October 2, 1927

I found your letter yesterday upon landing. How I wish I were more than a man so that I could reassure you and could heal the person you love so much.

As you know, I believe that the World is an immense plastic thing subject to the influence of Spirit. We shall band together our desires so that the principle, necessarily good, which animates all things, will restore your friend's strength. This desire, this hope, this supplication for immediate and tangible well-being is our first duty, as the Gospel itself teaches us.

But in our present Universe, as is all too clear, nothing can absolutely resist, but everything must sooner or later yield to the forces of death. Your love of Life is a healthy and magnificent power; and you must jealously guard this spirit of resistance to physical diminution which helps you to bear suffering. But there is still something missing in your attitude: you do not yet sufficiently love *all* of Life, *all* of the Universe to agree, once the inevitable moment has come, to diminish (in appearance) and to pass lovingly into it. We must struggle against death with all our force, for it is our fundamental duty as living creatures. But when, by virtue of a state of things (transitory, no doubt, but inevitably linked to the state of growth of the World) death takes us, we must experience that paroxysm of faith in life that causes us to abandon ourselves to death as to a falling into a greater life. To love Life so much, and to trust it so completely, that we embrace it and throw ourselves into it even in death — this is the only attitude that can calm and fortify you: to love extravagantly what is greater than oneself. Every union, especially with a greater power, involves a kind of death of the self. Death is acceptable only if it represents the physically necessary passage toward a union, the condition of a metamorphosis.

July 7, 1933

My physical self is at this moment riding over the Pacific. I left Peking June 22 with four geologists, and in three days we will go through the Golden Gate. As you know, I am going to the Washington Conference at the end of July. On September 8, I will take the *President Coolidge* back to San Francisco. In late fall and winter I plan to do some prospecting in Southern China. After that, I don't know, naturally. But I would be very much surprised if some reason did not eventually call me back to France again, if only to make a connection and transmit an impulse.

This, outwardly, is my position. Inwardly, I am not too sure where I am or where I am going. I think I told you that in May my Order requested me to turn down any offer I might receive of a position in Paris, because my ideas are not sufficiently "reliable." The more I think about this interdiction, the less it affects me (I don't think it seriously bothered me for a minute). On the contrary, I appreciate the advantages of having a clear road ahead and not being tied down in any way. On the other hand, it is no longer possible for me to have any illusions about the struggle in which, by an inevitable development of my nature, I find myself engaged. . . . There is only one course open to me: to develop what I believe more intensively than ever, and mingle more intimately than ever with the blood I dream of correcting. What is needed is not revolt, but greater love. I don't know if it is possible, but I want to try. One thing seems clear to me. In a cause like this, I am afraid of nothing.

. . . As for the present political situation, we are suffering one defeat after another. But on closer inspection one realizes that these defeats may be the best thing that could happen to us. In Geneva, as in London, nothing but conflicting egotisms. A World built on this slime cannot last. What we are waiting for must come from another source. I await more steadfastly than ever the coming of the Spirit of the Earth.

Peking, October 7, 1933

. . . Tonight I am leaving again for Tientsin, where I am going to spend all of next week. I want to get hold of myself intellectually and spiritually, and if I don't do it immediately, I never will. The work here is interesting but I am swamped. There really is Upper Paleolithic in the recent deposits in Choukoutien. It's rather fun and intriguing.

Peking, December 21, 1933

. . . One thing that might be important is that a letter from France seems to indicate a serious possibility of my having a conversation with my General in Rome. I will not decline the invitation if it really materializes. But you know my feelings: I am afraid that an interview of this kind might serve to bring out ultimate divergences. . . .

After I got back I went last week to spend three days in Choukoutien. Nothing new down there; the upper cave with the Upper Paleolithic is practically exhausted. The work of excavation of the top layers with Sinanthropus is well under way, and by next spring we hope to make real advances into the deposit proper. The other fissures (washouts with fish, and washouts with "salmon-like" rodents) are extremely interesting.

Peking, February 11, 1934

. . . Nothing new in my existence aside from the ups and downs of the laboratory. The work is just as interesting as ever. My daily program does not vary. . . . The sky remains an invariable blue, but the weather is growing milder: an exquisite time of the year.

Inside, no great changes either. An impression, however, that things are becoming more and more simplified without becoming fixed. Thus there is beginning to dwell in me a kind of great and large faith, relatively free of illusions as to any existing organization, but with sufficient sympathy for what is necessarily transmitted by the effort of the past. I entrust myself to the future. And I feel that I am ready to defend this faith, in all its logic, to the very end.

Peking, June 30, 1934

. . . As I was writing this winter at the end of a paper that I will certainly show you some day, when Man at last finds the means to control and utilize the formidable resources of the heart, it will be in his History like a second discovery of Fire. I cling madly to the conviction that this conquest is necessary and possible.

. . . Since Easter I have been traveling constantly, working toward Black's and my common goal of connecting the Tertiary and Quaternary of the Yangtze with that of the Hwang Ho. From Easter to May I explored the Nanking-Hangkow sector. From May to the end of June we did the Hangkow-Chungking part, and I pushed on as far as Chengtu, and the first foothills of Tibet. The gorges of the Yangtze deserve their reputation, and Szechuan is a magnificent garden disturbed only by the "military" and their insane taxes. The communists have just formed a new "pocket" in the northeast of the province. On a smaller scale this trip will have rendered me the same service as the Croisière Jaune (Yellow Crossing). It has shown me a world.

. . . Right now I am getting ready to leave again for a few weeks in Honan, where a political lull makes it possible for me to explore a region that is still blank on the geological maps. I expect to be back in Peking by mid-August, at which time I intend to devote myself to the writing of some necessary reports. Choukoutien continues to yield. We are gradually working our way down through the layers. An upper level untouched by the preceding excavations has yielded a very fine jawbone, very "Neanderthaloid" (probably still Sinanthropus), along with some remarkable tools. It is urgent that we have a professional anthropologist to replace Black as soon as possible. No one has been chosen yet.

So much for the outside. Inside, I continue to push forward, rather blindly, obscurely conscious of growing divergences, but determined to believe to the end that for the essential part I will succeed in making a synthesis. I cannot allow either my faith in God or my faith in the World to fail. So I try not to look too closely at what makes my present life a provocation or a challenge and let myself be carried forward, contrary to all probability. It seems to me that as long as I retain (and am therefore able to radiate) a passionate relish for "Being" and for its possibilities to come, absolutely nothing can represent a real loss for me.

Nothing particular to tell; still no idea when I might be returning to France. Black's disappearance doesn't help matters any.

Peking changes very little. Politically, things are marking time. Is it a lull, or the beginning of a better era?

"Have faith in Life." . . . May Life become for you not just some blind, favorable fatality, but a kind of living Presence or Benevolence in which it will be possible for you not only to trust but to confide. You know how deeply, by a combination of native inclinations, religious education, and independent reflection, I have come to be imbued with the conviction that the Universe in us and around us is *ultimately* a great birth, at the heart of a gradual quickening which nothing can escape. The more I explore this path the more convinced I become of its firmness and of the fundamental, unassailable joy to which it leads. Try it — that is, learn to love and to accept serenely (as the influence of a great loving power) those uncontrollable events which thwart your action — and you will see that you will come closer to peace. . . . I believe I have already told you that, basically, my whole "religion" can be reduced to this active surrender to a World which I understand less and less in detail (in the sense that the traditional explanations that people give of it seem more and more inadequate), but whose "divinization" or "personalization" seems clearer to me every day. That my existence has been as much as possible an act of fidelity to Life is the only thing that interests and reassures me from now on.

But what is an existence that is "faithful to Life"? Is it an existence that is *socially* successful, one with an outward continuity, recognized success, a tangible result, an acquired stability? Not necessarily. (Personally, I no longer concern myself with the outward "success" of my time on earth.) . . . But let me add this: Why do you assume that an existence that does not succeed in taking root or bearing fruit in the form of a tangible work is less valuable than another? Why might not the World, which has need of stable families and settled people, need also those mobile and wandering creatures whose action takes the form of a series of seemingly unrelated trials or tests cutting across all kinds of areas? . . . It is a great thing not to have a place to lay your head if you carry faith in the World in your heart.

. . . I have returned from a month of rather arduous but very interesting travel in Honan, which is now free of the bandits who have made it inaccessible for the past twenty years. I covered Tsinling from north to south, thus tying together the basins of the Hwang Ho and Yangtze rivers. The picturesque aspect of travel affects me less and less. But I feel more and more devoted to the "service of the World." I now plan to stay put until the end of autumn (at which time I hope to go and see those famous caves with fossils relating to human industry in Kwangsi). More and more I go beyond Northern China. Then Breuil will come. I wonder whether I'll be coming to France in the spring. From September to December I'll have to get a lot of work done at the lab. We are up to our ears in results to be published.

Tientsin, November 17, 1934

What to tell you in the way of news? My existence has been very calm since summer. Except for some very short trips to Tientsin I have not left Peking and its two labs: my "office" at the Survey in the morning and the P.U.M.C. in the afternoon (I even write at poor Davy's desk with pencils that he sharpened himself). I had to write a lot of reports, the most pressing of which are finished or even on the point of being published: the latest discoveries at Choukoutien for 1933–1934 (nothing new since summer), a report of my July trip, with beautiful specimens from the Tsinlings), and a note on Tienshan for an anniversary book of Sven Hedin's. Never, I think, has the scientific side of my life been more interesting. My plans for the immediate future are becoming complicated. I must combine the following elements: (1) a short trip to Canton and Kwangsi in December or January (inspection of the terrain and of two caves with well-known fissures); (2) Breuil's arrival in March; (3) Professor Weidenreich's arrival in April, to replace Black (Weidenreich seems to be a distinguished anthropologist and very congenial; as a Jew, he has to leave the University of Frankfort); (4) my own trip to France, where it is urgent that I renew contacts; (5) possibly a few months in India (Siwaliks), where de Terra is asking me to join his next expedition. It is this last factor, still undecided, which will determine whether I go to Europe in the spring or fall of 1935.

December 31, 1934

. . . What to tell you about the life of the continent? For a month (a long month) my life has followed its usual pattern under the beautiful cold sky. But now this beautiful calm is coming to an end. The day after tomorrow I leave with Young and Pei for Canton and Kwangsi, with the ambition of putting a little order into the Quaternary and Tertiary of that region (in five weeks!). There must be traces of human life in the country, but so far nothing seems to have been understood about the formations that contain them. We expect to be back by mid-February. Breuil arrives the first of March, Weidenreich the fourth of April. At the end of April I expect to go to France (I'll go back with Breuil, no doubt). In September I'll probably meet de Terra in northern India to work on the Pliocene and Pleistocene of the Siwaliks and the Salt Range. After that I'll have to get back to Peking right away, since the Cenozoic Laboratory still can't function by itself! It's a rather hectic existence, but since I love Life, I don't mind feeling a bit dominated and pushed by it. Still, I admit I regret leaving my life in Peking even for a few months.

Inside, too, things are moving along. I am taking the liberty of sending you in the same mail a copy of my latest essay, "Why I Believe." It seems to me that these pages are clear and that I have almost succeeded in expressing my present position. . . . I am now ruminating another "paper" on "The Discovery of the Past." I find it more and more deceptive to spend my life in the scrutiny of dead things, and I want to make an analysis of what is truth and what illusion in the study of what *has been*. I need to set this down so that I can clarify my ideas and justify in my own eyes the use I have made of a part of my life. "Why I Believe" was originally intended for publication, but as it has expanded it has taken on characteristics that may cause it to be considered unpublishable. In that case there is always private circulation.

Peking, April 10, 1935

. . . I am gaining more confidence in the spirit that leads me. . . . Storms are still possible, of course, and also, which is perhaps worse, dead calms. Still, I believe that when one has succeeded in penetrating to the essential and omnipresent element of things, these squalls or depressions do not go beyond the surface of our being.

Here, in spite of a wind full of sand which raged only today, we are enjoying an admirable spring such as I have rarely seen in China. Everywhere there are masses of pink, white, yellow: lilacs, apple trees, apricot trees. I write these lines in my little room in Peitang before going to bed. Outside the wind seems to be dying. Breuil is in the next room. Tomorrow we will resume the daily routine: at eight o'clock to the Survey; in the afternoon, I go to P.U.M.C. Weidenreich has arrived. Naturally, he can't take the place of Black, but we are really congenial and I look forward to a fruitful collaboration.

My plans are unchanged, except that now I can take a trans-Siberian train sooner, arriving in Paris the fifteenth instead of the twentieth of May. So my next letter will probably be from Paris.

Paris (undated)

. . . Somewhere in the Scripture, which I am not in the habit of quoting, there is this saying, which has always seemed to be the true solution to life: "It is faith that conquers the World."

Nothing can resist the person who smiles at life — I don't mean the ironic and disillusioned smile of my grandfather, but the triumphant smile of the person who knows that he will survive, or that at least he will be saved by what seems to be destroying him.

. . . Right now I am still a little dazed by my reimmersion in a Western world that I had really completely forgotten in the course of the last two years. I hope that the dip will be salutary. But I now want to live only by faith, "shamelessly."

Have seen the lab, naturally. The first time, I even showed up on Wednesday at 2:45 sharp for a lecture by M. Boule (on the Artiodactyls!), just like the old days. You remember: going down the big wooden staircase together at 3:00 to the room where the aging and immortal group of listeners waits. It took me back to 1924. I fought back a slight feeling of melancholy. Yes, life is elsewhere, and ahead.

Paris (undated)

. . . I don't sail for Bombay until the sixth of September, at Marseilles . . . I won't try to give you all the news that would interest you now. Generally speaking, the political situation here seems to be reaching a critical point. The "Popular Front" and the *"Croix de Feu"* are confronting each other, each party trying to enlist the majority of the country. I am more inclined to believe in the first, especially if it succeeds in ousting certain undesirable secondary leaders such as Daladier. The *"Croix de Feu"* have no positive program and are beginning to worry. Impossible to foresee what the France of tomorrow will be. At least I have the impression that beneath the chaos a certain common desire to and hope of building something is emerging. That would be an advance over the lethargy from which we suffer.

As for myself, for the past two months I have been leading a life of excitement that would be absurd if it had to continue. I can't say no to all kinds of friends who want to take advantage of the too short time I am spending in France. And this program becomes a little exhausting in the end. The best result from my own point of view is, through conversation, seeing my thought clarified and even discovering new areas of development for my ideas. In short, I will have done rather little science, and in this regard I sometimes wonder if my enthusiasm is as great as ever. I owe the best of myself to geology, but everything it has taught me tends to turn me away from dead things.

Paris, September 13, 1935

. . . We must, to a certain extent, look for a stable port; but if Life keeps tearing us away, not letting us settle anywhere, this in itself may be a call and a benediction. The World is understood and will be saved, as I have already written to you, only by those who have no place to lay their heads. Personally, I ask God to let me die (metaphorically, at least) by the side of the road.

S.S. Cathay, September 18, 1935

. . . We arrive in Bombay the day after tomorrow. . . . The trip has gone very quickly, with no other disadvantage than a very hot Red Sea, the hottest I have ever seen (because the wind came off the stern at this time of year). And now we have come into a cooler wind, with the last swell of the monsoon.

. . . I decided to write a few pages on a point that has preoccupied me for a year, "The Discovery of the Past," a criticism of the interest that there can be in digging up dead things. I am going to send Max this short essay, which may be used as a conclusion to his father's anniversary book. Tell me what you think of it. I am afraid it may upset several of my friends (Breuil, Miss Garrod, etc.) or at least annoy them. But in it, as in my other papers, I wanted to try to clarify my own ideas. The fact is that I cannot feel the same passionate interest I once had in the study of what is now finished. The big job was to prove that the world progresses, and it is this fundamental truth that has just been established. From now on, is not all interest in the future? I felt as if I couldn't breathe, those last months in the galleries of Place Valhubert, and I couldn't believe I was the same person who had filled his lungs there for so long. What is the meaning of these new inclinations, and where can they lead me at this late date? I really don't know, but I am inclined to follow them to the end as long as they whet, rather than dull, my taste for action. Meanwhile, if all goes according to plan I shall soon find myself in the field facing big problems. Don't worry. I'll do my best to solve them even if I am less convinced of their importance. First, because this importance still exists for other people. And then, to the very end I must set the example of an effort to discover everything, to try everything; and outwardly there is no other line of research possible for me but geology and paleontology. Without geology I would have understood nothing of the World, and now that I think I have understood the World, I want to work more directly from the *living* thing.

I plan to spend a week in Bombay, and then meet de Terra in Rawalpindi before the first of October. All this is unknown material ahead of me.

S.S. Tjinegara, January 22, 1936
(en route to China)

. . . Right now I am coming to the end of a period that is one of the most interesting of my life. In India (with de Terra) and more recently in Java (with von Koenigswald, another charming young German), I had an orgy of prehistoric finds. Never had it been my luck to collect so much untouched Chellean or Acheulean in newer or more unexpected regions: in the Punjab, in the wasteland of the Salt Range; in Sind, in the delta of the Indus; on the verdant banks of the Narbada; and finally, the crowning touch, among the coconut palms of Java. All this, of course, part of a stratigraphy which in some ways alters the problem of Fossil Man in southern Asia. What a shame that Davy Black is no longer here to appraise and inspire these developments in the plan to which he gave his life! I am returning to Peking with a much clearer view of the work to come, and with reliable collaborators in India, Singapore, and the Dutch East Indies. At the same time, would you believe it, never has "The Discovery of the Past" seemed to me more obviously a secondary thing which decidedly no longer holds the profound interest of my life. . . .

So everything is going well. I come out of this new experience with the strengthened conviction that we can do nothing better in life than take and follow the threads it offers us, step by step, toward something that we do not see but which must be there ahead, as surely as the World exists.

Peking, October 30, 1936

. . . Externally and materially, my personal situation has changed very little. I am writing you from the same office at the Survey. The biggest difference is that the headquarters are now in some imposing buildings in Nanking, which has caused a decline in activity and working facilities here. From now on we are only the "North Branch" of the Survey, which does not prevent discoveries and publications from proceeding as fast as ever. Dr. Wong is now an important political figure (First Secretary to Chiang Kai-shek), which does not prevent him from keeping a close watch on the Survey, of which he is still the director. He is fine, still cheerful in spite of his responsibilities, but was very shaken up by the untimely death of V. K. Ting (in December 1935), which was a great sorrow to me and a grave loss for the Survey. I still have a vivid memory of my months in India, then in Java — months that revealed to me a new area of research (related to the one I am exploring there) and resulted in the formation of a deep personal bond with de Terra in India and von Koenigswald in Java. I am forming ambitious plans for the systematic exploration of southeastern Asia with these new allies.

Since I got back in February I have not moved except to

spend a month in the field on the peninsula of Shantung, a real Brittany. The rest of the time I have spent finishing up some notes on various "Novitates," and have begun a more substantial report on an enormous Pliocene fauna recently found in Shensi. So that's where I am. The future is a little uncertain. It's possible that at the end of March I may go to an important symposium on "Early Man" in Philadelphia. If the international geological conference at Moscow really takes place in July 1937, I would stop in Philadelphia on the way to Europe, where I would then spend May and June. But what state will Europe be in by then?

But, as you know, I am less and less absorbed or even interested in the mere "Discovery of the Past." It is the extensions of the Universe into the Human that fascinate me. Like everyone else, I am anxiously trying to follow and understand what is going on in the West. But what strikes me is the necessity to bring about a general reorganization of forces, not on a "popular front," but on a "Human Front," and according to the following program: faith in a Future, faith in Universalism, faith in the priority of the Personal. "Futurism, Universalism, Personalism" must replace or complete the old slogan that stirred our fathers, "Liberty, Equality, Fraternity." . . . Then, no doubt, the "technical" solution to the immense problem of the material organization of the Earth would become much simpler, for people would be in agreement on the road to follow, or at least on the position to adopt. I am trying to write a few pages on this subject, for publication, if possible. Naturally, I have written other things. In the spring, a rather long piece, "Outline for a Personal (i.e., personalistic) Universe," which Max has probably shown you: a good synthesis, but still clumsy, perhaps. At the urging of L. S., I printed (for private circulation) an English edition of the *Spirit of the Earth* and of *Why I Believe* (I thought I had a perfect right to do it, but I know I'll "catch it" when it becomes known). It loses in translation, of course, but at least it is one way of reaching people. And I am constantly observing how easily ideas of this kind spread. In spite of the interest of my scientific work in China, I would like to renew contact with Paris in order to enlarge my views and keep them up to date. Everything changes so quickly nowadays.

Paris, May 6, 1937

. . . Since my arrival in Paris I have been living a frantic existence in which I can't do what has to be done. . . . From the tenth to the thirteenth of May I am going to Lyon to see friends and also to pay my respects to a new superior. He is really a friend, but I'll have to defend myself a little since Rome is alarmed by the repercussions in the American press (you know American reporters!) of my purely scientific lecture in Philadelphia. Imagine, the headlines described me as "the Jesuit who says that Man is descended from the ape"! I hope everything will work itself out without unpleasant consequences, since on this point at least I am on very firm ground. Here, for the writing of the "Studies," I find myself in a sympathetic milieu that supports me openly.

As you know, I will be in France until the fifteenth of July. I am thinking of going to the Moscow conference and on the Siberian excursion, if I have enough money. It is quite expensive.

Murols, June 28, 1937
Puy de Dôme

. . . Your letter reached me here the day before yesterday in the peaceful and rather dull countryside where I have come to rest at the home of one of my brothers for a couple of weeks. I feel perfectly all right now, and I am sorry I gave up the Moscow conference and especially the Siberian excursion. But I had to make my decision (to go or not to go) just as I was having a new attack, and now it is too late to change my plans. For various reasons my present plan is to leave Paris toward mid-August via Siberia (alas!). On the whole, these few weeks in France have been full of disappointments for me. And yet in spite of these disappointments (or possibly because of them) I have rarely felt as fundamentally alive. It is as if having been cut off from most of my activities in the area of the "Study of the Past" had made me freer to look to and long for the future. Actually, the only reality that can interest me — or excite me, to be more precise — from now on is the "Human Energy" to be measured, discovered, and developed, and I am surprised to meet in so many different circles in America and Europe so many people who, in the last analysis, perceive precisely the same goal and the same problems. My major work, if I ever get to it, will be entitled simply "Man." After one or two more preliminary essays I will probably try to write it. These preoccupations, together with the totally new welcome that was shown me in France (even within my Order!) tend to make me suspect that my life is changing and that the time may be coming when I will be giving more and more time to something besides geology. And yet geology must continue to be my root in the real as well as my platform, and I will not be satisfied until I have made the connection between Yunnan and Burma which must, I know, complete the stratigraphic work I have been carrying on in China for the past fifteen years. There is a vague possibility of plans that, without forcing me to leave Peking, would permit me to extend my periodic trips to France. I don't know. My natural inclination would be to settle down in China. But might this not be inertia, and the line of least resistance? I know from experience the fascination exerted by the Far East. But I continue to believe that ultimately the real battle is being fought in America and Europe, and that China will follow our lead. This leads me to explain my position on the idea that "in these days, only action counts." I have been thinking about this for a long time. (In Philadelphia I saw my friend de Terra troubled by this idea to the point of anxiety.) But when it comes to trying to decide how to carry out my aspirations, truthfully I see no other course (at least for the moment) than to continue as intensively as possible to hasten a Christian renaissance (revolution?). . . . I am speaking very seriously, with my full freedom of thought as it has formed for the past twenty-five years. You see, what now dominates my vision of Human Energy is that its totalitarianism (without which one understands *nothing*) must culminate in a maximum of *personal* consciousness which in turn is incomprehensible without the equivalent of a personal Divinity in which the personal elements of the Universe attain their maximum personality while losing what is separatist in their individuality through union. The World cannot endure, advance, or realize itself without the action of a power that is a species of love. This is why, much as I sympathize with the "totalitarian" faith of popular fronts, I am forced to acknowledge that their *impersonal* forms of ideal ("Humanity," "Society," *a fortiori* the "Race" or "Empire" of fascist doctrines!), without soul or "face," are going to nip the Evolution that they want to promote and save in the bud. This is why, just as I rebel against all desperate religious representations and attitudes that are proving powerless to totalize the World, so I am convinced that to show men (in a really universalist, human, and triumphant form) the love of a Universal-Personal (imparted, this is the blunt fact, only by the Christian phylum) is the most urgent and effective work to be accomplished. To advance this work, I admit, there might in fact be a necessary gesture, different from but comparable to those of Christ or Saint Francis. It is this which I await but which I do not yet see, but to which, I promise you, I will give myself as to the betrothed I have dreamed of all my life as soon as it appears to me.

. . . I have never known how to write anything but theses and dissertations. The highest pleasure must be to pour one's soul into a living creation: a novel, music, or better still, into another living soul. . . .

Not much news to give you. I am sure that Wong must have watched the military demonstrations in Berlin, so like the ritual of the Coronation, with an inexpressible inner smile: "It's curious," he told me, "to have seen this once in one's life." His affection touched me: his first visit in Paris was to me, and he was in my room (I was in bed) two hours before he took the train to Germany. Yes, there are treasures in China.

Paris, July 20, 1937

You must have received my letter from Auvergne. Here I am back in Paris preparing for my departure under conditions I did not then foresee. The fact is that shortly after I got back I had a third bout of fever (a brief one), the real third, in fact; and although they do not have absolutely positive proof, the doctors lean more and more toward malaria. Under the circumstances the trans-Siberian appears to be contra-indicated (not to mention the fact that it may not be possible because of events in China), and I now expect to leave France August 6 from Marseilles on the *d'Artagnan*, in a comfortable first-class (private) cabin kindly provided by the Messageries. I think that nothing will do more to put me back on my feet than knowing I am on my way again. I am anxious to get back on the spot in China, to see how things are working out at the Survey and give a hand if necessary. I still hope that if the Japanese win new "advantages" in the northern provinces, the authority of Nanking will remain sufficiently nominal that the Survey will maintain its "North Branch" in Peking and not withdraw completely to its base in Nanking.

Actually, as I told you in my last letter, I have the impression that, for a number of reasons, something is changing in my mode of existence. On the advice and urging of several friends (Piveteau, Leroy, Jacob), I am taking the first steps to obtain a laboratory at the Hautes Etudes (with a chair at the I.P.H.), a job that would be purely nominal but that would have the advantage of giving me a social position in Paris without keeping me from devoting the necessary time to China. In a sense it would be much simpler and more comfortable for me to settle more and more permanently in the Far East, and this is what I anticipated only three months ago. But in the course of this trip to Europe I felt more strongly that the moment had perhaps come for me to leave Fossil Man for the Man of Tomorrow. The tricky part is to negotiate this transition without losing the scientific platform that I will continue to need in order to be heard.

At Sea, August 15, 1937

. . . The boat is very crowded, and with people who are not very interesting on the whole (should I make an exception for

Miss Pondichery?). Still, since Port Said the ice has been melting (and no wonder). . . . Actually, I am keeping to myself rather, and am on page 22 of my essay on Human Energy. And I am feeling fine. Apparently Paris did not cost me anything, this time at least.

. . . It is very, very hot and yesterday, to make matters worse, the sky was obscured by a fine dust from Arabia. Tomorrow afternoon, at last, we are hoping for the first breeze of the Indian Ocean.

It would be useless as yet to comment on the events in China which we are following on the radio. Will the *d'Artagnan* be able to dock at Shanghai, or will I have to get to Tientsin by coastal steamer from Hong Kong or Kobe? We shall see. In any case my place right now is there.

Peking, November 2, 1937

. . . You will no doubt have heard that I had an easy trip via Kobe back to Northern China, which is completely overrun. The first few weeks I was lulled by the illusion that somehow or other we would manage to maintain the status quo at the Cenozoic Laboratory. But for the past few days things have been deteriorating, largely because of a sentimental and unfortunate policy of Nanking's which consists in clearing out wherever the influence of the opposing party takes hold. All my colleagues have gradually withdrawn to the South and for the time being I remain virtually alone to save what is left. Already the leaders of the opposing party are beginning to circle around the prize. We are trying to protect a center at the P.U.M.C., but Nanking is giving us very little help, and I am afraid we may see the excavations of Choukoutien fall into other hands. How long can I stay in the North without giving my friends the impression that I am deserting them? Meanwhile, I see my chances of joining de Terra in Burma, where he expects me in December, disappear. I must make my decision in the next two weeks. How can I leave here without the last remnants of the organization collapsing? It is a great disappointment for me to have to give up this little expedition which I helped to launch.

. . . I now live in the north of Peitang in a house of my Order that was just established to teach Chinese to new members. It's too far away, and this costs me some freedoms, but the situation also has some advantages, particularly the feeling of being among my own (up to a certain point!). I continue to think and write. And I am making preparations for a book on Man in which I would gather all the ideas that are dear to me.

P.U.M.C., Peking, February 9, 1940

. . . About myself I have very little to tell you that you do not already know. The situation is the same, and so is my routine. Every day I cover the ground that we have been over together: the Western Survey with its little office, the P.U.M.C., with the same chair Black used, and the Peking Hotel. You would easily recognize all this, in spite of an amount of traffic that is beginning to look like Mukden, the increasing rarity of "foreigners," and the painful atmosphere of a fine thing coming to an end (at least right now) at the hands of something less human and less fine. The same roofs under the blue sky. The same street cries (especially that of the man selling fragrant potatoes). Is it I, after all, who am in danger of getting in a rut?

The fact is, as you know, that at the moment I can hardly do anything besides what I am doing, and I still manage, I think, to go forward. Above all, there is the Cenozoic Laboratory, reduced to its simplest form, but surviving, I hope, like a seed. Will we be able to resume work at Choukoutien this year? We will have to if New York is to continue to support us, and I have some hope that we will. Meanwhile, I am publishing ten times more here than I could in France. And I am even making preparations for a basic work on the geology of China that I could not possibly make at any other time or in any other place. I had hoped to get away to Yunnan this winter. I have just given up the idea for good because of the situation at the Laboratory. Another thing that occupies me and keeps me here is the probable transfer to Peking itself, in an excellent location, of the Licent Institute transformed into an Institute for special research. I am not directly involved in the plan, which leaves me free. But I can't avoid a certain supervision of the metamorphosis. And finally, as you also know, my best thinking goes every day to the writing of "The Phenomenon of Man."

Deep down, I cannot help knowing that my physical stamina is no longer quite what it used to be. Since my return here I am too often nervously depressed. A phase, no doubt, and one that will pass. The main thing is that I can work. On the whole, naturally enough, I feel that the time has come for me to assemble and relate my best insights into the world of the heart and the spirit. Without feeling any less close to the World, I feel closer to "God." And without seeing any less clearly its rigidities and limitations, I realize that I am more wholeheartedly a member of the Christian movement, "the phylum of the personal and of what must become the true charity." In short, many things in me are at last becoming simplified and clarified. I want so much to "finish well" (whatever the desirable length of the end), to finish proving the value of the ideas I have defended!

Peking, August 5, 1941

. . . Externally and materially, my existence has been infinitely ordinary for the past two years. Arriving in Peking just a week before the war, I haven't left it since, so that I have no personal experience of the upheavals the West has undergone (just the opposite of what happened to me in 1914). I could have gone back to France before the *débâcle*. I'll tell you later why I did not. In fact, I found an important intrinsic reason for staying here in the necessity of keeping the Cenozoic Lab alive, and for the past year, of nursing along a second baby, I mean the "Institute of Geobiology" newly established in Peking. This Institute (born of the transfer and transformation of the Licent Museum of Tientsin) could become something new and interesting if I had two more men and some money with which to build real laboratories. Currently, with the help of an excellent friend (P. Leroy, a pupil of Cuénot and a zoologist) I am spending my time getting out a series of notes and reports in which I am putting the best of what I have learned or found in China for the past twenty years. The sort of work that is done at the end of one's career and that I was not expecting to start for several more years, but which the impossibility of going into the field obliges me to do now. I'll feel freer afterwards.

In a few months Peking has almost completely emptied of the international population that accounted for its liveliness and charm. Until a new order, I'll still have the R.'s. He is still just as nice and caustic, but basically very discouraged by the rise of an anti-Semitism whose odious imbecility his case alone would be sufficient to establish. It's work that saves me — as long as it lasts. Outside of the scientific work I have written quite a few things, notably a real book, *The Phenomenon of Man,* which has been under consideration in Rome (!) for the past three months, and some pamphlets (one of which I sent you a week ago). These Notes on Progress, if you receive them, will show you that my thoughts about the future continue to take the same direction. I am currently working on a new and more up-to-date statement which will be called "The Atomism of the Spirit."

Getting back to the events of the day, I would like to know what you think, you who have lived in the very heart of the storm and who saw it coming for a long time. A profound source of personal irritation is my inability to take sides in the conflict. You have often told me and you would probably tell me again, "one must choose." But on the contrary, I do not see what to choose between, because the conflict seems badly stated theoretically (not to mention that at this time the two sides include the most incongruous elements). Fundamentally, the only thing I believe in, the only thing I have chosen, is that one must believe in a Future of the Earth which will coincide with a "totalization" of Humanity. My "enemies" are those who deny Progress. And this, by the way, is why since September 1939 I have not cared for this war which, from the French point of view, was merely a defense of egoism and the status quo. The constructive idealism, however distorted, was "on the other side." For the last year, fortunately, things have been changing, and the democracies are beginning to understand that freedom is a thing that is won by means of organized effort. But the separation of the elements is far from complete. In the present conflict I see above all the unlawful clash of two complementary human ideals — the clash being caused by the baneful influence on both sides of those who, under cover of noble words, are only interested in their own immediate gain. No one will ever dissuade me from thinking that the real divide, the real human conflict of today, is not between democrats, fascists, communists, and Christians, but between those who do and do not believe that there is a Humanity to be constructed over and above man (to save and complete Man, to be precise). It is a struggle between Stability and Movement. If only this essence of the conflict could appear for what it is, then would we not have the courage to fight and the willingness to give our lives! And how the shape of the front would be transformed!

In the meantime, it is clear that we are surrounded by absurdity, and I have no taste for a pan-European serfdom that would lead us straight to the anthill (which it is biologically necessary to avoid). It seems that in the shadow of Vichy a sincere effort at reconstruction is under way which is not simply a reaction (that would be the end of everything!). Granting this, it seems evident from a distance that "honor is lost" on that side. And I have no confidence in reforms, however timely, that are built upon a foundation of cowardice. I think I cried a year ago when I read the famous slogan, "Work, family, country!" It is not with prudence that you make people move, but with a little passion. Where are our fathers of '89! Actually I feel as if for the moment I no longer have a country. But there is still the Earth.

Paris, October 16, 1947

. . . Thank you for making the pilgrimage to the Museum of Natural History for me. I'm glad you saw my friends; what you tell me helps me to clarify my plans for the future. I am thinking of writing to Weidenreich to ask him (just in case) for a letter of invitation that will enable me to obtain a visa of entry into America, if necessary. Incidentally, four days ago I ran into Henry Field and Wendell Philips. The latter formally requested me to join the Expedition. I had to tell him that unfortunately there could be no question of anything before next June or July; a matter of health. We shall see. Meanwhile I continue to do well and before the end of the month I am going to see the doctors again to discuss an unrestricted program that is to begin the first of December. In the meantime the days pass quickly. First, because my nights are long, and next, because I have started seeing quite a few people again. . . . In Rome they are applying the new measures even more strictly than my friends here had expected. They did not want me to publish, in *Les Etudes,* two carefully edited pages on Lecomte de Nouy, a personal friend! There is only one possible explanation: the General felt obliged (?) to make a formal commitment to silence me for the time being under pain of public condemnation. On the other hand, the ideas I believe in continue to make their way better than ever and the friends who are in the best position to know urge me to keep going with the means I have left just as straight ahead as before, advice that I have no difficulty in following, especially since circumstances seem to guide me comically (that is, providentially) and keep forcing me to take another step forward. So life remains completely interesting, even exciting, and I am happy, even in my uncertainty about what will happen tomorrow. I feel as if I have never seen so clearly or so passionately the vision of the future that I will have spent my life trying to apprehend, express, and propagate.

Yesterday, a very nice lunch with Max and Simone at Mlle. M.'s. Once again one had a chance to observe that convents are the refuge of good cooks and good cooking! A week before I had lunch with B. I liked him, and we promised to see each other again. Difficult to get a good look and come to an accurate conclusion at a lunch for five; but it was an interesting meeting. My impression is only that, with his strictly evangelical (as it were) ideal, B. is still much more attracted to an ideal of human *justice* than an ideal of human *progress*. And not for the world would I want to disturb a vision to which he has found the courage to devote himself as he does. But if the occasion arises I will try to give him a glimpse of something more. As I have been repeating constantly for the past year, the great event of modern times is the discovery that for Man, imprisoned within himself, there is a way out *ahead* (by self-development of something beyond Man), whereas previously the only way out we saw was *above* (by escape into God). It is the dawn of this "faith in Man" that appears about to eclipse the traditional faith in God. Under these conditions, my conviction is that if "ahead" (carried to the limit) cannot be understood without "above," conversely "above" is even less understandable without "ahead," which means that the Christian faith can recover and survive only by incorporating faith in human progress. And it is also my conviction that if this synthesis between faith in God and faith in Man were put into effect we would again see (and in much more universal and intense form) what has happened a few times in history (for example with Buddhism, Christianity, and Marxism); I mean the spreading like wildfire of a new state of mind. Is it not this climate and this new atmosphere that are necessary if our incredible technological resources are to succeed in producing their natural result of human unification?

I wonder if from America you feel you have a clearer view of the political, economic, and psychological condition of the World. Here people are still living as if they had fallen from the seventh floor, that is, as if it is inevitable that a radical transformation occur at any moment. But where, and of *what kind?* And there are still people who do not see that Humanity is the collective subject of a real evolution!

Listen to me holding forth the way I used to do. You see how true it is that nothing has changed!

New York, March 7, 1948

. . . I have barely started to look around in this great New York, where I have not yet seen half the people I have to see.

Actually, I don't really know yet what might eventually come of these various contacts. The most interesting result would certainly be to be able to prepare myself (since work in the field seems contra-indicated) to develop an anthropology worthy of the name, I mean a science of "Humanization" (rather than merely a description of the psychological and social particularities of Man). But I still don't see exactly how to arrange this. Not to mention the political clouds ahead. . . . I make fairly regular appearances at the Museum of Natural History. But I now have a kind of nausea of fossils. Explain that for me!

New York, April 16, 1948

I just received your letter. . . . My mind is still in a state of confusion. All I can find to say from the whole edifice of my experience, my reason, and my deepest convictions, is this: "Whatever happens, even in this apparent disaster, hold fast and do not lose confidence (however ironic it may seem) in the value, the interest, and even the fundamental and ultimate goodness of the World." For some time I have often had to think about this: In a Universe in which we find that we have awakened one day, without asking to or understanding why, and in a Universe which, however, really seems to be going somewhere, engendering something, after we have done our best to stay afloat and our strength fails, the great infallible and fundamental gesture is to abandon ourselves confidently (I think that with the whole Christian experience we must say, *lovingly*) to the current that bears us along. In this atmosphere of blind surrender, the absurd and the unjust are transformed and take on a meaning. This is the prayer of prayers. This is the first defense, the first response. In itself, it is a magnificent human function to resist despair by faith in Existence. After this you will perhaps understand that, in the formidable human conflict into which we are entering, you can immerse yourself as in a better and newer life. . . . Perhaps you do not belong to yourself. Have you thought of that?

Do not *brace* yourself against suffering. Try to close your eyes and surrender yourself, as if to a great loving energy. This attitude is neither weak nor absurd, it is the only one that cannot lead us astray — unless life itself is inherently a contradictory and stupid thing, which its very existence belies. It is still too soon, no doubt, for you to recover: try to "sleep," with that *active* sleep of confidence which is that of the seed in the fields in winter. . . . As I've said before, this is the true and great prayer of moments of great sickness.

May 13, 1948

I find your letter on my return from Boston, where I went to spend two days at Harvard at the home of my friend Movius. I am afraid you have too high an idea of me. Sometimes I feel terribly weak and helpless, especially these days. But what reassures me a little (for my friends and for myself) is that, as the great Saint Paul said again and again, what force and ardor I do have are not me, but deeper than me, and are the more active the more personally vulnerable and fragile I feel. I suspect that it is precisely from this profound source that little by little you will see the light reappear. . . . This is why the best thing I can find to tell you is always the same: trust blindly and wait patiently, for all things take *time;* indeed, this is the very reason for the existence of Time in the World. Trust and patience: borne on these two wings, you have a chance of seeing the face of a God appear within you. Also, do not hesitate to look for and recognize around you some influence of P. This is my sincere and rational conviction. A Universe that did not collect the individual, incommunicable elements of personality in the course of its progress toward Personalization — such a Universe, in the end, would collect nothing and culminate in nothing. The old idea of the "immortality" of souls (like that of the super-Personality of the divine source) appears once again as more necessary and better founded than ever from our modern perspective.

. . . How weak and vulnerable I feel at this moment! But as I was saying in my last letter, is it not one of the principles dearest to Christianity that God is all the more likely to act through us, the more aware we are of our helplessness? . . . Now that the veil of my person is beginning to wear thin (because I feel so vulnerable), I have confidence that God will take over for me somehow. . . .

Is not the world tending to become one so quickly these days that certain differences between countries are disappearing? Really, sometimes I no longer see much difference between being in Paris and being in New York. The main thing is to live in the direction in which everything converges (and consequently in which "God" arises): forward.

The meeting on Monday went well. I was in good form, and said what I wanted to say. The audience (ten people) was composed mainly of professors from Fordham. I got on very well with the President. This may have importance for the future, for he certainly has a great deal of influence in the Order around here. So everything would be fine if it weren't for this nervous weakness that paralyzes me in everything.

. . . What to tell you about myself? I am still in something of a nervous depression, but I am trying to think about it as little as possible. . . . I managed to write a short essay on the directions and conditions of the Future which I want to give to *Psyché* for an issue on The Destiny of Man; and I am now working on another piece (unpublishable) and on my general *Weltanschauung,* which may be of interest for private circulation. This keeps me busy. I must not have told you yet that the Collège de France is making overtures to me about filling a proposed chair in prehistory. I have written to Rome to find out whether or not they will let me do it this time. Actually, I would have barely two years to teach, but it would give me time to say certain things. I am still waiting for the answer (which is pretty normal — everything goes slowly in Rome). In the same letter to the authorities I spoke of the plan for lectures in America next spring.

Paris, August 13, 1948

. . . I beg of you, hold fast to "faith above all." Once again, in one of its outwardly simplest sayings (like "Love one another"), I mean in its reiterated recommendation to trust in the World as fundamentally and ultimately good (and even loving!). I am more and more convinced that the Gospel has touched upon one of the profoundest structural laws of the Universe. The Universe yields, it is plastic somehow, under the influence of faith; it comes to life and grows warm.

. . . Still nothing very definite here except, as you already know, that I am cordially invited to come and talk in Rome in October. These are obviously peace offers. But I have lived with opposition so long that this good will embarrasses me. The pretext of the visit is to settle the question of the publication of *The Phenomenon of Man*, and there have been hints that I will receive full permission for the Collège de France and America, and greater latitude in writing. I have no doubt about the sincerity of their sentiments, but I am somewhat dubious about the possibility of a real agreement. In fact, if I do go down, it will be primarily to take advantage of the opportunity to say to the head of the hierarchy himself exactly what I have not *on* my mind but *in* my mind. The fundamental question really at issue is whether or not official authority is willing to accept (and to integrate into the Christian faith) "faith" in a future (i.e., a superevolution) of Humanity on earth. . . .

Meanwhile, I am going to leave August 16 to visit my brother in Auvergne, where I plan to spend a month. Paris is almost empty right now while awaiting the invasion of the O.N.U. in September. Since my return to France I have written two things, one of which is a rather long essay entitled "How I See," divided into three parts, a "Physics" or "Phenomenology," a Metaphysics, and a Mystical theology. In it I have tried to present the totality of my *Weltanschauung* in its most recent formulation. It certainly isn't publishable (although perfectly orthodox, in my opinion), but it might be useful to "professionals" or selected intelligent people. Another semiclandestine publication, probably. I'll send you a copy when I have one. This work has distracted me, and I needed that. I still can't manage to completely shake off this form of anxiety (whose origin is purely physical, that has become quite clear) which began in New York. I have told you that it is something I have had before. I must be patient. I have a good doctor friend (now on vacation, naturally). . . .

You heard about the death of Weidenreich, which grieved me very much. I still don't know any of the details. Neither do I know who will be entrusted with finishing the almost complete report on Java Man.

Paris, December 3, 1948

. . . In our souls, as on the sea, storms subside gradually. Hold your course toward confidence, not exactly in the World, but in the "Heart" of the World, that is, in the center of convergence toward which I am convinced that we fall, by an attraction more irresistible and just as universal as that imposed on the heavenly bodies by the Einsteinian curve. This is almost all that I live by myself these days.

. . . You already know the result, so far negative, of my visit to Rome. On the whole I have a good memory of the place (the country, the golden light, a very sympathetic welcome from the authorities of my Order, etc.). But I was forced to observe that if on the one hand the main axis of the World's Faith in a superpersonal and loving God really passes through Saint Peter's, on the other hand the Vatican and all around it is characterized by a radical lack of human faith and fervor. And this experience, which I was expecting without really being prepared for, has had the advantage of confirming me more definitely than ever (if possible) in my resolution to devote what time and energy I have left to developing and disseminating the rationally and biologically established conviction that Man is not complete and that under the appearances of the social phenomenon it is still the World that is unfolding in and around us in order to give off more conscious light and heat. On this point henceforth nothing could make me retreat or weaken my position. The only question is the purely technical and strategic one of how to behave most effectively in the World. To break with my Order could only hurt my influence, and in fact I have no pretext for doing so except minor harassments which are obviously inflicted on me reluctantly (because in Rome they are forced to consider the "impression" everything makes on other Romans). The Collège de France has fallen through. But there is still a ghost of a chance for the book, and a little better than that for America. We shall see. In any case, remember that I am by no means crestfallen, but rather heartened by the turn things are taking. I only wish I felt more robust physically. I have not yet recovered my inner "euphoria," which may not be essential, after all. And then I ought to find a "primary occupation" to replace work in the field. As far as the laboratory goes, it's hard to see what I could do that would interest me, at the point I've reached. The study of the "human social phenomenon" is just about the only thing I really care about. But it is hard to see how I might tackle that subject at my age without remaining in generalities. I count on events to guide me and show a solution. As a last resort I can concentrate on a new "book" dealing with the structure and progress of Humanity (a sketch for a treatise on Anthropogenesis).

. . . Max and Simone must be leaving Paris as I write. I found them unchanged, that is, just as affectionate, luminous, and strangely healthy in spite of their fatigue or thinness (Max). . . . Breuil recently sent me some details on his summer campaign (or winter campaign, if you prefer) in the West: a lot of painted rocks. He plans to come back in the spring. I wonder if the political defeat of Smuts and the new spirit now prevailing in Africa won't hinder him a little.

. . . Personally speaking, I am more and more struck by the tragic condition of a Humanity that is sufficiently reflective to raise the problem of the Future and the beyond but not yet sufficiently enlightened to be able to answer it. Pascal and many others have already felt this, but they probably did not see as clearly as we do how closely this situation is linked with the successive and inevitable phases of the appearance of consciousness in the World. This is a phase of half-light, in which one must know how to wait and trust.

For I don't see anything else to say to you (at least to begin with), or to myself for that matter. What can really allay our anxieties about the meaning of the World and of Life is total confidence, not blind confidence, but a confidence based on the fact that the Universe exists, that in spite of everything it succeeded in producing a thinking being, and that consequently our most intelligent and safest course is to continue in the same direction and according to our new stature the movement that produced us. Therefore, "no retreat": no capitulation. You talk about convents. I know that in certain cases they can serve as sanitoriums. But this is neither their true origin nor their true function. Normally the monk and the nun are persons who have decided that life has a precise meaning, even to the point of often underestimating the role that Mother Matter (*Materia Matrix*) must inherently play in the genesis of Spirit.

Confidence then, to begin with, in a World that presents itself to us as a process of genesis. And as an inevitable consequence, in one form or another, the sense of a Presence. This is the kernel, the germ to which you must cling patiently, persistently. This is what must gradually take form in your reason and your heart. This is how the Christian Christ, the most adaptive and progressive form of the Divine, grew in the womb of human consciousness. Above all, look for and rekindle in yourself the fundamental spark of faith in the World: this is how the fire bursts forth. And don't forget, of course, that faith is nourished and fortified by action.

I am in the midst of writing my fifth and final lecture, "The Socialization of Repression."

. . . These few lines to wish you *bon voyage* and a speedy return, although I hope that we will see each other in America before that. May these last days in Paris finish giving you the vitality you recovered in June! I hope that now, with the help of Brittany, the evil spell is broken and you are turned toward the Future. This is the order I give myself, this "no retreat."

Actually, for the moment I am not too sure where I am going. I have a clear vision and I feel the same great passion for what I call "my gospel." But I have no clear picture of the forms of a possible action, except that I would need some event to get me moving. While waiting for the thing to happen I console myself by thinking that it may be the day-to-day germinal activity that is most effective, if the force of the virus is there. So it is "the virus" that I am working on. For lack of anything better, I shall try to give some "seminars" at the I.P.H. this fall and winter.

. . . In a scattered way I have been rather busy of late, except that a recurrence of that nervous anxiety which is more or less my birthright (and which returns a little with age) has slowed down my activity a little. But everything passes except the fundamental taste for life, which is the main thing, or, as the Gospel says, "the unique necessity."

More and more, what counts for me is the elaboration and diffusion of a certain sense or vision of the Universe, Man, and God which it will have been my life's work to define, comprehend, and express. I can do without field work if it is beyond me and official positions if they are forbidden me, as long as I am able to see and help people to see what seems to be the next step in the advance of things. For the moment what fascinates me still, and more than ever, is the study of what I now call the "ultra-human" (as in "ultra-violet"). By this I mean the probable forward curve of a "humanization" whose mechanism appears to me more and more clearly to be biologically defined. I have given several private talks about this lately. And the manuscript of a book on the subject is even now on its way to Rome to try its luck once more. This new manuscript is a shorter and better focused version of the long *Phenomenon of Man* which is still held up by censorship (and of which, by the way, I made this fall a limited mimeographed edition of two hundred copies not for circulation, exactly, but for "preservation"). I suppose that its chances of success (permission to publish) are fifty-fifty.

To occupy myself in a more Platonic manner, I am contemplating another essay (not for publication) in which I would try to describe the actual psychological process by which, ever since I have known myself (seven or eight years), a certain obscure attraction for the Earth and Matter has, in conjunction with my religious training, gradually changed into a well-defined and all-consuming love for some "Universal Center" whose type and reality are provided for me by the Christian God. There is a whole evolution here that is perfectly recognizable and whose analysis might be of general interest. But to find my place and follow myself through these subtly overlapping phases would take me time. No matter, the work is interesting.

Outside of this underlying work, which proceeds pretty constantly in my daily encounters and in chance conversations, my life goes on in a rather ordinary way, interspersed with interesting meetings, as always in Paris. No plans on the horizon. As I have told you, my interest is concentrated more and more within. But who knows whether external events will not come along and call everything into doubt? Not that I believe in war; but one way or another the present tension must be resolved. This is why it is so important that Man rediscover, in a new form, the "sense of Species."

Paris, March 31, 1950

. . . These few lines to wish you a sunny Easter (without and especially within). . . . Here, nothing sensational. The winter has gone smoothly for me. A series of lectures at the Sorbonne (technical ones on the Pleistocene and prehistory of the Far East), and two or three longer speeches (the last of these at the *Cité Universitaire* was rather amusing; it was on "the phases of a living planet"). I think I'll write this last one up. Incidentally, my second book, which I sent to Rome for consideration at the beginning of February, seems to have some chance of getting by (?). The council of examiners (unintelligent on the whole) is only asking for a series of easy minor alterations (mostly a question of dotting the i's). I am constantly sending the text back to Rome. If only they don't take it into their heads down there to submit it to a "supercensorship"! For then it would never get published. Meanwhile, I observe with satisfaction that the ideas are circulating and spreading a little like fire, and that makes up for everything. We *all* need a new face of God to worship, and I am more and more convinced that this face can appear to us only through and beyond an "ultra-human." It is still the study of this "ultra-human" that absorbs the best part of my time. Several interesting meetings recently: for example, lunch in Place Beauvau with the head of the Criminal Investigation Department! (a graduate of the Ecole Normale Supérieure who is very much concerned with human problems). It reminded me in another field of that time in '48, when I had to give a speech on original sin at the Ecole Supérieure de la Guerre.

. . . Editions du Seuil has just accepted a book on (or more precisely by) my younger sister, the invalid, who died in '36: primarily things she wrote herself. I wrote a very short preface for it, but one that suggests quite a few things. I think the book will make its way and leave a trace.

Paris, May 29, 1950

. . . By a series of unforeseen circumstances, I have just been elected to the Institut (Académie des Sciences). What with the decoration, I'm getting to be a regular "grand old man." What would dear old Boule say if he were still here — what scorn! Actually, the chief advantage I anticipate from the business is that after this Rome will think twice before "banning" me. On the other hand, they may think more than twice before letting me publish. So the advantages of the operation are still uncertain. The Father General is still thinking it over (for the past month!) to decide whether my last book (the "five lectures" on Man) can appear or not. . . .

R. very shaken by the death of her brother. . . . [She] is supersensitive to the pain of the world; the suffering of others affects her almost as much as her own. This is an immense (although painful) force, provided it is not tinged with pessimism. The future belongs to a faith (or religion) that will place Hope above Pity (without diminishing the latter, quite the contrary!): this is what I think.

Paris, July 25, 1950

. . . Thank you for your good letter of the twentieth. I wrote to Mme. de la B. immediately, telling her that I would go to see her as soon as she let me know of her return to Paris. Another person who is looking for the face of a God great enough to be adored. . . .

I understand the poignant quality of your consciousness or perception of the World. But for me, as you know, this poignant quality, which is only increasing, always tends to take the form of a formidable and irrepressible metamorphosis of "matter" into "spirit," the former being the stable form of the transformation. In other words, the vague impressions of my youth are now invading everything in the form of participation in some immense energy which is a curious blend of Hindu "totality," Western "technology," and Christian "personalism."

More and more I see growing in me the evidence and the human consequences of the great thing that is happening right now. Not "God who is dying," as Nietzsche said, but "God who is changing," so that, as I am in the habit of saying, the Upward movement is now reinforced by a Forward movement never before considered by the religions.

. . . Take advantage of your sea and your rocks. And try to believe in the World's future more than in its end.

. . . These few lines to send you my best thoughts . . . at the time of your redeparture for America. Another visit in which we have seen too little of each other. More and more I find that one of the most painful aspects of life is that it keeps us from following so many things to the end. No doubt (according to my philosophy) we are still too far from the point of convergence toward which I am "scientifically" convinced that the Universe is inevitably rushing, psychologically and biologically speaking. I hope that you will have a good school year, with the rise of some light up ahead to guide your way!

About myself I have nothing to tell you that you don't already know. Scientifically speaking, the "dream" of South Africa is the only interesting work I can still do. I am being urged to do it from several sides and I would like to prove that I am still active, not just at my desk, but in the field. Not to mention that a temporary disappearance from Paris would allow things to cool off in Rome. We shall see.

In other respects, you also know that for some time now the principal interest of my life is no longer Fossil Man, but the Man of tomorrow; or, more exactly, "the God of tomorrow," since I am more and more convinced that the great event of our time is a kind of change in the face of God in which the pure "God of above" of yesterday is being combined with a kind of "God of ahead" (in extension of the Human). I seriously believe that all this is completely in the mainstream of the Christian "phylum," and I know that hundreds of people around me feel it (hence the success of the books I've circulated privately).

. . . Naturally I'll keep you informed in the months to come of developments in all these plans and ideas. It is a little like building a house on the side of a volcano. But I often tell myself that if, by chance, an eruption did occur, certain molds would be broken and what I desire would happen. Still, I cannot believe in a world war, and I hope with all my heart that it will be avoided. In which case it would be a serious proof that something in the world has already profoundly changed.

. . . About two weeks ago I sent you *The Heart of the Matter.* I hope you received it and that you recognized me in it.

Actually, as time goes by, I have a curious impression of liberation and simplification: interest in old evidence, and an intensification of this evidence along lines that are so fresh that I feel as if I were discovering a World that is radically enlarged and transformed. For the moment one realizes that the Universe flows (and always has flowed) in the direction of "ever greater order and consciousness," a whole group of values is introduced into things which, without making one blind or insensitive to Disorder or Evil, give everything an extraordinary savor, warmth, and limpidity: a superior and synthetic form of "mysticism" in which the strengths and seductions of Oriental "pantheism" and Christian personalism converge and culminate! Impossible for me not to pursue this vision in a series of essays that keeps getting longer without my yet having managed to grasp exactly and fully what I feel: fortunate situation!

Finally, and in spite of a few alarms (notably, some imprudent articles written by friends), 1950 has ended for me without major difficulties. It even looks as if Rome has almost forgotten me, partly, perhaps, because I've talked up my plan to go and study Australopithecus. Even so, Paris has become a little hot for me. It is time I disappeared for a while, if possible, or else (Heaven forbid!) that some big political upheaval diverted attention elsewhere.

Like everyone else, I feel the shadow and weight of the threats of war. But at the same time I cannot help feeling *with greater intensity than ever,* the reciprocal warmth and intimacy of all peoples. Ultimately, I am convinced, it is always a little more "planetary unity" that is being purchased at the expense of these frightful battles. Another threshold to cross. As far as the conflict in the Far East goes, I do not agree with those who already see a rising supremacy of Asia over Europe and America. In my opinion the new wars (of the modern type) are no longer for the possession, but for the leadership of the Earth. Now, in the present business, though Asia presents a supremacy of *mass,* it has no human "ideology" to offer. So it will be a long time before Asia will dominate the world. On the other hand, it is urgent for the West to develop its *Weltanschauung,* or simply its *Faith.* And it is certainly remarkable that people as positivist and "agnostic" as Julian Huxley feel and proclaim the biological necessity for this. I have had a very interesting correspondence with him on this subject and even talked with him in Paris recently.

Socially, my life remains very much the same. I plan to give five lectures at the Sorbonne this month on "the phyletic structure of the human zoological group," a sort of "seminar" outside of the regular courses in paleontology.

Still no news of Fejos (Viking Fund). He is too reliable a friend for this silence to worry me. But I am beginning to need definite advance information. Meanwhile, reservations have been made on the Union Castle Company for the end of July.

Johannesburg, August 12, 1951

I feel very happy here, free again in this vast milieu. Of course, the exhilaration I once felt for exoticism and rocks is no longer the same. Here I am vividly aware of how the interest (the quick) of the World has passed from the background to the foreground of my life. No matter; it is salutary to lose oneself again for a moment in the bedrock of the continents, and in those old fissures where the process of humanization once occurred.

Marvelous weather. Sky invariably cloudless over fruit trees in full bloom, like February in Peking. But nearby the bare hills are covered with pink aloes. And for a hundred miles the white slag is piled like a row of ghosts: dust from the Rand quartzite, where they are digging over a mile into the earth in search of the auriferous conglomerate. An extraordinary expression of Life in all its degrees (even the human), springing from Matter!

. . . These lines to send you my deep sympathy, my prayers, and my wishes for a quick recovery. May the calm of your letter have been illuminated and warmed for you by that sense of Confidence and Surrender which we should all feel for the vast and powerful movement of the Universe which, at first approximation, is a "process" in the eyes of science, but which upon the *complete* study of Man reveals itself as necessarily belonging to the species of a Life and even of a Love. Not the "black pit," but the burning center, whatever it is.

May you and I grow in the Vision and the Presence of this Unique Necessity through all the successes and failures of our lives.

LETTERS II
1938-1950

Maison Chabanel, 1 Shih Hu Hutung,
5 Ville Intérieure, Peking 9, June 5, 1938

Since my last letter, things have been going smooth and just a bit monotonous for me. After the rush of the first days [after his return from Burma], I have come back to the normal routine: laboratory work morning and afternoon, social life between 5 and 7 P.M., and from time to time a small party (very little cocktails . . .). Peking is pretty much "deflated"; and yet there is still a nice circle of good friends, surviving in the midst of the Japanese atmosphere.

Scientifically, I am busy enough, with two paleontological memoirs. In addition I have just finished a "mixed paper" on Burma which I will send to H—— as soon as I know where to address it safely. Impossible to make excavations this year in Choukoutien, because the place lies just between the Japanese soldiers and the Chinese Reds. Should I not have the chance to work in the field this winter, I would find the time long and dull in the laboratory! And yet, my presence is rather useful there for keeping the Cenozoic Lab alive as long as the Sino-Nippon "incident" is not settled. I am still needed in China, and I feel that I need it still more. That does not make my position easier, on this *ground* also, so far as the balance is concerned between Peking and Paris. From Paris, I have just heard that I have been definitely elected to the Laboratoire des Hautes Etudes, and with a somewhat flattering and touching eagerness — three institutions wanting to shelter my *laboratoire* (of course I will join Boule at the Institut de Paléontologie Humaine). My plan is, as I have told you, to go to Europe in October, via America, and to stay in Paris up to next June; then I will come back to China, for several months — and so on. So many unexpected things may happen, in the meantime.

In the meantime, too, I am slowly but steadily preparing my essay on Man, which I will probably start writing this summer. I feel more and more attracted and absorbed by this part of my activity. And it seems that this last winter has brought me a new harvest of clarity and certitude: I have an impression to perceive more and more distinctly the few central points which, if better understood and conquered, would change the face of our fascinating world. I believe that the next winter in Paris will have a decisive influence on the final maturation and the possible spreading of whatever may be good in my "gospel." . . . Here, in my pious Pekinese house, I feel much more comfortable than in the fall, partly due to a new direction, partly because I make more and more interesting connections with several of the young people here. Something is growing, most evidently, in the spiritual atmosphere of the world — and something is dying, accordingly.

Physically, I feel perfectly all right. Another result of Burma. This year, the Pekinese weather is moist and gray. People accuse the war!

Peking, June 22, 1938

My American friends are really those who are impressing their stamp on the depth of my life, largely because they are so alive themselves. It is not so simple a matter to keep "young" and warm after fifty-five years. . . . You can and you must help me in preserving, and even in increasing, the particular faith which is the real fire of my life. Concerning the impression you had that it might be unpleasant to fall back the next year with the black "pongies," don't worry. Of course the Burma life was better. But, at the same time, the Paris atmosphere is so tense psychologically that the sense of the fight will obliterate for me many other feelings. To keep very strong *the fighting spirit:* this is the essential thing for being happy under any circumstances. As I told you, I am *not* specially attracted by the prospect of the next winter in France. But I see more and more clearly that I *have to go* through this experience. The letters of my friend B—— are full of the exciting news about the diffusion of the views which are the most precious part of my soul. I feel that a kind of last (or fore-last) touch will be given to my "gospel" by this fresh contact with the Occidental world.

Nothing interesting to tell you, since my last letter. The life goes on, along the same routine. The summer is rather rainy and moderately warm, so far — and the conventual atmosphere positively more bearable, as I told you, under the new influence. Besides one does not mind so much to cover long distances by rickshaw when the trees are richly green and the sky dark blue, above the yellow tiles of the imperial city. I am very busy with my two paleontological papers. But I hope to finish both of them at the middle of July. That would give me a long time before my departure from China for starting the redaction of "Man." The frame of this work is now approximately clear in my mind. I have also several interesting schemes of lectures for the next winter.

Socially, too, things are going well, gaily and smoothly. A few interesting tourists or newspapermen are visiting us these days — for instance a young R——, who has been traveling in Abyssinia and Spain during the wars. In spite of his traditionalist views he is an interesting man, not blind at all on the fascist weaknesses. I suppose that you are fretting, as myself, when you read the papers. Personally, I would forgive the ruthless ways of fascism if fascism did not shelter and foster antiprogressive forces and reaction. But maybe they will not do it much longer, even in Spain and in Italy.

Peking, August 3, 1938

I begin to realize that it is easier to burn than to keep the spark always more alive, more easy to start one's life than to end it nicely. In other words, I become aware of the fact that I have come to the difficult part of my existence.

Things are essentially the same as described in my last letter. Work goes on, rather monotonously, in half-empty laboratories; and social life is not yet entirely dead, in spite of too many friends on furlough, or at the seashore. We are in the midst of the worst of the hot rainy season. Something like Singapore, in the middle of the day. But the nights are cool. Rain, this year, was terrific. Walls, and even houses (they are built mostly with mud) have collapsed everywhere in the more primitive districts of the town, and consequently in my own "convent," where we lost a goat. Some days, I had to navigate the streets, the water reaching the middle of the wheels of my rickshaw. Now the sun is glorious, and the trees full of cicadas — but everything still pretty hot. I can work nevertheless. Two paleontological memoirs are in the press. And I have definitely started writing "Man," with interest, and even with pleasure. I proceed slowly (one or two pages the day). But the whole thing seems to develop easily and naturally . . . so far. And yet I am busy with the most difficult part: *La Prévie.* The further I advance, the clearer are the things in my mind. At such a rate, I may finish the manuscript by the end of 1938.

My plans otherwise are the same. I still think of leaving Peking in the middle of September. . . . As you know, I have to force myself a bit for leaving Peking. I foresee many clouds ahead. But I see very clearly too that life expects me there; and I must go. This year may be the decisive one. I wish only that I should feel myself closer to God.

15 Rue Monsieur, Paris VII,
November 12, 1938

Here, in Paris, I experienced a very warm welcome from my colleagues, and I am now fairly well settled in my monastery. A "nice" invitation to pay a visit to my superiors in Lyon (next week) seems to indicate that the high officials of my Order are slightly scared of my presence in France. But I hope to go on without major troubles. Officially, my situation in Paris is now well fixed and definite; and I have even the prospect of a small sum of money to support my work. So, everything seems O.K. materially.

Scientifically speaking, my next steps are not yet very decided. Yet, from a few casual conversations, I feel that there are great possibilities ahead, in the way of organizing and developing a new study of continental deposits. With the young B—— (son of a prominent Italian man, you saw him, probably), we are already planning a spring trip in Italy to the places pointed by H——. Luckily, I will not be asked for too many lectures. In the meantime, I will try to keep to my plan to stay home every morning. Maybe I will succeed in finishing *"L'Homme"* before summer. Mind is not so quiet here as in Peking; but more active, perhaps.

In any case, a large part of my activities will surely be absorbed by "parascientific" efforts. Along this line, I believe to see more and more clearly the aim: to develop *a new psychology and ethics of research* or, if you prefer, a new type of scientist, who would carry on his task with the consciousness of his function, which is to achieve the World as a faithful servant of Evolution. I am more and more convinced that this new spirit is essential to the future of Man. This future is obviously bound to be more and more under the spiritual and material control of research. But so far research is still egotistic, meaningless. Scientists have a narrow soul, a short sight, and generally an underdeveloped heart. They are dry and inhuman, and so often ugly. All that because they are burrowing without looking at any sky. I dream to open this sky, right in the line of their tunnels! And I have precisely met here, a week ago, a group of brilliant youths who are going the same way, instinctively. Something is going on, in Man — I am so sure of that. . . .

One thing I envy you: to be in New York.

Personally, I am now quite busy — thinking, and talking. People are swarming around me, searching and asking about a broad and idealistic representation of life — in the most various and unexpected corners of society. So many contacts give me a new life, and require a continuous improvement, in my "gospel." In fact, I find myself, more and more, in the paradoxical condition which has been mine since years. In France, the best part of my colleagues back me and support me. But, in Rome, I look more and more suspicious. In Lyon, I was confronted with a very strong letter of my "General," complaining of a new paper of mine which has leaked out (not a bad one, but not the type I would have selected for Roman criticism), and complaining also that I should disturb the minds of my younger colleagues of China (?). Naturally, that means new restrictions. Fortunately, my French superiors are most understanding, so that I have serious hopes to get through practically unhampered. I guess easily your first reaction: better for me to resist and break. But, this is precisely, I think, the thing *not* to do. I am a hundred times more active inside than outside. And, in addition, my own "philosophy" obliges me to stick to a religious movement which I regard as the true seed of the things to come. A "descent on the marketplace"? I don't see how to make it, at least just now. My feeling is that it would be unwise to force the things *as long as they keep growing.* And they are *growing* in France (I don't mean the external and political France, of course) in a stupendous way. My conviction is that, if really a break of some sort has to happen, the natural breaking point is not yet here. My plan is to finish my paper on Man in such a way that I may start the real fight on the question of its publication. In the meantime, I have just written a few pages on *La Mystique de la Science* for publication in the Jesuit Review edited here. If they are printed (as I hope) that would be the most polite indication to Rome that I am still alive. And maybe they will understand. At bottom, they do not dislike me: they are only bewildered and anxious to defend "tradition."

Rawalpindi, India—1934.

Facsimile of letter dated Tientsin, October 12, 1926.
Written in French.

Burma—1938.

Burma—1938.

Burma—1938.

Burma—1938.

roar ahead. —/ In the meantime, I try to read more clearly
in myself, and to focus better my views. — My leading
idea, just now, is that the true crisis of the world, today,
does not lie exactly in a conflict between Totalitarians
and Democrats, — but between mobilists and fixists. If
th. Democracies were not hampered by the heavy load of
fixism which hides, and /excuses itself, glorifies! among them under the unexpected
name of liberty, they would swallow in no time th. powers
of th. Axis, — or at least they would soon find a ground
for mutual achievement. A progressive Democrat is not
fundamentally different from a really progressive Totalitarian. — Consequently, th. main thing today, on th. field of
sound propaganda, is to make a campaign for the faith (a
passionate and rational faith) in a well-understood human
Progress. To my opinion, th. world of to-morrow will be
born out of th. "elected" group of those who (arising from
every direction, and class, and confession, in th. human world)

ℭ.

INSTITUT DE GÉO—BIOLOGIE

私立北京地質學生物學研究所

RUE LABROUSSE
LEG. QUARTER
PEKING

MUSÉE HOANG-HO-PAI-HO
RACE COURSE ROAD
TIENTSIN

Peking................ 194...

will decide that there is something big waiting for us
ahead, and give their life to reach it. People have to
decide for or against Progress, — now. And those who say
no have just to be stopped behind. And those who say
yes will soon discover that they speak th. same language and even worship th. same God. — These are th.
things I should like to tell, in N.York. — And these
are th. things which I am decided to fight for, as long as
I live, anyways. —

Facsimile of letter dated February 9, 1941.
Written in English.

Glacier Park, Wyoming—1952.

My precious mornings have been dangerously encroached, since a fortnight, by an increasing number of visitors: very suggestive and useful talks, in the course of which I had the feeling to advance deeper in the understanding of my own thoughts. I cannot regret such meetings, which are perhaps the best part of my work. And yet, when one has seen three people between 8 and 12 A.M., there is not much space left for private writing. . . .

I enjoy watching the results on you of your last experiences. Just trust Life: Life will bring you high, if only you are careful in selecting, in the maze of events, those influences or those paths which can bring you each time a little more upward. Life has to be discovered and built step by step: a great charm, if only one is convinced (by faith and experience) that the world is going somewhere.

Since my last letter, I went for a week to my native Auvergne, where I spent a week with my dear "holy" brother and his witty wife. A very cold weather in a cold old country place. But it was so pleasant to crowd around the fireplace, despite the fact that clods of snow, introduced by the wood shoes, did not melt in the staircase. My sister-in-law is very busy grouping the country girls in one of the professional Christian associations which are spreading so fast over France since a few years. It is really amazing to observe how quickly those previously shy and sullen girls turn into active, direct, and even enthusiastic young persons, as soon as they awake to the pride of their condition and to the esteem of "good earth."

And now I am again in the midst of the Parisian life. New contacts almost every day, amongst which, curiously enough, I have not the feeling to lose, but to find myself. Yet it would be excellent if, next year, I could have six or eight months isolated in China. I need such a period to assimilate and to write down what I see now; and, for some obscure reason, the Far East is the climate where I get the excitation to write. With Rome, tension (as far as I am concerned) seems to settle down: I am well supported by my French friends and colleagues. Yet I foresee that, if I am allowed (as most probable) to go back to China, I will have to locate my headquarters in Tientsin rather than in Peking (where I am frankly undesirable to the Canadian director of the new "monastery"), at least for a while.

Toulouse, February 26, 1939

Just now I am stranded in a passage room of the monastery (or rather a college) of my Order in the sunny, brick-built, strongly provincial town of Toulouse. I came here three days ago, and I am leaving tomorrow to go back to Paris. And in the meantime I will have delivered four lectures — one of them before the local Société de Philosophie. For the circumstance I am dressed in a long black gown: and in spite of your preferential taste for this kind of dress, I feel completely unnatural to myself. Anyhow, people are perfectly nice to me, and, thanks to my lantern slides, I have been quite a success. And nobody seems to have been scared, neither by my philosophical utterances, nor by the ape-like face of great-grandfather Sinanthropus.

Concerning my "gospel," I realize more clearly that my possibilities and tendencies are not exactly to start any definite social movement, but to help to create a kind of spiritual atmosphere in which the whole of each life should be enlightened, transformed, just as a precious stone by a ray of the proper light: suppose the feeling that the whole world is permeated by a creative love. This is, of course, essentially the Christian attitude, but made richer by a confluence with the best and subtle essence of what is hidden behind the various pantheisms. I will send you the paper you ask me. The last part of it will help you to understand what I mean. (The first part is unsatisfactory, because too schematic: a mere catalog.) Anyhow, my views become more definite, day by day, in the course of innumerable talks, which are always, more or less, concerned with the same subject. My lecture in Nancy (*La Mystique de la Science*), which approaches the question, will be published before the end of March. And I have two other short things under preparation. But I must as soon as possible come back to the main work: Man.

In Rome things are apparently much better for me. Rather providentially, a colleague of mine in Tientsin went to Rome a month ago. And, as a consequence of several hours of serious talks with the "big ones" there, atmosphere seems to be much improved in my favor. People are not so bad there: but they do *not* know what is happening really outside of their precincts. So, it seems that, just now, the sea is almost open ahead. I will take, and try not to waste, my chance.

Besides, nothing much new: writing, talking, lecturing. Very little left to scientific research: but I do not mind. I plan to spend a few days in London — Cambridge at the end of March. So far as I can see, I would leave Paris for New York at the end of June. I do not think that anyone will prevent me now to go back to China. A few days ago, I met in Paris some American friends, and had lunch with the Lindberghs. Is that not funny? America and France are interlocking in such a way in my life, that I wonder sometimes where I belong.

114 Mount Street, Grosvenor Square,
London, W., March 30, 1939

As you see I am in England. That will account, at least partly, to explain you why I have been so slow to answer your letter of March 8. Well, you know, I am groping myself for my way, and I do my best. But sometimes you wonder where the right path is. In fact, I must confess (and you have been extraordinary quick, quicker even than myself in perceiving) that I am probably feeling closer to my Church and Order just now than I was a year ago. *Not at all,* I sincerely think, that I am slackening in my line of progress. And because, for the first time in my life, I have felt and realized, during the past three months, that my people really needed and wanted me, I feel a bit more certain possibilities, and certain responsibilities. And it seems to me that since I don't want (and since it would be a mistake) to break off, I have logically to "adjust" myself somewhat more in the possible things. You know, I have got, recently, so many evidences that people (outside as well as inside of what they call Church) expect me to be, if I dare say, another type of Christian *in* Christianity, that I do not see how I could do anything useful and true, except by pushing in some way Christianity above itself. . . . I am not yet absolutely sure of what has been decided in Rome concerning my going back to China. (I have told you, I think, that, in November, I heard that the new Peking superior of my Order did not like to see me there so close to his youngsters — Tientsin wants me back, on the contrary.) I am practically sure that the thing is settled now in my favor. But I have not yet the final answer (it will come in a few days), so that all my plans were hanging. In the meantime I have published a rather good article (*La Mystique de la Science*); and I will soon finish another one, rather good too I think, on a new way to understand the question of human races; so that I come slowly on the stage. I have the feeling to have understood a lot of things more, this winter.

I am in England since a week; but tomorrow I will be back in Paris. I had a most impressive dinner with the staff of Trinity College in a huge Elizabethan hall, amongst I don't know how many "Nobel Prizes," etc. England is surely a funny, but pleasant, mixture of dignity and progress.

And, as you know, we are hanging between war and peace. I bet for peace. But the situation is tense — and it is queer not to be able to make any definite plans a fortnight ahead. . . .

May 7, 1939

I am ashamed and sorry not to have answered earlier your letter of April 15. I have been more busy than ever since Easter. Any kind of people stick to me, including unfortunately such unexpected customers as Catholic dreamers, young geniuses, and even a feminist "spiritual association of Women." . . . I get mixed with matrimonial affairs, and tomorrow I must christen a baby. Well, it is almost time for me to escape — one thing which I plan to do about June 24, provided *S.S. Champlain* should not burn in the meantime.

A first thing I must tell you is that I had a long interview with my chief superior in France, since I wrote you. He arrived rather in a low mood, since another one of my papers (a rather strong one) had reached Rome since last November. But, thanks to my friends here, he left in a better spirit. In fact, although he does not understand much about ideas, he is a very fair man, and he likes me. So that presently everything is practically O.K. I am allowed to go back to China, and back to Europe, according to the old routine. In the meantime, I try to express my views (my *real* views) in a printable shape. Another article on *Races* will probably come out by the end of the present month. I get a real fun from the game, and, at the same time, I improve distinctly my ideas concerning Man. A third paper on the meaning and value of human education is ready, to be used as a conclusion for a book edited by a friend of mine. So, you see, I am not inactive. Your proposition that "rebels accomplish the most" is one of the worst paradoxes of life. I wonder whether the solution has not to be searched in a definition of what means exactly the word *rebel*. Of course, I do not feel exactly as a prodigal son. Simply, the very development of my mind brings me to a *new* understanding of several things which I would have been inclined formerly to dismiss too simply, "the child with the bath."

Nothing much new, besides. Because of lack of time and of material, I do very little scientific work. And the worst is that I have a distinct feeling that I am losing the thrill of geology. And yet geology is my real platform. What to do? . . . Maybe that I am just needing to be back somewhere in the field. Something is sure: I must get some feathers in my cap. An expedition to the Hundes Basin would be a blessing: but I have no news from this side.

Useless to tell you anything about political considerations. Everybody talks and talks; and nobody in the world, even Adolf, knows where we are shifting to. The general feeling, just now, is that there will be no war — or rather the war will not go further than the present type of war: a "tension war," without actual bombing and fighting. My secret hope is that, in the meantime, a deeper evolution, toward some sound internationalism, is going on in the masses, so that a new world will emerge. A mass experience (and unfortunately a mass suffering) seems to be the condition for a mass transformation.

Berkeley, August 2, 1939

My stay here was definitely a pleasant one. I saw lots of interesting people in my line, and my interest for science has been distinctly rejuvenated. C—— was awfully kind and friendly; and so many others. At the same time, I gained fresh evidences of the need amongst scientists for a higher understanding of their scientific effort. Most of them are positively working by mere instinct — and they do not realize how deeply their activity is hampered, or even undermined, by their incomprehension of the meaning of research, and sometimes by an explicit mistrust of human value. Really "Moral Rearmament" is the fundamental need today. But it has to be based on a more consistent ground, and to be planned along more constructive ways than those broadcast by the Monterey Buchmanites. Yes, I know what you think. Some day, perhaps, I shall see. . . .

I am leaving tonight. Plenty of clouds, west. But I feel, in an unmistakable way, that if I do not make the step to China, I shall *not* know where to put my foot next. There are links in life. My next position depends on the way my situation is going to mature in Peking.

Kobe, August 23, 1939

I am leaving Kobe tomorrow, on a small Japanese boat, to Tangku, under rather ominous conditions. The German-Soviet pact, disclosed today, does not make the human atmosphere clearer, in spite of the far-reaching fact that it breaks, a second time, the Nazi creed (along the anti-Comintern dogma) still deeper than did the Czechoslovakian annexation (contradicting the races theory). I wonder how much this spiritual loss is going to be compensated for Hitler by any material advantage. Anyhow, we are facing troubles everywhere. We shall see. In the meantime it seems easy for me to reach Peking, which, after all, is a rather good and safe place to watch things. After these weeks of incessant moving, I feel the moral and physical need to settle for a while. And, as I told you, I perceive clearly that I have to make this new tentative contact with Peking, in order to know where I shall put my foot next. Unless I get somewhere a letter suggesting a different method, my plan is to avoid Tientsin, flooded and blockaded, and to go directly to Peking. I will write you from there.

Peking, September 17, 1939

And now, what! . . . Such a terrible mess all over the world, with so many clouds left perhaps to burst (Russia? Italy?). I wonder what you think, what you feel.

So far as I am concerned, the situation is as follows. From Kobe, I succeeded in reaching Peking almost easily, if you except one night spent on the floor of a room in Tangku (the harbor, coming from Japan), and an uncomfortable eight-hours trip on a crowded tender between Tangku and flooded Tientsin. Impossible to stay in Tientsin. I went straight to Peking, thus being forced by the "facts of God" to reintegrate my Pekinese house, where I got a perfectly nice welcome from the famous Canadian superior. Things are all right from this side; and I am glad for it. I am therefore well stationed in the imperial city for the time being. In Tientsin, the water is receding. But since a part of the city stands *below* the level of the river, remains of the flood will have to be pumped out. I plan to go, by the end of the month, to look for my friends and my things there. Presently, the university shelters some eight hundred refugees, and there is no place for me.

Consequently I have resumed my old life in a Peking which, in spite of a small core of friends (mostly Americans), is far from being the old Peking, except for its glorious autumn sky.

Morning and evening I go to my almost deserted laboratories, where I have still by chance a lot to do with the undescribed material (no more excavations in Choukoutien, of course); and in the meantime I progress slowly, but steadily, in the redaction of Man, my best and only way to fight for a better world. Here, one can scarcely realize that there is war in Europe, as long chiefly as no letters have arrived, describing the new situation. The past war has made me. I would like to think that the present one will achieve me. But I don't know how that might be possible so far! In any case I prefer that the war should have surprised me here rather than in Europe. Being too old for active service, I should have been terribly embarrassed what to do best. Here, at least, I have no choice, but to wait, to watch, and to work. No news so far, from my family nor from my various friends.

Besides nothing new. My plans are just as vague as the development of the war.

Peking, October 6, 1939

I wonder what is going to be your next step in life: I think of it, and even I pray for it. May you find the path which will lead you to the highest and the truest of yourself! Keep the right direction upwards — and the hope for perpetual discovery — and trust Life. That's all.

Personally, I am still in a rather "mixed" condition. For some obscure reasons I do not feel yet exactly myself, physically, or if you prefer, nervously. A mere temporary accentuation, I guess, of some dispositions which I had to live with since childhood. In the meantime I keep my old routine, with this only difference that there are much less parties now, which of course I do not mind. Social life is somewhat reduced in Peking; and in addition I have to be specially careful not to scare the people in my monastery. Things will gradually adjust themselves, I am sure. Provisionally I do not see anything better for me than to keep the lab and my personal work going. I write several scientific papers (rather interesting notes, for our Bulletin), and chiefly I try to advance my paper (or rather book) on Man. And, at the same time, I am wondering whether I should not do something more adapted to the present conditions of the world. But what? . . .

In fact, I have the greatest difficulty to understand and to *feel* the present war. Is it because I am too far geographically from the European atmosphere, or too far psychologically from the military clashes and methods? But I do not react to the crisis as I did in 1914. Even I have the suspicion that in Europe, in spite of being decided to bring the Nazis down, people do *not* have any *spirit* of war. Would it be possible that we are gradually getting "vaccinated" against spells of mere brutal violence? Maybe I am all wrong, because my perspective is distorted by the Peking air, where everything is going on practically unchanged (nobody here, practically, has been recalled so far to Europe, from any country!). But I have a kind of feeling that we are going toward tremendous political and social changes through an *abortive* war. And by the changes only I am interested. When they come out, an internationalistic (and really "Earthy") objective and ideal will be required. Along this line of research I can perhaps do something. And in this spirit I try my best to finish my book. In the meantime, if I can see something to *do* with my life . . . well, we shall see. Help me to see.

No news from France, so far. I have not the slightest idea what my two brothers, and so many friends are doing. Waiting for new developments in the conditions, I do not see any reason, and even any pretense to move. What could I do in France, just now? . . . Just to be in the hot spot of the living world? Yes, after all, that might be a real reason. I always felt anxious to stand at the border of the moving things. What do you think?

P.U.M.C. Department of Anatomy,
Peking, November 20, 1939

Such a long time since I wrote you, and since I heard of you. It seems that mail is desperately long these days (two months to get a letter from France!). And then one gives up the hope to receive, and the hurry to write, any letter. . . .

So far as I am concerned, no change, except that I feel distinctly better. Days are slowly following days, in a most "regular" life. From time to time I have lunch in town, or even, as yesterday, a delightful picnic in the barren beauty of the Western Hills. I write a number of scientific notes, to be published soon in our Bulletin. And I go on, step by step, along the long road leading to the end of my dreamed book on Man. In February, I may have reached the middle of the work; and then, I feel, the second half will be like going down a gentle slope. Writing this essay has become the axis, and the most serious part of my activity. Something has to be said (or at least *prepared:* who would listen these days? . . .) clearly and strongly *for* Man. It is so easy to be pessimistical or cynical, like dear Hooton, about the present and the future of Earth! I must show the other and truer side of the things. If I can do it, my life will be full and fulfilled. And if, in order to do it, I have to stay here in the quiet Peking, instead of taking my part of the European troubles, I will not regret it. When the storm is over, in the West, then people will need some constructive hope.

Of the Western war, I have scarcely any more news, so far, than those read in the newspapers' propaganda. Sometimes, looking from here, the impression is growing that the whole thing will end in a kind of huge readjustment, without any great fight along the old style. Funny to observe how things grow invincibly different from what we had sowed and planned. . . . But, in any case, I think that the readjustment will be great and deep — and *not* conservative, I think and hope. Many things can be hated and fought against, in this world. And yet, there is only one foe against whom I should fully like to give my life: immobility.

Here, my life is going mostly along the same routine. But the occupations begin to be pretty thick.

To begin with, I am gradually more and more involved in the scientific side of things. We have just sent to press a new number of our Bulletin, entirely written or rewritten by me. And now, in addition to more paleontological descriptions, I have decided to write an outline of the Continental Geology of Eastern Asia, where I should condense the best of what I got in the field since almost twenty years. On another hand, it seems that our Tientsin Museum is going to move, during the spring, to Peking — under the shape of a Research Institute, for the idea of which I am responsible. This change might turn out to have a considerable importance for the development of geological and human researches in China. Of course, I do not belong to the staff of the institution, directly and officially; but I act very much in the thing as an adviser. Such a transformation would give me a much more independent and pleasant situation in Peking. But at the same time I would not like to get more tied here, in case something more important would call me elsewhere. In fact we are building here on a very moving ground: nobody knows how much an Occidental Institute is going to be tolerated here in the next future. It may well happen therefore that I get free, from this side, even faster than I should like.

And, now, so long for science. As you know, the axis of my life is running somewhere else above. The book on Man is progressing steadily. Not specially fast, but, on the average, a page a day. After two months, maybe, the most intricate part of the work (Life) will be over, and I will stand safely on Thought and Man. Then I shall feel on the safest and descending side of the journey. In fact, I am more than halfway, already, because the scheme of the book ahead gets more and more elaborated, even for the details, at the same time as I am writing the definite text. Now the four parts are definitely these: *La Prévie* (Matter), *La Vie, La Pensée, La Survie.* The fourth is my pet.

In the meantime, I went to Tientsin to make what we call a

retraite. Eight days of self-recollection are pretty long. Yet, that was a useful time, and in Tientsin I had a very comfortable and sunny room. Well, I tried to perceive more distinctly and practically a loving influence at the "alpha" and mostly at the "omega" of our World and lives in the making, and I hope not to have too much deceived myself. . . . Externally, Tientsin had apparently recovered from the flood. But the blockade was just as bad. The French are relatively well treated. But it is a sight to watch the long "queue" of Chinese waiting hours and even days before being admitted in the concessions, and the procession of cars loaded with vegetables, and the coal or eggs unloaded for examination. The problem is to know who is going to get tired first, the British or the Japanese. And both seem to be perfectly stubborn.

Finally I have gotten, a few days ago, a bunch of letters from France. One of my brothers is mobilized (in a safe place), and the other not (but his twenty-year-old son will be called this winter). At the time the letters were written (in October) the question was how to keep the national and private life going on, in spite of extensive mobilization of people and material or supplies. I think the situation has been improving since then, decidedly. Reading these letters, I felt a little more the spell of the events, and a kind of longing for joining home. And still I cannot yet be really excited by this war. I realize its urgency, and its drama, and even the great Object it is to repel the reign of material force. But I have an obscure feeling that the Allies are fighting too much for quietness and stability (or rather immobility); and this point becomes always clearer in myself: the only fight in which I would like to mix and to die should be a battle for construction and movement ahead. In the same line, historians ought to distinguish more clearly two very different types of crusaders or martyrs: those who were killed for keeping, and those who were killed for changing, an old thing. I suppose that the mutual positions will become clearer in Europe after a while, and I still hope that some agreement may be reached without any major clash. So strange that Russia should have turned enemy no. 1. Whatever should be the end, the world needs a thorough readjustment under a more definite human common ideal. That is the only thing I believe to see.

Well, for the present time, my existence, I am afraid is overregular. Due to the geographical location of my North Pekinese monastery, I do not see much of the world — and more specially of the evening world. But, for a while, and because I am busy inside, I do not object essentially to the situation. Since my last letter, I wrote another scientific Note; I sent to my Parisian Review (the austere *Etudes*) some pages on the meaning of the present war, which will probably be printed; I made a long recension of the H——'s memoir on India (with a few friendly criticisms to P——); I built an incipient scheme for a book I dream on the Continental History of China; and finally I wrote every day a few paragraphs more of Man, which brings me rather close to the half of the whole redaction. Since I have every day one hour and a half to sit in my rickshaw, gazing at the icy blue sky and at the Sino-Japanese crowd, you will agree that I have some excuse for keeping on my table a heap of reproachful unanswered letters. To be true, by cross-examining me, you would perhaps detect by times in all this a touch of feverishness. But, on the whole, I feel much better than last autumn. And really, since my mind feels clear and alive, I think that there is nothing better for me than to go on along an interesting and creative line. In spite of what I told you above *à propos de* my monastic life, occasions for relaxing are not so rare. Two days ago, for the seventieth birthday of Dr. Grabau, we had a very merry evening, in a beautiful Chinese house, with fantastic cocktails and food. I was toastmaster (!!) and the first one to talk after me was the American ambassador (!!). Several pleasant meetings for Xmas too.

I forgot to tell you that I am (or rather was) planning to spend February and March in Yunnan, in order to get in touch with things and friends, down there. But some material difficulties in the lab seem to prevent me from leaving now. Besides, I have no plan for the middle and the end of 1940. As for everybody, everything depends on the evolution of the war. Here, in the Far East, invasion is going on. But no indications so far of any real reconciliation between yellow cousins: the gap in the feelings was never deeper, I am afraid. And yet, there is no possible peace without sympathy. In spite of all these troubles, I am always more convinced that the present crisis is for the birth of a new world. I should like it if my book would be ready (and allowed . . .) for publication just when the fight is over.

P.U.M.C. Department of Anatomy,
March 4, 1940

Well, February went on, with its usual cold spell, and the red lanterns of the Chinese New Year. Very little snow, a beautiful and dry powdery dust, evanescent under a bright sun. Chinese were as merry as possible; but this "possible" was limited by the food question, which, for the natives, if not for the foreigners, becomes acute. Prospects are bad, for the next month, up to the next crop (if there is no drought and no flood . . .). No export, very little import, and the money falling down. And no indication whatever that we are approaching the end of the Oriental "incident." . . . I was planning, you know, to go to Yunnan this winter. As I wrote you already, perhaps, I had to give up the trip, because my presence was supposed to be necessary at the lab here. Consequently, I went on along the same routine. In fact, I never had such time to work peacefully, since years. Several scientific papers already printed, or under preparation. And "Man" is proceeding, too, at the regular speed. Now, I am decidedly along the slope down. Maybe, before July, I shall reach the end. Good, I hope. But I am so much immersed in the subject, since months, that I have no more perspective. Anyhow, I must finish — and now I hope to.

From France, news are coming regularly now. My impression is that the end of the war will come from the side we are expecting the less. We think still of a final battlefield. But in the meantime a new order is gradually forming itself and developing *under the strain.* And when the order is born, maybe an impossible and useless struggle will stop by itself. In France itself I am struck by the mixture of people and social classes brought by the evacuations, mobilization, and general pressure: a complete stirring up and recasting of the nation under a generous spirit. The same is true, I guess, for other nations.

Socially speaking, I live very moderately. Yet, I get a pleasant afternoon, or a merry lunch, from time to time. Last Sunday, we had a nice picnic in a temple of the Western Hills: a marvelous "Mongol sheep," which you roast yourself, with long chopsticks, on a grill — I enjoyed the walk in the barren hills. But I felt sick to be in the field again. Since Burma I did not properly come in close contact with Mother Earth!

Nothing to tell you, so far, concerning my plans for the future. Eventually, I will have to go back to Europe, and I suppose I need it. But it should be useless to make any decision before spring gives (perhaps) a new turn to the war. And in the meantime I am stuck here. Weidenreich does not come back before July. And decidedly we move here the Tientsin Museum in April or May.

Peking, April 8, 1940

It was sweet of you to send me the Ugly Duckling and the nice Easter card, which arrived almost exactly at the proper time. . . . Clearly, after having been left for years practically loose and free in my Order, I feel gradually tightening on me (at least as long as I am here, in my monastery) the frame of "regularity," which does not fit at all my type of activities, but which, for a lot of higher reasons, I feel obliged to accept and to some extent to respect — because I have no choice between breaking (which would be egotistical and foolish) and being as much *régulier* as I can manage to be. Probably it is difficult for you to understand the problem. But the problem exists. This time again I hope to go through just by being as much as possible responsive to various and apparently contradictory sides of reality, at the same time. But I can not yet foresee exactly where is leading me this complicated evolution. One thing I know, is that this evolution is just going always straighter to the aims of more comprehensive and more human Truth which are since years the only reason and soul of my life. I know what you think, the duckling with the ducks, and the little swan with the swans. . . . I did never see so far, and I will apparently never see, the *real* reason (for which I have been often instinctively longing) which should allow me, in the face of Life, to return to freedom. . . .

Nothing much new, since the last weeks. Spring has come, a typical North Chinese spring: clear, dry, windy, dusty. Cherries and apricot trees are everywhere like pink clouds mixed with clouds of dust. Yesterday I spent my Sunday afternoon in the hills. A pleasant time we had. But always this feeling that long trips on the field are impossible, and impossible for a long period, now. At least we have some solid hopes to resume before long our Choukoutien excavations, for more Peking Man. If so, that would be a new life and blood running in the laboratory.

I told you, probably, about the plan of moving here in Peking the Tientsin laboratories, and to have in town our small private institute. If it does materialize (as I still hope), the scheme would solve automatically a lot of my domestic difficulties. But, just when everything was ready, some authorization has become necessary, which is not yet there. Thus, we are still hanging on our old position. If things turn well, transfer should begin immediately. Lot of troubles. But after them, peace.

From Europe, nothing, except what you know from the papers in America. And the propaganda is so confusing and awful, almost from both sides equally. What I am still afraid of is that the Allies do not seem to understand that no end and no peace — a real peace, I mean — can be expected except from a complete readjustment. The trouble is that the readjustment should include an intellectual and moral change in the men themselves. Maybe that will come out of the long and terrible pressure we are undergoing now.

Peking, April 18, 1940

Today I am rather in a hurry, because tomorrow I am going to Tientsin, for several days, and I have to make many things ready before. The reason for this trip is (I hope, at least!) the transportation of our Tientsin labs to Peking. But there is a little flaw. At the last minute, the head of my Order was a bit scared by the prospect of such a change under the present world conditions. And we are still expecting the cable giving a final answer. A positive answer is expected, but still nothing is absolutely sure. . . . Let us hope for the best. If the worse happens, that is if I have to stay here in my monastery, instead of moving to a more merry place, well, I think I will take the thing philosophically. After all, this is a heavy business to transfer a whole library and innumerable collections. In my next letter, I will tell you.

Nothing new, besides. Spring is marvelous, and I enjoy just facing my Chinese window, two large apple trees covered with flowers as by a heavy snow. Not too much wind or dust. These last weeks my writing has been going on tolerably, so that I begin to feel the end of my book: in two months, maybe. . . . I feel that it is going to be for me a relief to get free for thinking in a less strenuous and less limited way. I need to face other problems, or the same problems from a different angle.

These days things seem to move faster in Europe. I feel, as you do, the scandal of the whole situation. And yet, at the same time, I am so convinced of the bigness of the change which Earth needs and expects, that I feel ready to accept any perturbations and any pressure. For a new world we need new mass feelings, and the feelings of the masses do not evolve except under world-wide reactions. The question comes always back to the same dilemma. Either the World is absurd; and then, of course, nothing to do; we have just to retire. Either the World is going somewhere. Then he will find his way through any emergencies. And World cannot be absurd: otherwise, how could we be here, criticizing him? . . .

Peking, May 29, 1940

I have well received your letter of April 9. In fact, I would have answered it much quicker, but for the rather hectic time I am having since a few weeks — first on account of the transportation of our Tientsin labs, and also as a consequence of the dreadful things which are just now happening in France. It is not easy to keep exactly one's balance in such occurrences. I am sure you feel the situation deeply, too.

Well, coming to my Chinese life, I told you that I was busy. To sort and to pack the Tientsin material was a job. Now I have only to wait, for a few weeks perhaps, till the boxes cross the blockade, and find the railway trucks to cover the 80 miles separating Tientsin from Peking. In the meantime I hope to be settled, in a week from today, in our provisional home, decidedly too dark, but so well located in the Legation quarter. In the meantime, too, I have finished writing my book, a part only having still to be typed. Now that the thing is over, I begin to wonder what it is really worth. Anyhow, it is over, and I will not change it any more. Possibly, after a few weeks, when my mind has settled down, I will discover that what I was trying to express is still something else. In any case, I am decided to try my best to have the present essay accepted and printed. But then I must wait for the end of the war. And what is going to be the peace? . . .

I should like tremendously, to talk with you about these things. On the whole, I am still optimist, but mostly on a long range. Since the beginning, I was positively afraid to see how "conservative," only, was the Allies' position in war. To keep a situation, they were fighting, and not clearly enough, to make Man and Earth better. If only this awful shock would awake us to the sense of construction and progress, then, in any turn of events, we should profit from this war. But, by all means, Man must emerge out of this devilish condition to have to spend his whole resources in building more tanks and bombers. I am sure we will emerge, some day. But then the face of the world will be terribly different from what it is now. And *we* have to pay.

Peking, June 18, 1940

Just today, after the French final defeat, you can suspect what I am thinking. In fact, I can't say that this provisional end of a part of the World's transformation took me by surprise. Since three weeks, the situation was pretty clear; and, since the beginning, I did not like this war; because I felt (maybe I told you) that, on the Allies' side, there was *not* any spirit of conquest and renovation: only fighting to keep going on an old-fashioned, "bourgeoise," conception of Man. There is something dreadfully primitive and narrow in the Hitler's religion and ideal. But the Germans had an internal flame, and *this* was too strong for us, much more than the tanks. So, I am just there, facing what was bound to come.

It is much too early, of course, to appreciate the magnitude of the collapse, and chiefly the span of the impending changes. But one thing is sufficiently clear. It should be absurd to decide that the world is definitely lost or bad. The problem is to find the right place where to apply the right kind of force. And that is what I am mostly thinking, these days: to repress useless and sentimental reactions, and to search how a new Man may rise out of the crisis. My hope is that, from awakening to the threat of a mechanized Earth, we shall be forced into the conception of and the belief in a spiritual structure of the world. This is the very moment, paradoxically, for Man to discover the biological value, and the possible extension, of the only energy which can group and achieve individual Man, without turning him into a gadget or a slave: a mutual form of love, based on the consciousness of a common Something (or rather Somebody) into which all together we converge. Am I true? To spread this half-scientific, half-religious faith of my all life is the only and the best thing left to me ahead, I guess. I am not specially afraid if people think me dangerous, or naïve, or mad. What I should like to know, next, is who amongst my friends in France are still alive — or dead. No news of course, so far, about any of them. And, for the coming years, how much is going to be left out of France? Shall we escape revolution? Everything is possible, after such a shock. If sometimes you are doing something like praying, ask for me spiritual and physical strength. This is not the time for a breakdown, just now. Nothing really bad, with me; but an unpleasing feeling of depression, the reverse of myself.

Since a fortnight, I am living rather pleasingly in my new

home. The bulk of the Tientsin material did not yet arrive, on account of the blockade; but some day we shall get it. In the meanwhile, I have plenty to keep busy. The book on Man is finished, but has to be retyped in three copies, and here the typists are not easy to find. I hope to succeed. And then I must go through the censorship. I do not forecast any special difficulties in this line, chiefly now.

Don't let you be disturbed by the world's events, but excited to do still more. This is the time to sow in a newly open field.

Institut De Géobiologie, August 3, 1940

I hate to think that the present mess of the world makes you unhappy. And yet, at some extent, I rejoice that you should feel an attack of *Weltschmerz*. Is this not a divine pain? Provided, of course, that you get not finally depressed on account of it, but in some way excited and driven to the best limit of yourself. In fact, the great pity is that too many, just now, are only weeping over their own small losses, and do not experience the real magnitude of what is going on, for evil or for good. Personally, I stick to my idea that we are watching the birth, more than the death, of a World. But the scandal, as you point it exactly, is that England and France should have come to this tragedy because they have sincerely tried the road of peace! But did they not precisely make a mistake on the true meaning of "peace"? "Peace" can not mean anything but a *higher process of conquest*. And, since 1919, France at least did scarcely do more than to stick comfortably to the old routines. World is bound to belong to its most active elements. If we are defeated today by sheer brutal force, the reason is, I believe, that we did not, after the last war, find a spiritual and constructive outlet for force. Just now, the Germans deserve to win because, however bad or mixed is their spirit, they have more spirit than the rest of the world. It is easy to criticize and despise the fifth column. But no spiritual aim or energy will ever succeed, or even deserve to succeed, unless it proves able to spread and to keep spreading a fifth column. To incorporate spirit in Force (or either to sublimate Force into spirit), this is the problem, and this ought to be our dream.

From France, since the collapse, I have no letters, and nobody has. And I do not expect news before long. So I am left completely in the dark concerning the fate and the present life of my brothers and friends. In fact, I am even unable to understand what did really happen in June, and what this funny Pétain government really means. Looking from China, the whole thing seems to have been rather a shame. A most curious and unpleasing feeling to have the impression that there is no more France. Still I hope for some kind of revival. The sad part of the thing is that, as I told you the last year, I had left France with the conviction that something was growing there which could have been a ferment for the world. Maybe the seed is not crushed and killed, but ready to develop in a rejuvenated ground. But I long for news telling me those things which are not to be found in any newspaper.

In the meantime, I am really enjoying our new house, in the Legation quarter. We are four friends living there, with our books, the best of our collections, an excellent cook, and a dog. I expect two kittens very soon. I am finishing two scientific papers, and my book will be finished retyping next week (3 copies). But where to send it for censure (!) in the present condition of Europe? . . . I have no definite plans for the future. This should be the time to do *something*. But what? . . . I don't see. I must first know who is left in France, and in what conditions. And first, too, we must see whether the whole situation is not going to be changed by England.

P.S. Just to explain you what I feel, I send you the few here included pages (in French, alas!). They are still true. They were sent to France, but never published, possibly because not optimist or patriotic enough? !

August 18, 1940

For me, as I told you, this year was somewhat difficult, physically speaking. But do not worry about that. To be true, I do not know (nor did any doctor understand exactly) what was the matter with me. A kind of mental dizziness and anxiety ("psychasthenia," told me with a smile the best clinician of Peking): in fact, an old acquaintance of mine, since I had touches of it since I was a boy. Very unpleasant. But the best remedy, I was told and I had already found by myself, is to go on as if nothing happened. To have my book to write was the best cure. Now, I feel much better. But I think that this is something you have just to accept to live with, as to become old and farsighted. The essential thing is to keep interested thinking and doing things. And for this you will help me.

As far as the book on Man is concerned, a good friend of the American Diplomatic Service is going to bring a copy of it to Washington, and later to forward this copy to France, by the American Embassy, as soon as I know something about my friends in Paris. I can't do anything more in the present circumstances.

. . . By the way, this letter was interrupted just here by a visit I paid to the diplomat above mentioned. He and his wife have been extremely nice. And they urge me to come to America to preach my "gospel"! I do not yet see how that should be possible. But I tell you this, because you will like to know that you are not alone thinking as you do. If only the book could be published, I would have a good platform to start. The first objective, I think, is to have the book out. In the meantime, I have several scientific papers ready, or almost so, which are not bad, I think. This is another platform which I must not neglect.

No news from France since the collapse. . . . I have not the slightest idea about the conditions there. Who is alive, and where. . . . The "Vichy government" and the would-be fascist regime seems to me a puppet comedy. If the British are not submerged, I suspect de Gaulle will be the chief the people really want, unless we go to communism. In any case, a new Europe, and perhaps still more, will be born before a few years.

Now, I suppose you are back in New York. Have a good and fruitful year! You are lucky to live there. My own plans are just in the clouds. I cannot decide anything before I know something of France. Here, in our new house, life is rather pleasing. But this is not real life.

So far as I am concerned, life is the same, except that the Far East might turn some day, not far away, to be a hot spot too. Yet, do not believe the "transocean" reports too easily. In fact, very few Americans are thinking of leaving China, so far; and we should be very surprised that a real clash should happen here. Still, the Pacific area is bound to undergo just as much readjustment as the Mediterranean one. The present distribution of the Earth is far from being such as to make a status quo possible, and still less advisable. But why not to adopt another form of readjustment than sanguinary fighting? . . . I am more and more convinced that the real battlefield, today, is not in Dover, Egypt, or Rumania, but in Man's mind and soul. We are striving to discover and express a new "Spirit of the Earth." To be true, this is the only type of activity and research which attracts me any more, and to which I would like to devote the rest of my life. The clipping about Einstein's statement on God which you sent gave me a real kick. I don't have the hundredth of the Einstein's mathematical brains. But I am dumbfounded that such a man should not realize that a single particle of consciousness present in the Universe makes it physically necessary that the Universe should become all-conscient eventually, at the end of the transformation; and what finally is Consciousness, if not Personality? . . . And what about the "Religion of good"? . . . Is there any religion without devotion and love? . . . and is it possible to love "good"!! The trouble with Einstein, and so many others, is that they still imagine a "personal God" as a sort of super-Man, and not as the focus and center of a cosmic-personalistic Evolution. At least, I feel satisfied in observing that, by concentrating my effort on this very question of the "personalistic nature" of Universe and Evolution, I hit the exact point on which everything depends, ultimately in the present human conflict. Well, I should like that my book could be printed, as a platform (or as a declaration of war). But I have not yet any idea to whom to send the manuscript for censure. I heard recently that one of my best friends and most helpful supporters in France is a prisoner. I told you that a copy of the book is in Washington, in good hands, ready to be sent to France by diplomatic (!) channel. In the meantime, I am ruminating the substance and the shape of a small confidential memoir, for Rome (if possible). Christianity *has to* take a constructive standpoint, *now,* based on a rejuvenated presentation of God, Christ, and "charity."

From France, news comes slowly (yesterday I got two letters, of the middle of August); and everybody seems to know very little about everybody else. Relatively few casualties (no one in my close family). Pétain government is full of good will; but, I am afraid, it has no spark, and the reforms it promotes have no clear root in the country. It is all right to "repent," or to pour oil on the wounds. What we need is a burning sense of creation and conquest. To sail towards the new, and not to retract inside of the old shell! Anyhow I am hopeful. The great present crisis obliges everybody to face the major problem of constructing the World as a whole. Provided we escape the temptation to take refuge in the old shelters, nothing better could happen to drive us ahead.

Here, I go ahead in my routine work. Several interesting scientific papers are in press. *Vaguely,* I am thinking to tour South America next spring, in order to collect a little money for our new institute. The idea is not mine but belongs to my friend and colleague L——, director of the institute. I would just follow him, to back him. The idea should be to make a scientific tour (in the line of the institute's researches), and *incidentally* to look for funds. If this ambitious scheme should mature, I would try to turn it into something useful for the development and the propagation of my own views. And obviously New York should be on my return trip. But all this is still most uncertain.

Goodby. Today I begin my eight days' retreat.

Peking, November 11, 1940

I suppose you have not taken too seriously the evacuation of American citizens from the East. The gesture is possibly perfectly wise. But I cannot personally visualize the chances for major troubles. For the present time we are chiefly sorry here to have to part from a number of dear friends. So far most of the nonofficial residents do *not* move. But they *might* some day be urged to leave, too. On the other hand, the French Embassy is coming back to Peking, with full forces, so that the city is not yet dead. Still, on the whole, the situation is gradually becoming more and more uncertain here. Absolutely no danger, but the feeling that, after one or two years, conditions and life may be here entirely different from those we knew since 20 years. Thus, simultaneously, France and China are sinking or shaking under my feet. As a result I feel more and more inclined to concentrate on the development of the kind of "meta-biology" (*no* metaphysics, I hope) in which I try since years to include Man, Life, and World. I was wondering whether, by writing my book, I had not exhausted the spring in myself. On the contrary, I have the impression that fresh water is pouring again. I see better and deeper the important points, and I have more to write. As far as the book is concerned, I cannot think of any edition in America before my French manuscript has been censured; and I don't know where nor to whom to send it for "revision." My best friend and supporter in Paris is a prisoner! Two days ago, I have written to another friend, who is perhaps in Rome. On the other hand, my colleague L——, here, is more and more decided and eager to tour South America, in order to collect the pesetas we need to build a definite house. If Rome agrees (we are still waiting for an answer), we might go there next spring, the tour ending necessarily in North America. But what is the World going to be after six months?

Just now we are enjoying a perfect autumn, bright and cool. I hope that in your broadcasting you will discover the right touch. Yes, it must be terribly difficult to be at the same time crusading and entertaining about democracy. Sometimes one has the feeling that limited and selected audiences, "esoterism," is the proper atmosphere for great truths and revelations. Presented to the mass, such big things are exposed to look ridiculous. And yet can we expect anything, finally, except from mass movements? . . .

. . . What we need, all of us, today more than ever in the past, is to discover the way toward being *more* ("super") *human*, without becoming *inhuman* (this is the danger of many religions, and especially of Christianity, on account of its special "ascensional power," to confuse the two notions!). As you know, this research for a new spirit is the very soul and the very meaning of my life.

Nothing particular has happened, during the past weeks, except that the South American project had to be dropped, because Rome (for still undisclosed reasons) did not think it was opportune, for the time being. Consequently I am following, presently, the same routine. After all, since the field work is impossible, the wisest thing is perhaps to liquidate the few important or interesting scientific laboratory work left here, so that I should be free, if some possibility comes along from another side, to take it. A new memoir is almost out of press, and I start a summary of my knowledge on Early Man in China. But, at the same time, I keep on trying to focus the essence of my Creed or "gospel"; and, along this line, I have the feeling to go always further on. Like a huge snowy range emerging, clearer and clearer, from the clouds. Five times, since two months, I had the opportunity (in lectures or in written exposés) to try my wings. Did you hear (and did I write you already?) about the September 1940 Congress on Religion and Science, in New York? Recently I got more details, and I felt together sick and excited at the inability by the speakers (*both* sides) in spotting the two points of divergency and of (possible) convergency. Well, a fortnight ago I have written right to Rome, asking for the publication of my book ("revision," first) and for my participation to the next sitting of the N.Y. congress. We shall see . . . In the meantime, I am preparing a concentrated exposition of my views on the subject, to be sent there, if I cannot actually be present at the meeting. In any case, unless the Pacific should be closed and mined, I should be surprised if I had not to go to the States next year.

From occupied France, still *no* news; a few from unoccupied

France. Breuil is in Toulouse. Nothing has been damaged in his Paris personal and scientific belongings, and a newly discovered painted cave in Périgord supplies him with an interesting field of activity. But, where are we shifting to, in France? . . . and are the Germans not going to force upon us nefarious *auvergnat* Mr. Laval? . . . I strongly believe with Anne Lindbergh that this present war is only "scum on the wave of the future." But no organization is finally possible under mere compulsion. That is where England and America will eventually save the world in the unavoidable course of its totalization. I admire tremendously England, and I hope that France is not so low as she seems to be.

Here, in Peking, the life is going on, in spite of the departure of so many American friends, and of new military restrictions at the gates of the city. In fact, since two months, I have spent almost every Sunday in the Western Hills, doing some unexpectedly interesting field work before or after picnicking with thoroughly ungeological, but most pleasant, people. Funny how the Pekinese life and these barren picnic landscapes are, for everybody, bewitching.

I am really sorry for H——. I have received a letter from him, very anxious about his future, but I did not realize he was feeling so lost. I don't see that he can do anything but stick to his little job. At least he can think and write. How to give him, not exactly a faith (he has one), but a constructive expression of this faith? . . . I will do my best.

February 9, 1941

As far as I am concerned, things are going the same way — rather smooth on the whole, too smooth, probably. I enjoy a rare opportunity to advance a series of synthetic scientific papers, where I can summarize the so far scattered results of the past eighteen years of field work. But I wonder whether I should not be better somewhere else, where I should find myself on the edge of the present human wave. For the first time in my life, I am not at the hottest point of the world; and that gives me a feeling of inferiority. But where to go, and what to do? France, I am afraid, should be simply a trap for me. And how reach France, even if I decided to go? I am eagerly expecting the letter from Rome answering the questions I told you (How to have my book revised? could I go to the N.Y. congress in September?), and I am *not* much optimistical about it. In any case, yes or no, the answer will clear the road ahead. In the meantime I try to read more clearly in myself, and to focus better my views. My leading idea, just now, is that the true crisis of the world, today, does not lie exactly in a conflict between totalitarians and democrats, but between mobilists and fixists. If the democracies were not hampered by the heavy load of fixism which hides, and excuses (glorifies) itself among them, under the usurped name of Liberty, they would swallow in no time the powers of the Axis, or at least they would soon find a ground for mutual achievement. A *progressive* democrat is not fundamentally different from a really progressive totalitarian. Consequently, the main thing today, on the field of sound propaganda, is to make a campaign for the faith (a passionate and rational faith) in a well-understood human progress. In my opinion, the world of tomorrow will be born out of the "elected" group of those (arising from any direction and class, and confession in the human world) who will decide that there is something big waiting for us ahead, and give their life to reach it. People *have to* decide for or against progress, *now*. And those who say no have just to be dropped behind. And those who say yes will soon discover that they speak the same language and even worship the same God. Those are the things I should like to tell in New York. And those are the things which I am decided to fight for, as long as I live, anyway.

Life in Peking is going on, within its always more restricted circle. The new French diplomatic crowd (all concentrated here now, with nothing to do) has however infused a new and comforting blood into the social body. Several of the newcomers are positively pleasant, and even positively interesting. During the past weeks, weather was cold, but bright, so that I spent several pleasant Sundays with good friends (and my hammer) in the Western Hills.

From France, news is scarce and unsatisfactory. I still hope that something is burning underneath. But, looking from outside, the perspective is simply disturbing. "Neither external nor internal impetus," would say Dr. Grabau. I envy the Britons. . . . Not only do they save themselves. But, since Dunkirk, it would seem that they have stolen from the Nazis the moral leadership of the world. Some atmosphere to feel comfortable in!

Peking, March 21, 1941

Life here is going on pretty much the same except that some kind of crisis is evidently approaching every day, together with the growing feeling that personal projects are just now rather futile. Two weeks ago, I have received an answer from Rome. Half, half. . . . Evidently the Number One down there, is just as suspicious about me as before. Number Two on the contrary (to whom I have written) seems more understanding: even he confesses to have read "with great attention and keen interest" a rather radical memorandum I had sent to him. Practically: (1) They do *not* like the idea of my participation to the N.Y. congress (they had too much of Philadelphia, I guess); but they agree to my sending a written communication, which I am preparing now. (2) They agree too that I should send to Rome the manuscript of my book for a sympathetic (?) revision (in fact the manuscript has been mailed to them a fortnight ago). This is not much; and yet it is not so bad as I could fear. I know that, from your point of view, these limitations (and my not fighting stronger against them) are hard to understand; and I feel it myself to some extent too. And yet, I do not see any other logical (or even biological) way to proceed. According to my own principles, I can*not* fight against Christianity; I can only work inside it, by trying to transform and "convert" it. A revolutionary attitude would be much more easy, and also much more pleasant, but it would be suicidal. So I must go on step by step, tenaciously. I know that the tide is rising, which supports me. For the present time I believe that the most strategic effort is to promote in the world a strong and rational faith in the power imparted to Man to raise the world above its present stage. As I told you already perhaps in my last letter, I am convinced that the present war is, at bottom, a conflict between "mobilists" and "immobilists," and that it will stop the minute the mobilists, in each camp, will recognize each other and drop the political *and* religious immobilists. I was therefore greatly pleased by the booklet of Anne Lindbergh, "The Wave of the Future" (you know it, certainly). And I could not resist making a lecture on Human Progress at the French Embassy, two weeks ago. Did you see also, by chance, a rather thick book, *Pain, Sex and Time,* recently published in America by a certain Mr. Heard (or something like that)? The background and platform of the book is exactly mine, meaning that Man is now confronted with the evolutionary necessity to find (develop) a higher stage of consciousness; and to this extent, the book is quite suggestive and inspiring. Where the author fails, in my opinion, is when he tries to explain what should be *the way toward* more consciousness. He tries to sketch a kind of Yoga. But he does not determine the precise type of mystic (the precise "spiritual effort") to develop out of this Yoga. So far as I can see, the solution of the problem requires a new and clear definition of the notions of "Spirit" and "Spiritualization" along the three following lines: sublimation of Matter, synthesis of human mass, recognition of a supreme Center of Love and Personality. And I do not think that Mr. Heard (?) expresses himself clearly on any of these points.

Socially speaking, life here is quite reduced with so many people going away. My best distraction is a weekly excursion, on Sundays, to the Western Hills, where I find always more geological questions to solve. Because so close to Peking, the area was somewhat despised and neglected before the war. Spring is bursting, these days, as an explosion of green and pink buds on a background of yellow earth. A fortnight ago, it was still freezing.

I hope your holidays are a success. But I still more wish that you should gradually discover, as you say, "what you really want of life." Concerning this point, do not forget that the value and interest of life is not so much to do conspicuous things (although we must have this ambition) than to do ordinary things *with* the perception of their enormous value. This, I think, is the mystic to come.

Peking, May 9, 1941

Did I tell you, in my last letter, that Rome (remembering perhaps Philadelphia?) did not like the idea of my going to the New York congress. I am only allowed to send them a written communication (provided of course that this communication should be approved beforehand). I have sent, six weeks ago, a proposed text; but I don't have so far any answer, neither concerning these few pages, nor concerning the manuscript of my book. Everything takes so long now! In the meantime, I am printing here (privately) two short Notes on the idea of Progress, which I think to be *good*. (I will send you a copy, eventually); and I have reached, it seems, a new and perhaps deeper way to express my views on Man and the World. So that, if by chance my book should be stopped by the censors, I would not mind so much, because I have found something better to do.

Scientific papers also keep me very busy. Since I can scarcely go in the field, I have been gradually brought to give a little synthesis of my work in China; and I am just caught now by the interest of doing it, without forgetting the American Museum. But how to make any definite plans for the future, these days!

Peking is gradually losing more and more "feathers." Still, life is fundamentally pleasant, even now, although always wrapped in a kind of shadow. Everybody enjoys the good hours of friendship, and the spring flowers, as a most precious and fragile thing. . . . Spring was awfully windy, this year, and yet, to me, the gray dust and the pink-blossom trees were never so dear.

From Europe, letters are rare. Nothing tragic in the food question, so far. But France is so humiliated, and so little, now. People say that a healthy revival is developing underneath, socially speaking. I hope it is true. And I hope, chiefly, that some day, the spark will come. Life is fire, not wisdom.

I have well received your long and so good letter in which you urge me to force more strongly my way toward a freer expression of my *Weltanschauung.* You must be sure that I understand perfectly your point of view. The only and great difficulty, as I told you many times, is that I am convinced that my best efforts would be useless if I should break with the religious current which the problem is *not* to fight but to transform. On such a battlefield, I can only act *from inside,* and this not by politics, but by sheer conviction. Let us hope. So far, I have no reaction from Rome concerning the book. But I know that the manuscript has reached its destination all right, so that it is now under study. In a way, it is a faintly favorable symptom that I should hear nothing. At least the thing seems to have been taken under serious consideration. In the meantime, a short pamphlet (in French) is probably finished printing in Shanghai (almost three months for thirty pages!). I will send it to you, as soon as I get it. I have the feeling that my perspective is getting rapidly more simple and more focused. I will try a new expression of it after a month, when I have finished two rather thick scientific papers, about ready now. All this work keeps me busy, and luckily. Because Peking is more and more deserted, every day. A last bunch of American friends is leaving in August. If I were not partly tied here by the care of the residual Cenozoic Lab and of our newborn institute, I don't think I would stay. And in fact I don't think I will stay if some occasion arises to make a trip abroad anywhere. I suppose that the answer of Rome will show me the road ahead.

I shall tell you nothing about the political situation which becomes acutely painful for any Frenchman as fond as I am of Anglo-Saxon people and culture. I still stick to the hope that we are going toward a really new Earth, a preliminary form being found for the necessary synthesis of collectivization with personal freedom. Nothing can save us except the awakening of Man to interhuman affinities. Biologically and physically, the thing is overwhelmingly *evident.* The difficulty is to find the match which will light the fire.

Do you realize how old I am, now? . . . And yet I hope to keep young up to the end, for God. . . .

P.S. Today, a beautiful day, I go to the Hills with my hammer and a good French friend; and day after tomorrow to Tientsin (for two days). A year since I did not take a train! Can you imagine that? In fact I feel happy here, in my new surroundings: my first *home* in my life. I am perhaps getting old, really?

August 5, 1941

Peking was never so empty, and in some way life was never so blank ahead, as they are now. Just a period to go through before something else comes out, I suppose . . . don't think that I am depressed, however. This is just a material situation to face, and to transform, if possible.

Since my last letter my daily routine has been exactly the same: writing papers, and correcting proofs. With the hot days, and so many people going back to America, or simply to Peritaho Beach for the summer, chances for Sunday trips in the Hills have become scarce (and now they talk of cutting gasoline for private cars!); so that the immediate interest of my life gets more and more concentrated on the study and the publication of our material. I have the feeling that I will be more free to turn entirely toward other more important tasks if I can first put down clearly, in a few synthetic papers, the substance of what I think to have understood in the course of twenty years of field work in Asia. In the meantime, my chief preoccupation remains the problem of living Man. I sent you, a few days ago, a short pamphlet (in French!) expressing the present trend of my thoughts. I am slowly busy now with a new and better focused development of the same views. Man cannot become really Man unless he becomes practically conscious of the "cosmic" process of which he is a part and even the responsible apex. Did you read the last book of Julian Huxley (*Man Stands Alone*)? Although Huxley stops too short, I think, and although his book is not constructed into a coherent *Weltanschauung*, I have been delighted to discover that our minds were working so closely. And the same is true with Sherrington (*Man on His Nature*). Unquestionably we are approaching the critical time of a great spiritual revolution. I should like so much to see my own book out (although I am now thinking somewhat ahead of it)! No news from Rome, except that the manuscript is well under "revision." With the present conditions of the mail, I scarcely expect an answer before months.

Just now the main question is the development of the war. Less and less I am able to make a clear internal choice between the conflicting forces. I hate the coercion; but, at the same time, I am convinced that we need a complete panhuman adjustment. In other words, the real problem seems to me *beyond* the present clash — so that I cannot be really interested in the clash. Meanwhile, I think that the extraordinary (and *never* witnessed so far) tension of human energies which we are undergoing now is bound to develop into extraordinary constructive effects. And here I am, waiting for some chance to do something more active. But no outlet so far. From France, nothing comes out (judging from the papers) except a depressive feeling of old-fashioned wisdom, and a puzzling lack of "sense of honor." I still hope for the spark under these ashes; but I do not feel especially attracted to force my way home. America is still the place where I would like best to go . . . something deep, and strong, and free.

September 24, 1941

I hope you have well received my letter of August 5 (did also the French pamphlet reach you?). It seems that the mail has been seriously disturbed, this summer, on the Pacific. Since that time, I went on along the same routine: writing, and printing, full speed. This is the only way to pass the time. If only I could have the feeling that our new institute is a really growing seed! Unfortunately, I am not convinced that our destiny will not be simply that of a shooting star. We are steadily consuming our capital of geological and paleontological data, and I do not see anybody to take the place left empty on our staff by a friend of mine who has recently left the Order, when he was in France. At least a good line of escape remains to me, since, if geological possibilities become exhausted, I can still try to develop and to spread my "ideas." I have just finished a new paper (better focused, I hope) on the same general subject of human phenomenon and human progress. But I get tired to write. I would like to talk and to act. But where? In France, not a breath of intellectual freedom is left (even in the "unoccupied" part): I know it from direct and excellent source. So I am playing with the idea to go for some time in America. But the visas are terribly hard to get. I may try to make these days the preliminary steps: a matter of months.

Peking is terribly empty. And yet, life remains quite possible, thanks to a few good friends left. Gasoline becomes rare . . . I would miss the Sunday trips in the Hills, with the little field work I can still do there.

Tell me what you are thinking and planning.

August 10, 1942

Will this letter ever reach you? Good friends of mine, who leave tomorrow by a "diplomatic boat," will try to mail it somewhere, on their way.

As far as the external life is concerned, almost nothing is changed for me, too little, in fact. Following the break of December 8, I have been out of my lab in town (most of the collections are safe, but I cannot use them any more!), and I am living now in our little institute, busy with the publication of everything I had still to write about my researches in China (we are publishing now our *own* paper, in a special series of memoirs). Nothing very exciting in that; but at least I can do something. These last months, I could also (quite unexpectedly) do some interesting field work in the close vicinity of Peking. But, with the restriction of gasoline, even the small trips become increasingly difficult. At the same time, the town is becoming gradually empty: the twilight of the White Man (but the Dawn will come). For us, here, a kind of overwhelming dullness is the most dangerous enemy. Still a small number of good friends are left here; but so few really inspiring!

Inside, I try to keep as alive and wakeful as possible. My great fear, being here, is to *lose the contact* with the new spirit which certainly is now in making all over the world. On this point, at least, the last events did not change my mind. We are witnessing the birth of a new Man. This I believe more and more. But this new Man is still so much diffused among the conflicting human groups that it is less a matter of speculation than of direct and living trials to discover and recognize him. For this reason, I regret not to be in Europe or in America, really merged in one of the main currents which will combine together tomorrow into something which we can hardly foresee. Here, of course, we are caught in a current, too: but this current is *not* ours. We are externally surrounded and drifted by it: we do not feel it from inside. . . . You, on the contrary, I am sure that you feel intensely alive.

Your last letter received was of September 26. And I was to mail you a letter (already written) on December the eighth! I have no plan, of course, except to escape from China at the earliest opportunity. . . .

October 10, 1945

Mr. Horace J—— is leaving tomorrow for New York. I give him this letter, and maybe you can meet him in N.Y. if you want to have a visual report on the present conditions of Peking.

For me, these long years have been paradoxically quiet, much too much in fact. Except for two or three small trips to Shanghai or to the seashore, I did not move from our small institute of Peking. Cut as we were from the big world (and submerged in a practically nonthinking mass of yellow mankind) we did not have any other escape but to develop a kind of mostly French microcosm, a rather warm nest, in fact, but only a nest. You could not fly very far. . . . Well, I took this chance for writing a rather long series of scientific papers, and a good number of private essays. As far as science is concerned, I have practically exhausted the whole material at my disposal and printed everything essential I have in mind concerning Asiatic geology. I think a few of those papers are really good. But they have been so far scarcely distributed, by lack of mail. Along the philosophical or religious line (the most important for me, as you know), I have been going along the same groove, but deeper, I hope. Presently my two "pet ideas" are what I call the psychical "planetization" of Mankind all around our round Mother Earth, and the spreading of a kind of new Mystics based on "the Love of Evolution." The book I wrote in 1939–1940 on the *Phénomène Humain*" was stopped by censure in Rome, I heard, but rather mildly, so that I hope to get a printing permit eventually. I know that I am now in favor, in France. Time is ripe perhaps, at last!

I have been officially invited to go back to France without delay. But communications are not easy, chiefly if one needs to carry a little more than sixty pounds of baggage. I hope to find some boat at Shanghai before spring. And then there are some serious chances that I shall travel by America (the other ways are closed except by plane), and then we should meet in New York?!

Physically, well, I am four years older, past sixty-four. My hair (what is left of it) is quite gray, now. But, on the whole, I don't think that you would hesitate to recognize me. The body is still strong. But getting older does not make my nerves as calm as I would like. On the whole, I have been spared by the war. Too much, I think. I have been living here in the backwater; and this is not so good for a would-be "prophet." I trust God and Life that nevertheless I can still accomplish something in this newborn world of ours.

The town, since two months, is rejuvenated by a flow of Americans. Everybody likes them: they are so full of vitality, so generous. A succession of parties. I met five or six of them who were *really* interesting.

I must bring this letter at once to J———. So I stop here. But this is a new beginning, already.

S.S. Strathmore
April 12, 1946 (near Colombo)

At the end of February, a cable reached me from my highest superior in France (a great friend), urging my return to Paris. I had already waited too long; and I could not afford to risk major delay. Let us hope that I will be repaid for this "obeissance." In Paris, I am assigned to my old place (15 Rue Monsieur), the stronghold of "progressive Christianity," a good indication that I am wanted in France precisely for the reasons which formerly made me there rather an undesirable. I will write you longer from there, as soon as I have settled. Anyhow, I did not close behind me the gates of China (where the Geological Survey keeps me as an adviser). I must keep the world open to me for further journeys. I don't think that I could bear a purely French life any more.

The *Strathmore* is a beautiful and fast boat, the pride of the P. & O., but half-turned into a military transport. We are rather crowded (some four thousand aboard), and sleeping in "hammocks." Impossible to concentrate and difficult to develop close friendships. Still I can think and have some interesting talks with a few old acquaintances.

Soon I will write you again, from Paris, and let you know my first impressions of Europe and my prospects.

15 Rue Monsieur, Paris VII, May 26, 1946

Since my return here, three weeks ago, I am still submerged: people calling, telephone, letters piling up on my table. Rather exciting, but also bewildering. Like the Buddha, I should like to have ten pairs of hands, ten heads, or only a good and efficient secretary. . . . The journey on the *Strathmore* ended just as it started: no troubles — but no real pleasure. . . .

I feel it difficult to explain to you clearly, in these hasty lines, the substance of my position. In short, I can tell you that, if the political conditions in France are still a maze for me (and everybody) one point is clear. From the philosophical or religious standpoint, there is here a tremendous fermentation, precisely in the direction which has so much attracted me since years. Except for those (the dead ones) who still cling to defeated positions, everybody is craving for a new *Weltanschauung,* or as Huxley puts it, for a "minimum working hypothesis" in which every man anxious to face and control the new world might agree and collaborate with the others. And, as a consequence, I am surprised (and just a little scared) to discover how widely my small papers have spread, and impressed people of every kind, during the seven past years. Something like a rising tide. The problem for me is to keep going ahead, that means to keep my "internal fire or light" always brighter; and this can only be a gift of God. In the meantime, the daily contacts with so many eager souls and brains is a powerful incentive for the further development of my thoughts. So, everything is all right, and even quite exciting, so far. By and by I hope to concentrate on a few selected channels the best of my activities. A first step should be to get the ecclesiastical permission for publishing my book on the "Human Phenomenon" and a few selected papers. A few good articles have already been published or are in printing since my return. As far as science is concerned, I will give two series of lectures the next year (*à la* Sorbonne, and *au* Musée de l'Homme), and, after that, it seems that I can easily get the money sufficient for some scientific trips abroad (China? South Africa?) including a visit to America.

Socially speaking, I have naturally found here a crowd of dear friends, many of them being, like myself, just returned from China. Atmosphere is warm here, and I feel like reborn in the intensity of Western life. Breuil has somewhat aged, but remains as indomitable as before. On a ground of so-called collaborationism (a true psychosis) he has cut V—— down, a situation which does not make life easy at the Institut. I keep carefully outside the conflict which does not interest me. Past is past. We must build ahead.

Material life is quite sufficient here, and, externally Paris is quite alive and pleasing, everybody being surprisingly quiet and smiling, and polite, in the streets, in the Metro, etc. If however you could manage to send me a *few* cigarettes, I would appreciate them very much. . . .

15 Rue Monsieur,
(undated but sometime in July, 1946)

. . . all the last weeks, life kept on being so busy that I scarcely find the time to write any letters. In addition, I had to write, recently, two short articles (one of them on the psychological effects of the atom bomb . . .) which took an appreciable part of my leisure. Now, however, so many people are leaving town that I can breathe more freely. At the beginning of August I plan to leave Paris myself, for Central France, in order to meet some friends near Lyon, and to visit what is left of my family in the Auvergne. On September 18 I must bless the wedding of a niece, not far from Vichy; and on about September 20 I shall be back here.

On the whole my life and my general plans remain the same. Life, here, is terribly exciting and interesting, so many people being on this quest for a thorough readjustment of the world and of their own thoughts. And I am positively amazed, a little more every day, by the spreading, everywhere, during the war of my clandestine papers. During the vacation, I will try to repolish somewhat the manuscript of my book on *Le Phénomène Humain,* with some hope that a new examination of the work will be O.K. But, to be true, I am only half-interested today by this expression of my thought, which I regarded as so *final,* five years ago. . . . Now, I would prefer to write something new, less historical, more concentrated on the structure and the biological behavior of present mankind. But, probably, both points of view are necessary: and I will do my best to salvage the old thing. From the purely scientific side, the situation is less bright — meaning that I do not accomplish much. Next year I will give a few lectures at the Sorbonne, deliver a few "communications" at various societies. But what I need, obviously, is to be back sometime somewhere in the field. Maybe, after a year, it will be possible to make some short expedition in China? Maybe also I will succeed in promoting a small (but efficient) symposium in South Africa (for which I would ask H—— to come: I never found a more congenial coworker in the field). Much depends on the benevolence of the Rockefeller Foundation, which kindly elected me recently as an "associate professor."

Do you know that, thanks to old Weidenreich (still at the American Museum of N.Y.) the two K——s are to spend the next year at New York. . . . My impression is that Mankind needs to be "psychoanalyzed" these days: everybody, I think, is longing for the same Something, today (everybody: technicians or workmen, white or colored people) — but nobody so far was able to give this "Something" its proper name.

Yesterday I got your precious parcel of cigarettes. Magnificent! The only trouble is that the French Customs (very unkind of them!) charge them with such a heavy taxation that I am obliged to ask you to stop your munificence. Anyhow, I got the first lot O.K., and I will enjoy it accordingly.

15 Rue Monsieur, September 21–24, 1946

Your letter of September 17 has just arrived, for my first day in Paris, where I came back yesterday after six weeks of very good holidays. The first weeks I spent in the Lyon area, talking the most part of the day with various old or new friends (mostly belonging to my Order). But, since the beginning of September, I stayed comfortably at home in the nice, old-fashioned country house of my Parisian brother, in Auvergne: a wonderful landscape of meadows and woods, with the whole chain of volcanoes on the skyline against the setting sun. After so many years spent in China, I did not realize that I am still so much rooted, spiritually, in the native ground. My brother is irresistibly sweet and attractive (even for the peasants); and in spite of his living most of the time in Paris in the deep of big business and social circles, his heart remains in the country where he keeps planting oaks for his grand-grandchildren. . . . There is something deeply human and instructive in this faith and attachment to ground and familiar trend, something which has to be preserved even in the biggest transformation of human society. This experience came to me as a good warning, at the time when I am more and more involved in the discovery of the true outlines of Humanity.

Here, I am already caught by the whirl. Since three days I could not finish this letter, always interrupted by people, all of them anxious, in one way or another, to make some sense of Life and Man. This summer, I had four, and even perhaps five, short articles published in various reviews; and I must find the time to write another one (longer) on the Structure and Future of Mankind. Somehow the same old story, but better focused, I think, and much improved. Incessant talking obliges me to go deeper in thinking. I am still surprised, and vaguely anxious, by the way people keep hanging on my small papers, *clandestins* or not. The affair of the publication of my book on Man seems to take the right way. But nothing is decided, yet. Moreover, to be frank, I am less interested in the work than before: the manuscript is already six years old! I would write it a little differently by now. But I have no time and no taste to recast it. I must do something else. If I get the O.K., I will print the thing just as it is, with only a few retouches, and possibly a "post-face."

I am glad to have H——'s address. The possibility of having a symposium in South Africa seems to increase, and I should like to have him in the field. For the next future, I have no plans. I am asked to give lectures in Belgium, Switzerland, and Italy; but I will probably not go, except to Bruxelles. I have plenty enough to do here, and I need also time to work and concentrate with myself.

15 Rue Monsieur, Paris VII, November 1, 1946

Now I am back in Paris, since six weeks. During that time I was mostly busy writing a lecture supposed to be delivered in Bruxelles next week, in which I have tried to focus and concentrate my newest and latest ideas concerning the making of Mankind. Unfortunately, as I will explain to you below, the lecture will not be given this time. But it remains that the paper is there, well written; so that I hope to publish it this winter in a decent review; and this is the main point. On the whole, the demand for my "gospel" is just as big as before, or even it is still increasing. But, as a consequence, some anxiety concerning the whole business has been recently rising in some official quarters; and this is the very reason for which my going to Bruxelles was decided to be, not exactly "undesirable," but "inopportune" and unpolitical. Don't be afraid for me on account of this slight handicap. Following the general meeting recently held by my Order (for the election of a new "General") it seems that I am much more in sympathy with the new government than with the precedent one. I may even hope that the question of the publication of my book on Man will be favorably decided before a few months. You know, since I feel that the best of my ideas is now spreading all around in some irresistible way, I feel much more philosophical about books and printed matter. But at the same time I am passionately decided to go on, always further, along my line. Each time I expect to approach the end of the trend, something new and bigger seems to appear. A very fascinating life, which you certainly experience yourself along your literary road. Just to be able to bring out what one is made for. . . .

As far as pure science is concerned, I am doing very little, because I have very little to do: no material at hand. But it may happen that I should go next summer, for a few weeks, to South Africa in order to study the "Australopithecus" fissures. Thanks to Dr. Weidenreich and the Viking Foundation it seems that money can be found for the trip. I am not so much excited by the prospect as I would have been ten years ago. But the work down there is so much in my line that I feel that I must do it. I need to keep my scientific platform, even for other purposes.

Socially speaking, my life in Paris is highly interesting. Almost every day I come in contact with new and curious personalities interested in the building of a new world, new economics, new ethics, etc.

Since my last letter, life has kept busy, along the same line. More lectures (to rather large audiences of students and even priests!), and a rather crowded social life. The last event was, two days ago, an extremely select dinner at UNESCO House. Huxley took me in a corner to ask me to write down my views concerning a new redaction of *The Rights of Man* to be promulgated, in the next future, under the care of UNESCO. First I did not much react to the proposal; but now I begin to feel positively interested. . . .

The South African business seems rather to materialize. The money is there, at the Viking Foundation; and Camp accepts my association with his expedition. So that I must, one of these days, approach Cook for a prospective reservation in July. I hate this whole business of tickets, money, visas, vaccination, etc. But I think *I have to go:* the call of Life. . . .

I have finished, two days ago, retouching my book on Man. Better than I thought; and decidedly "bettered" by a series of clever (?) touches. Now I will have to send the manuscript first to Lyon for "official" approbation (by friends), and then back to Rome for the official permit to print. Concerning the final decision I am not quite optimistic, but I feel at least quite philosophical.

15 Rue Monsieur, April 9, 1947

Here, my life has been relatively quiet. No more lecturing for a while; and just a little too much evening social life. During these Easter holidays, most people had left town. But now they are coming back. Day after tomorrow I am going (by car) to Beauvais for a semireligious, semiphilosophical "symposium" (managed by a colleague of mine, I could not refuse) which I am supposed to open with a talk on "Human Thought in the World."(!) It will be the turn of the scientific symposium (on genetics and evolution), with Mr. Simpson. I will have to speak twice. Naturally, I will be glad to discuss a lot of theoretical and practical points with Simpson. I can not understand on what grounds Weidenreich could decide that I was not happy in Paris; but at least he wrote me that Mr. F—— was still hoping that I would eventually study his large fossil material from China: and that, of course, has to be kept in mind and carefully considered. All the more so since Rome, friendly but firmly, has finally discouraged me from competing for a professorship *au* Collège de France; for which decision I am unable to feel sorry, since it means for me the continuation of the present regime of complete independence and entire liberty. As a kind of compensation, it seems that the same people in Rome are rather inclined to back me, in full sympathy; so that it might be possible that my book will pass, after all. The manuscript is still being typed. I hope it will reach Rome in May.

15 Rue Monsieur, April 30, 1947

I have just received this morning, on the very eve of the first of May, your letter for my birthday. In fact a birthday has ceased for me, since a long time, to be a particularly cheerful day. Really time is flying too fast, and faster, it seems, precisely when one has the feeling to be able to fill it at the best. Don't believe, however, that I feel especially sorry for myself. Just something human to face, and get the best of it.

The South African plan seems to develop all right. I have received nice welcoming letters from down there. But I have not really started so far on the awful work of material preparations, visas, reservations, vaccinations, etc. I must do it during the coming month. In the meantime, my book is in Lyon for approval (by a group of friends who have read it already). Then, (before June 1, I hope) it will be transmitted to Rome. And then we shall see. In fact I remain rather (with a few others) at the spearhead of the fight for a "new" Christianity, a position that renders my superiors shy whenever it is a question of me. But I find, for me, this situation quite interesting. And, after all,

I am not so excited about the publication (or the nonpublication) of the book. The only thing in which I am *really* interested is that the ideas should spread, helping the conjunction between the two faiths (in God and in Man); and they do. So that I feel really happy.

Paris is simply beautiful: looking from above, the avenues are a green and white river of blooming horsechestnuts. On the whole, my life remains the same. The symposium between biologists and paleontologists kept me rather busy the last week; but the whole thing was rather a success. My mornings are somewhat more free, now, and lectures much less frequent. But now begins the South African business. . . .

15 Rue Monsieur, May 23, 1947

Here my life remains substantially the same, except that more and more new people come on the stage, with the result that I keep talking and thinking more and more. On the whole, the past year (since I came back from China) was probably one of the most interesting periods of my life. In any case it has brought me to perceiving more distinctly than ever what was for me the meaning and the value of life. Now, I think, I know, almost exactly, what are my faith and my "gospel"; and I know also that they can (that they ultimately must) win. Incidentally, the manuscript of my book has been favorably examined in Lyon, and it will soon be forwarded to Rome. But don't be too much optimistical: it is a matter of fifty-fifty — and perhaps still less.

The South African project seems to mature. But I could not settle here, so far, the question of transportation, or at least the question of the date of departure. I would like to leave around the middle of July, so as to be back by the beginning of November. But things are still somewhat uncertain.

When I wrote you the last time, I was reading your book. My final impression is that, from an artistic and psychological point of view, it is decidedly a very good book, which catches the reader and obliges him to criticize his own philosophy of life. Now, as far as *your* interpretation of life is expressed in the novel, you already know my reaction. In one way or another, I think that the "magic" circle must be broken: there is an escape toward an ever growing love. But then one "dimension" more has to be introduced in our experience, the dimension of the "divine" (of the *true* divine, the one, I mean, which does not suppress but transform).

15 Rue Monsieur, July 4, 1947

This is the first letter I am trying to scribble, in a month. A proof, to you, that I am out of my bed and moving in my room. On the whole, I am and feel much better. But the doctors are adamant: I must still stay more or less in my room for a month (July), and then rest somewhere (in the vicinity of Paris) up to December 1. After that, I may go on, with some "precautions," of course.

In the meantime, I have to reconstruct (or to think over) much of my internal life. I doubt that I will be able to be a man "of the field" any more. Then, I must concentrate somewhere else my effort. This incident, I suppose, must be used as the beginning of something constructive and new.

15 Rue Monsieur, Paris, July 17, 1947

I shall try and tell you exactly how I feel. Physically, I am getting better, fast, it seems. Since a fortnight I spend a part of the day walking in the garden of the clinic which is relatively beautiful, for being in the center of Paris. Day after tomorrow, I am going back for a day *aux* Etudes (the next block); and the following day I will go to St. Germain-en-Laye (near Paris) where I am supposed to spend a month in a resting house (well attended by nuns), just next to the St. Germain forest, on the plateau. After that, nothing is clear, so far, except that, up to December 1, I must keep to a somewhat reduced type of life (twelve hours of sleep, as few staircases as possible, no physical strain, etc.), which will apparently keep me (up to November at least) outside of the Etudes house (where there is no elevator!), and possibly in the outskirts of Paris. Morally, I do not yet know exactly where I am standing, except that the springs are still good. I think. Evidently, I still feel sore about the African trip, which was apparently *so exactly* the next step to take for me. And also nobody can tell how much I shall be able to resume the real field work, after six months. . . . Scientifically, I feel a bit afraid to be largely "out of the circuit." But there remains the whole field of Modern Man and Social Biology, the main thing, in fact, which has kept me busy since I am back from China. Is that the "meaning" of the whole thing that I must now concentrate on this new side of my former activities? I can't say positively, so far; but the natural development of things will decide. In any case, one thing is sure: namely that the Human Problem, in the course of these few weeks (I mean the problem of the future of Man) has definitely taken first place in my mind, much above any other scientific preoccupation. I cannot say that I feel particularly cheerful, these days. But I keep a perhaps growing interest in life, which is a lot.

4 Place Louis XIV,
St. Germain-en-Laye (Seine-et-Oise),
August 6, 1947

. . . Yes, I think that there is something to say about the simultaneous shrinking of life and money. Money (just like love and science) is one of those energies (so-called *material* energies) out of which we are gradually brought to discover that there is no possible spiritualization in this evolving World. The only trouble is the way in which this particular money energy has a tendency to freeze and to stick where it happens to accumulate, instead of flowing as it should do.

I write you from a little clinic, right on the border of the St. Germain forest, where I spend a quite comfortable time under the care of extremely attentive nuns (in white and blue dress) who seem to have decided that I should leave their house fat, something, of course, in which they will never succeed, although I must recognize that I am already less thin than I have been in months, and perhaps years. Days are passing pretty fast: first because I stay late in bed, but also because my mind is rather active, with the help of numerous books and also of many dear friends: in spite of the distance from Paris, I get some visit almost every day. So, you see, I am still a *privilégié*. On the other hand, the family got a terrible blow. One of my nephews was drowned in Auvergne, when taking a swim in the pond: caught in the weeds. My brother came to see me last week; he is broken but at the same time so quiet and so strong. Going on. It pays to have a faith. . . . And, really, quite seriously speaking, I don't see how we can escape the alternative: either the world is developing, through good and bad chances, something "adorable," and then we must serve and love it; or it is simply absurd, and *haïssable,* and then we must reject it as much as we can.

Physically, I am quite all right (by the way, what I got is labeled, in barbarous French, *infarctus du myocarde*). But I have to keep quiet, just the same, up to December 1. I will certainly stay here up to the end of August. But afterwards I have no definite plan. The main question will be to readjust my life after December. Apparently, the answer will be given by the circumstances. If it proves at that time that my views on *present* Man are just as much in demand as last year (and if at the same time it becomes clear that extensive field work is no more for me), I may have to say goodby to old mother Paleontology. She brought me internal freedom, and she introduced me to a new science (still unnamed) of Man. But now I am likely to get sick among fossils, mostly if the fossils are in a drawer. And yet, at the same time, it was so comforting to feel a solid ground of material facts under one's feet. . . . We shall see. In the meantime, I don't worry. I just watch things in and around myself.

I did not mention to you the fact that I have been awarded the second degree of the *Legion d'Honneur* (*la rosette*) because, except for the kindness of the people who gave it to me, I would have refused it, by lack of modesty. . . . Decorations are so stupid, and each *vieux monsieur à Paris porte la rosette.* More interesting for me was my election (in June too) as *membre correspondant de l'Académie des Sciences.* But even that did not much interest me. I had the impression to be stronger and freer being nothing, and having nothing. A super-form of pride, probably; but also the disgust to see so many people hunting for "distinctions," instead of giving their life to a bigger Life.

August 18, 1947

Here, my life is just the same. Nothing really exciting. But I have the feeling that my mind is maturing; and it seems to me that the few really important points in my *Weltanschauung* are getting better and better focused. Thus, I keep interested in life; and even I am gradually developing the subject and the plan of several new papers. Well maybe I will soon bless the circumstances which may oblige me eventually to say goodby to geology. . . .

September 2, 1947

Nothing new in my life. I simply keep on reading and thinking, and even writing. Did I tell you that, a fortnight ago, I went to Versailles, to address a rather important (but rather mixed, too) meeting of foreign and French Jesuits? In fact, my paper was read by somebody else; but I directed the discussion without being tired at all. Friends are coming here almost every day. On the whole, the place is good; so that I might stay here until the beginning of October. Nothing is decided so far.

Since I wrote you the last time, life went on here just the same: a magnificent weather, beautiful trees, plenty of good books, a number of friends coming to see me, and a satisfactory growth of thought, inside.

The only drawback during this period was that I am once more in trouble with Rome. Apparently I have offended more people than I realized by my old papers. On the whole, the fundamentalist offensive of last year has been repelled O.K.; but someone has to pay something for it. And, in order to protect me from something dreadful (probably to be inscribed on the "Index"?), my "General" Father has decided that I should keep quiet (that is refrain from any publication) for the time being, in the line of philosophy and theology. On scientific matters, no restriction. But where does the limit lie for those people? . . . Well, I feel quite philosophical about the whole thing, because I know by experience (for the third time, at least) that such handicaps, if well managed, do not stop, but on the contrary help, the progress and diffusion of ideas. And, in addition, I have got so many devoted friends in good strategical positions that I feel quite safe about the future. Nevertheless it is a pity to have always to fight against some enemies inside. No wonder if Christianity looking from outside looks so backward and so slow. . . . In the meantime, of course, I keep thinking, talking and writing just as before. But that, of course, is quite fair play, and recognized as such even by my General.

Paris, December 23, 1947

I hope that your trip back to New York was a smooth and pleasant one. And now here is my Xmas letter, just a little delayed because I tried to avoid that our messages should cross each other — which of course they will do. May these feast days be as radiant as possible, for you and for N——! My deepest wish, as you know, is that a few more rays (light and heat, that is interior warmth) may penetrate the deep of you, coming from the main focus of love, above and inside of you. Don't be impatient however: just keep your mind and your heart open in the right direction — the direction of what is bigger than you.

No answer from Rome so far. But that does not mean anything I suppose. In the meantime, I had my passport fixed from the French side, which of course is already one step toward America. Life in Paris is quite normal, for the time being.

Last week, I gave two lectures in half-private circles: one at the Normal National School of St. Cloud (a rather anticlerical stronghold), and the other one to a group of advanced students, not far from here. Very seldom did I have the feeling to express so well what I felt and what I wanted to say; evidently many things have matured in my mind since two years, and I feel that there is some strength there. "With the help of God," I am quite confident for the future. In the meantime, I have written a new paper these days (I have a faint hope, now, that the one written this summer will be published); and I am planning to write more. My impression is positively that my *Weltanschauung* is getting focused very fast, since a few months. We shall see.

Socially speaking, I have nothing to complain of. Last Sunday I went to a tea party at B——'s (Canadian Embassy). Lot of writers, painters, etc., in the crowd (Maurois, Lacretelle, Gilson, etc.) and also a dear friend just back from Mexico (UNESCO). Yesterday I saw Ella Maillart (the girl who traveled Asia). You know that during the war she stood at the feet of an Indian guru, where she found a kind of peace. We had a long talk on Vedant mystics, which I distrust more and more (because I think that it solves incorrectly and even sophistically the fundamental problem of Unity, and logically destroys Love).

Paris, January 3, 1948

Last week my niece was officially *fiancée;* and for the circumstance we had a family dinner at my brother's. It really seems that the two young people are starting on a durable and happy union. The absence of the brother, of course (who died in July), was there as an undertone of melancholy . . . but not a real shadow. You know, that is one of the strongest points of Christianity, and a reason why it is bound to win somehow and some way: no other type of faith that has so far been developed in mankind is equally able to make the World around us (in spite of its immensity and apparent blindness and ruthlessness) sweet and *warm* inside (because it is personal, lovable, and loving at its upper term and in its essence). The real threat for Man is not a refrigerating Earth, but an "internally" impersonal, icy World. And, if I am right, this is not a question of "wishfulness," but a strict, biological question of survival. Anyhow, what I wanted to say is that sorrow was not sadness, at the betrothal of my niece, last Sunday; and that's much. . . .

Paris, January 25, 1948

These few lines to tell you that everything is coming along satisfactorily. I had my smallpox vaccination. The question of the visa is going more slowly, on account of the routine formalities.

Nothing much besides; except that I still gave a small series of lectures in half-private circles, yesterday especially in a restricted group of Marxists (professors, mostly). I have the feeling to master more and more my own point of view and to reduce it more and more to its clearest possible essence. I like this type of work.

A week ago, in the course of a meeting of the "Congress of Faiths" (which I am usually asked to attend, you know, although it's not exactly in my line), I was simply aghast when unexpectedly there entered a true and real Burmese "pongi," in full yellow attire (no rice bowl, however). The yellow bird was talking English; and he explained that he was the first of a flock sent to Europe in order to bring the West in genuine touch with the East. Touching, but not convincing. I told you, I think, what I am thinking of the so-called spirit of the East. The appearance of the pongi was the result of a sort of mistake. But I was thoroughly amused; and, in a *raccourci*, I saw the whole Burma, 1938.

February 6, 1948

Nothing new. Yesterday I gave a lecture to the Ecole Supérieure de la Guerre on Man and Mankind, before an impressive number of stars and *galons*. And the most funny part was that, after the lecture, I was driven to develop lengthy considerations on . . . original sin! Just the burning subject which I am supposed to avoid by all means. I really believe in Providence.

Georgetown University, Washington, D.C.
Friday, April 2, 1948

Nothing special along the way down here except that between Philadelphia and Baltimore, I had an interesting talk when I tried to open the eyes of a rather openminded Catholic student of the Pennsylvania University on the true nature of the present spiritual conflict in the world.

Yesterday I paid a visit to Mrs. and Ambassador Grew in the most charming residence in the woods: an exact replica of my visit to them in Tokyo in 1937. This morning I am going to the anthropological meeting at the National Museum; yesterday I met Weidenreich with two anthropologists, both of whom are to come to the Viking Fund talk. One of them told me that, starting from an atheistic base, he had the impression that he had reached the same conclusions as I have reached, concerning Man. That seems interesting.

Paris, June 22, 1948

. . . I have succeeded in writing a few pages (not yet absolutely finished) on a subject which occurred to my mind in New York ("On the directions and the conditions of the Future"). I am not particularly satisfied by the product. But it is already something to have been able to express decently a new aspect of my ideas. I wrote, as usually, these pages, paragraph by paragraph, in the morning between several "visits" and many telephone calls. A lot of people are still in Paris; and I am still far from having reestablished the most necessary contacts. Three days ago I had a dinner with Malvina Hoffman (Mme. de la B——— was also there) in her Parisian studio, which I had not seen since more than twelve years. Nothing was lost during the war! My *buste* (the head only) was there, for improvement (less pious . . .); but I did not see the new version, still under a veil.

Tomorrow I will write Rome in order to get an answer, both for the "six lectures" and for the Collège de France, for which I am now positively asked to be a candidate (by the people of the Collège). To be true, I am not specially tempted by this proposal. The number of lectures (at least twenty) seems to me too big; and, as you know, I am no longer so keen about prehistory. Anyhow, it will be interesting to have Rome's reaction.

I do not make any summer plans so far. Vaguely, I intend to spend a month with my brother, between August 20 and September 20. Just now, Paris is all right: green and almost cold.

15 Rue Monsieur, June 30, 1948

Here, I am gradually living again the old life, too much dispersed perhaps, without enough of a definite central work. I have finished the short essay I told you about ("On the directions and the conditions of the Future"); but I am not sure whether I will be able to get it printed. Nothing yet (but this is quite normal) from Rome, concerning the lectures in America and the Collège de France. Last week I had quite a pleasing talk with the administrator of the Collège. As I told you, I feel quite (perhaps too much) philosophical about the question. One reason to be calm is that, putting everything at the best, I could not be named to the professorship before spring 1949!

On the whole, as you see, things are going sufficiently well for me. Yet I need God to pour in me a new supply of spiritual energy.

15 Rue Monsieur, Paris VII, July 5, 1948

Life is going along rather the same. No answer from Rome, so far. But this is normal: things always go along rather slowly down there. I keep seeing a rather large number of people; and yesterday I had a private talk to some forty or fifty "sympathizers" in a most charming frame: the studio of an artist who designs the most astonishing modern tapestries I have ever seen. To deliver this talk was a good thing for me; because that gave me the proof and the feeling of realizing something. What I need probably, just now, is a definite line or prospect of activity in the future. Practically, I am still living *au jour le jour*. Each day is sufficiently full and interesting. But I need something clearer and bigger ahead. Let us wait for the answer of Rome.

I was rather distressed by the letter from I———. Well, the conclusion is always the same: love is the most powerful and still the most unknown energy of the world.

Now that I have finished the small essay I told you about (about the Directions of Man's Future), I will possibly write a short synthesis of my whole *Weltanschauung (Comment je vois)* not in a very developed way, but as a series of short and clearly connected propositions — just as Mr. Leibnitz did in his "Monadology." I tried it once already in China, and I liked the result: shorter, and more efficient, although less artistic than an "oratory" exposition. To do this work would not be so extraneous as you think to the composition of the six lectures.

15 Rue Monsieur, Paris VII, July 11, 1948

Yesterday I got a letter from Rome: very good, essentially, but at the same time quite troublesome. In two words, F. General thinks that everything will probably be O.K. (including perhaps the publication of my book), but beforehand, he wants me to come to Rome, for conversations at the beginning of October, for "one or two months." Following these conversations, he is confident that he will permit me everything (not aware — as I wrote him today in a most respectful answer — that both Dr. Fejos and the Collège de France want an answer *before Octo-ber* . . .). The whole thing is still a mix-up. And yet, objectively, this invitation for me to go to Rome is perhaps the chance of my life, and the turning point for a broader and more direct type of activity. Everybody agrees here that the thing sounds like a success for me. And the *ton* of F. General is distinctly pleasing. As soon as I get complementary instructions from Rome, I will let you know. In the meantime, I will probably write to Dr. Fejos that "most probably" I will get the permission for the six lectures.

Nothing new, besides (this is enough!). I am slowly, but steadily, advancing the paragraphs of *Comment je vois.* . . .

P.S. Just received the answer of Rome. Extremely kind in *ton;* and exactly what I should have expected. Namely, I have to express frankly (both to America and the Collège de France) the reason for the situation, and to tell them to wait (if they can) up to November, or to decide on a probability. If they cannot wait, then I have to give up. As I told you, I would not weep over the Collège. As for America, the lectures could be postponed.

Les Moulins par Neuville, (Puy-de-Dôme),
September 2, 1948

Here, I am still contemplating the rolling woody hills, the *plaine de la Limagne,* and the volcanoes on the skyline. After finishing some ten pages in which I have tried to compress (as an Introduction to my Bibliography: some 125 notes or memoirs) the most substantial results of my scientific work, for the Collège de France, I have decided to make (rather *less* than more strictly) what is called, among us, my "retreat": meaning that, for a week (to end on September 7), I mostly try to keep in touch or contact with the Existence and the "Omnipresence" of God. Not much external change in my life, in course (everything is so quiet and silent, here): but mostly a slight and continuous effort to live a bit more *inward,* closer to the universal Center of conscious convergency which I am so eager to defend and to prove, but whom I am so far still (unfortunately) from experiencing as a *real* thing. I feel certainly better and stronger for this kind of contemplation or prayer. And, at the same time — because I cannot think of God without the World, nor of the World outside of God — many of my old views on the structure and the future of Man become more clear and vivid, at the same light. *Physical* anxiety still hangs over me: I try to forget it. On the whole, I am certainly recuperating slowly here. Perfect weather: clear and cool. Grapes are turning black. But I will leave (on about the fifteenth) before they are ripe. I am reading a little, scribbling notes, and mostly wandering under the big oaks.

Les Moulins par Neuville, (Puy-de-Dôme),
September 7, 1948

I am approaching the last days of my stay in Auvergne. Nothing is decided exactly concerning my return to Paris: but it certainly will be on about the fifteenth. In the meantime, I have just finished the kind of "retreat" in which, as I told you, I had embarked: a rather simple and mild effort to live more closely in the all-embracing presence of God, the common and living Center to which we are converging. I think I was right to take my chance, and to profit by my last week here (an especially calm week) for this performance. When I come back to Paris, I will have very little time to be busy inside.

You ask me what I think will happen in Rome. Well, the idea of F. General is apparently to have a personal "contact" with me, and to leave me relatively free to publish and talk under certain conditions. But how far this meeting will bring us to a true understanding, or merely to a "compromise," I have no idea. I know that one of my best and truest friends (F. P. C——) has just passed through Paris (coming from Rome) last week, and that he left to O—— and J—— some suggestions as to how I should act. But I think and I feel that (just as with the "American" and Fordham people) I will follow my own inspiration, and speak (nicely) exactly as I think. I am not going to Rome to ask anything, but rather to let free, out of me, at the head of my Church, whatever has become evident to me, in the course of the years. What we need, all of us, is a clear statement of the religious conditions of the world. And I am decided to speak, quite nicely, but *clearly* (with the competent people only, of course). I think I can do it without any undue risks. I have always noticed that you can say about everything, provided you use the right *ton*. And in this case I have not to force myself to keep some unnatural *ton*. Quite sincerely, I am deeply attached to Christianity: but I simply think that, in the present conditions, Christ *is kept too small* (as compared with the World): this they *cannot* resent (the only trouble is — and may be — that they do *not see the real* size of the World . . .).

Les Moulins, September 13, 1948

Tomorrow, I am leaving the dear Moulins, and back again Rue Monsieur. I feel some slight melancholy at the prospect, because I have developed a kind of habit, being here, in the quietness of the fields and of the woods. But I suppose I have gotten as much rest as I could. And also I have some idea that too much protracted relaxation is not exactly the best for my nerves.

In a week or ten days, I must address in Versailles a large audience of priests (those in charge of the Young Workmen's Association). But this is a very sympathetic group of men, so that I will only have to speak quite openly and naturally what I think and feel about the "new Christianity" and the "new Humanism" — an easy task, on the whole.

Two days ago, we paid a visit, on the very border of the Allier River, to my sister-in-law Caroline. I am very fond of her. To see her, and the old house (still so full of my brother's presence) moved me quite a bit; and so many *souvenirs* rose up in my mind which I thought were completely dead. . . . But at the same time I realized once more how impossible it has become for me to look in any direction except forward.

15 Rue Monsieur, September 18, 1948

I came back here, with my brother, last Tuesday. And it seems very probable that I will leave for Rome during the very first days of October (I am expecting an answer from Rome), provided that there are no strikes or anything else. In the meantime, I have a good many small things to do: equipment, visa, money, a talk (in Versailles, the twenty-first) to a large gathering of priests working among the "proletarians," the last touch to my Bibliography, some visits to the Collège de France, etc.

I was quite interested by the clippings included in your last letter. As far as the Pope's speech is concerned, you know that I express things somewhat differently: the conflict is not between Christianity and atheism, but between the old and traditional faith in a celestial escape *upward* and another new faith, in an evolutionary escape *forward;* and the capital thing to see is that between *upward* and *forward* there is no contradiction but essential complementarity. This is the very core of my "message" to Rome. Concerning Huxley's book, it's really strange how close we come to each other. But I got "angry" at the reviewer, when he criticized Huxley's warning that in the near future we shall be able to control genetically the products of human generation; because, the reviewer says, it is impossible or dangerous to decide what should be the "best" human type. A very stupid criticism (probably expressing some anticommunist feeling), underestimating the fact that, if Man really succeeds in controlling his own heredity, no force in the world will prevent him from using his new power. I recognize that planning is always dangerous. But the question is not there. The question is to decide whether Man can avoid being forced to plan, by the very process of cosmic evolution. And the answer is that he *cannot:* because planning is the essence of Life.

I have on my table since two days, *The Heart of the Matter:* I will read it as soon as I can. *La Porte Etroite* is a clever but extremely unpleasant book: this idea of a value of sacrifice and pain for the sake of sacrifice and pain itself (whereas the value of pain is simply to pay for some useful conquest!) is a dangerous (and very "Protestant") perversion of the "meaning of the Cross" (the true meaning of the Cross is: "Toward progress through effort"). I am sure you will not like this face of Gide's genius, expressing his native Protestant education.

15 Rue Monsieur, Paris VII, September 25, 1948

So far no answer from Rome, concerning the best time for my departure. So, if nothing has arrived next Monday, I will make a reservation for the first days of October.

Tuesday last, I went to Versailles (I was almost stopped at the last minute by a strike), on a beautiful day. The audience was certainly interesting and *sympathique:* some three hundred priests, from everywhere in France, all in charge of workmen's associations, or even working with the workmen themselves. I think I was all right; in any case, I spoke to them from the deep of my heart; and I know that I was understood. Certainly two such hours repay for many weeks, or even years, of silence. In the meantime both the social and political world are more and more tense; and financially, in spite of an increase of production, people are rather gloomy concerning the future of France. A new spirit is obviously necessary, and very soon, for our changing world! I was quite interested by your reaction to Gide: but this is precisely the whole question, on which we have been and shall again discuss: how much can Man (endowed by the very process of development of consciousness with the fearful power of foresight) live any more in the present only?

Maybe this is the fundamental point on which modern Mankind has to make its choice. As far as Kafka is concerned, I regard him simply as a sick man, and his admirers are weaklings, to be swept away by the next human wave.

15 Rue Monsieur, October 2, 1948

I am leaving this evening, due to Rome. According to a letter just received, it seems that I may not be back in Paris before November 10 (the last limit for the Collège de France): they want clearly to settle the question of the book, and (for some reasons) they think that this process might take some time (which I personally think an error: either they will require deep changes, and I will not accept; or the retouches will be slight, and then things will go on fast). We shall see. As I told you, I am leaving without pleasure, but with decision and "conviction": because I must "deliver my soul" (*délivrer mon âme*). Religious dissatisfaction and hopes are too big in the world, just now: something has to be told and done.

My friend A—— B—— (the prehistorian) is now in Paris; but he will be back in Rome long before I leave Italy. I saw him yesterday, and he gave me a lot of important hints. According to him, Spirit is now blowing, even in Rome!

Borgo S. Spirito, 5 Rome, October 10, 1948

Since almost a week I am here, so that I am in a rather good position to give you a reasonable account of my first impressions in and of the "Eternal City." On the whole, they are good; and (probably on account of both the change and the relaxation) I feel much better physically than ever since May. Now let us come to some details. The journey was very easy (and beautiful: you certainly know the descent from the Simplon to the Lake Majeur), because, in spite of the inconveniently late time of the arrival (midnight), a friend was waiting for me on the platform. Presently, I am located at the headquarters of the Order (but not in the F. General's wing), on the border of Place St. Pierre. Just behind the house, I can enjoy an extraordinary look all over the Tiber and Rome, far up to the Mountains Albins, etc. — so much for the landscape. In spite of the fact that I knew very few people here (no *real* friends) I was quite nicely welcomed; and I must say that the Great Chief (I had only one talk with him so far, day before yesterday: he is very busy of course) — I must say that the Great Chief is particularly pleasing: I don't think that we see the world exactly the same way, he and I. But he is extremely open-minded, frank, and he wants you to speak frankly. So that the general atmosphere is decidedly good. But everything takes time here. First I have to wait for the last critics of my manuscript (they are expected this coming week, I hope). And then we shall see. Even if I give up retouching my book (because I should have too much to alter in my text) I am pretty sure that the climate will be sufficiently clarified and sunny at the end of my visit to guarantee me a serious increase of liberty, both in writing and talking. In the meantime, I am writing a tentative Summary (or "post-face") to my book, which may prove useful to avoid misunderstandings, and, at the same time, express my point of view (better focused since ten years) in its "up-to-date" shape. One of the main reasons for my being summoned to Rome, I can see it clearly now, is that I should meet people (officials and professors), in order to convince them *de visu* that I am quite an honest and tractable person. Along the line of meeting people (outside of my Order), I did not go very far up to now. But the rate of contacts will probably accelerate geometrically, by and by. Just now, I enjoy to be calm and take quiet walks in town, a little before sunset. Yesterday I went to the dark shadows of the Pincio, thinking. Artistically Rome gave me absolutely no shock (I feel curiously immune to the Past). But one of the most powerful spiritual axes of the world is certainly passing here. If only it could be set to move! . . . By and by I will let you know the next development. But probably no decision, in any direction, will be reached before a fortnight.

P.S. I have read *The Heart of the Matter* by Graham Greene. A study in despair. Why never a study on hope? Very clever, anyhow. We shall discuss the case. Incidentally, the Graham Greene title would be wonderful for me (although with a quite different meaning) for an essay I am dreaming to write since some time under a name which occurs to my mind in English (untranslatable into French): "The Golden Glow" (meaning the appearance of God from and in the "Heart of Matter"). I shall explain this to you.

Borgo S. Spirito, 5 Rome, October 19, 1948

Since my last letter, nothing particularly new, except that I have got (two days ago) the first of the two critics ("revisions") of my book which I was expecting (the most dangerous of the two, I expect). Well, after the first reading of these ten long pages, I felt rather discouraged by a decided "incapacity of seeing" Man and the World, too much obvious in the mind of my censor. But, after a while, I collected my forces; and, by the way of a series of rather clever retouches and footnotes, I hope that my original text will now look more printable, or even clearer and more interesting than before, *without* any distortion of my thoughts. I would be astonished if, on account of the second set of criticisms, I should have to make any more changes. And then the time will be ripe for the final decisions (Collège de France, etc.). Nothing new so far in this direction.

In the meantime, the program of my days remains the same: work during the morning, and a walk during the two last hours before sunset. So far I did not see much of the important clerical people (except a few): but, along this line, I do not make a step without being introduced by the man (a friend) who advises me *de la part du* Father General. On the whole, days are passing rather fast; and I can easily foresee that before long they will be more and more crowded.

Physically, I feel all right; and intellectually very much alive: things seem to me more and more simple and clear, along the same trends.

15 Rue Monsieur, Paris VII, December 27, 1948

Nothing yet from Rome. . . . I am going to write, tomorrow, to my friend the No. 2, asking for an answer. In the meantime I keep busy enough: two talks under preparation (for January), and the "recension" of a book on "animal tools" which gives me a chance to focus and to present some pet views on the development and nature of Life. I have a feeling that my *Weltanschauung* (whatever its value may be) is taking rapidly a more definite shape; and still more I see more clearly every day that the great event of our times (somewhat comparable with, but much more important than, Galileo's discovery that Earth was in motion) is that we become aware of a movement of Mankind as a whole toward increasing arrangement and consciousness. I experience almost every day the power of such a simple *constatation* on the mind of people around me; and I like to do it.

January 2, 1949

Nothing from Rome! I have written a few nice lines, asking for a quick answer. In the meantime a rather nasty and stupid article was published (next to one equally bad on Maritain) in a fundamentalist monthly of France, against me. The paper (*la Revue en question*) is notoriously reactionary, so that I consider that this attack (at least the third one in the course of two years — they ought to pay me for supplying them with something to say!) acts rather as an advertisement. Still, we have decided with O—— to take this opportunity to make Rome observe that the best way to stop such criticisms should be to let my book out: so that the opponents will have no more excuses left if they understand me the wrong way. We shall see. In fact, I understand perfectly the fundamentalists' anger. Just now, we are once more, exactly in Galileo's position, except for the fact that it is no more the Earth's physical, but Man's mental, motion which is presently under discussion. And to be involved in such an affair is certainly the greatest fun of my life.

Last Thursday I went to an elaborate lunch, . . . in one of

the nicest hotels of the Boulevard St. Germain. Mr. Bidault and his most intelligent wife were there. A very good chance I had, and did not miss, to say a few strong words about the present condition of religion.

Breuil wrote me from Johannesburg. He is still planning to be back in Paris for the spring, but not so sure not to go back again (for good?) to South Africa.

15 Rue Monsieur, Paris VII, January 10, 1949

As I wrote you, the week was rather busy for me. First (this was not on the program) I received an entirely uninteresting letter from Rome, written (in order to be nice, obviously) by the General himself, but with no mention of the pending questions (I am expecting an answer on this subject from my friend the No. 2, any day). The General was only anxious to have some explanations concerning an address of mine to a meeting of the priests in charge of the Young Workmen's Association (in Versailles, last September): a rather clumsy report concerning this address had been published in December by the archclerical *Osservatore Romano,* and some important people (the Pope??) were growing disturbed. . . . I sent back a very respectful, but just a little terse, answer, pointing out incidentally that everything I thought was in a certain manuscript now in Rome, and that the shortest way to cut any misinterpretations of my *Weltanschauung* might be to have the book published. Well, I have not the slightest intention to be rude, or to make things tense between me and my Order. But, since I am back from China, I can clearly notice that I am becoming more and more clear-cut and adamant on a few dividing positions: and that cannot change any more. Yesterday again I had rather strongly this feeling when discussing at L——'s (before a group of priest-scientists) what I call "the new Galileo's case," that is, the question to know whether Mankind is still moving ahead (not in Space, but in Consciousness). In the occurrence, I confess that I reached the limits of an academic behavior. . . .

This coming week, I will give a semiprivate lecture for *Psyché* on *Les conditions psychologiques de L'Unification Humaine*.

Not a word yet from F. de Gorostarzu! Since he is certainly a good friend, and very free with me, I have good reason to believe that, before answering me, he is just waiting for something which he is expecting to get any day. Still, if nothing comes out, I am decided to write again before the end of the week.

Last week went along rather calmly. I gave a lecture for *Psyché*, before a rather large, but most funny audience. Outside of a reasonable number of personal friends *de tout plumage*, I had to address a group of professional psychoanalysts, who, judging from their remarks, seem to be rather narrow- or confused-minded type of people. Fortunately, everything went off all right. After the meeting we had, some ten of us, a merry drink at the nearby Café de Flore. An extensive summary of the talk will be printed in *Psyché*. And just now, I am preparing another lecture, to be given on January 29 at the Musée Guimet people (Union of Faiths) on "the fear of Existence."

On a more social ground, I had lunch at the *duchesse de la* R—— and a dinner with Siegfried (the economist) and Professor Leriche (a famous surgeon), both of them on their way back from South Africa or America. Interesting talks; but I was struck by the fact that neither Siegfried nor Leriche apparently considered the fact that no human problem (and specifically the problem of colored people) could be conveniently approached before accepting some fundamental views concerning the structure and the biological trend of Mankind. Decidedly, it might be of some general interest that I give and publish the famous "six lectures." . . .

Tomorrow, I am going to meet the new director of UNESCO, Mr. Torres . . . , the Mexican, a quite intelligent and efficient man, I was told, but of diplomatic training. His first speech, in Beyrouth, was rather or even remarkably good; except for the fact that he too seems to rely too much on negative conditions, and not enough on a common faith to build a peaceful world.

January 25, 1949

. . . still nothing from Rome!! As I already told you, there is certainly no ill will toward me down there. But then what? I have refrained so far from writing a second time to Gorostarzu. But I will certainly do so before the end of the week. Putting everything at the best, I do not see how I could possibly get to New York this spring now. In any case I am taking the first steps to try out the lectures here, *à la* Sorbonne, before Easter. No better way to have them fully ready for America. . . .

Last week was rather interesting and busy. First I wrote down the lecture on *La Peur de l'Existence* (the real expression I use is *La Peur Existentielle*), which I am supposed to deliver next Saturday, in a private salon, Place des Vosges. I will try to have the text printed and published somewhere. Besides I met a good number of people, including the new general director of UNESCO (Mr. Torres Bodet, a Mexican) who was very nice; and a curious young Belgian lawyer and medical doctor, a determined but bold Catholic, who has started (in a very courageous little book) a campaign against the narrow and perverted way in which sex questions are handled in Catholic circles. . . . Evidently, in spite of every kind of barrier, the flow is moving everywhere. This is one of the reasons for which I do not think that I shall ever be really muzzled. Sorry for the Trappist monk. . . : but it becomes more and more evident every day that no religion will satisfy Man henceforth, unless it combines together both the faith in Heaven *and* in Earth. In other words, no force can attract Man to God, unless, and by the same drive, it pushes Man to the last limits of what he can discover, experience, and conquer. I am surprised at times to observe how much this conviction has become the soul of my life. . . .

15 Rue Monsieur, Paris VII, February 1, 1949

Still nothing from Rome. O—— has written to the Chief some ten days ago (insisting upon the printing of my book); and I have sent myself a word to de Gorostarzu asking for explanations. In despair, if I may say, I have asked and gotten from the Sorbonne the permission to give, in March, a series of five lectures (*cours libre*) on the structure and evolutive trends of the Human group; an excellent rehearsal, I suppose, of what I will be allowed to say, some day, in America. I could not wait any longer, as far as *la Sorbonne* is concerned.

Last Saturday, I gave (in a beautiful private drawing room, Place des Vosges) my lecture on *La Peur Existentielle* before a rather large gathering of distinguished, but rather mixed, people: and the audience was apparently much more moved than I expected. Evidently, my very simple, aphilosophical, almost experimental *Weltanschauung* of a "converging Universe" appeals considerably to the modern mind. I had of course to emphasize once more my belief in the fact that the World would be a failure if anything both "incommunicable" and "personalistic" in it should disappear; which means that, according to cosmic structure, each loving center, and each loving association of loving centers is *irréversible,* that is, "immortal," as far as the love it contains is concerned. Looking from this angle, Love is, biologically and physically, the principle and the measure of immortality. I think I will write something on that next spring ("The Heart of Matter," you know). I have the funny impression never to have been so "fragile" in my body (and yet I feel very well) and at the same time so "strong" in my mind as since I got this health business two years ago. I tell you: we have to rely on Life and on what is behind Life. The greatest and the most efficient form of spiritual life is *la confiance* — which is nothing else but another side of Love.

I hope that I—— will excuse me for not having written to her for such a long time and yet I want to do it every day. With my broken mornings and a good many things to prepare (I wrote entirely my two last lectures, without, of course, using my text for talking) my time is full up. I am finishing, just now, a few pages in answer to an *enquête* of UNESCO on the meaning of "Democracy." The questions were put down in a quite political and juridical way; and I try to uncover the biological and anthropological side of the matter.

15 Rue Monsieur, Paris VII, February 8, 1949

I have to tell you that I have finally gotten a letter from Rome, and that (as was to be expected) the letter is not good: no lectures in America (the Superiors in America have objected to the plan, which, I am afraid, was proposed to them in an "unpolitical" way, not insisting enough on the limited number and dominantly technical subject of the lectures; but what could I do . . .); no printing of *Le Milieu Divin* (rather badly treated by a Roman censor, in spite of the fact that it was unanimously accepted, in 1930, by the theologians of Louvain, and extensively read and used, since twenty years, by a lot of priests and religious people of all feathers); the shadow of a chance is still left to the *Phénomène Humain* (still under a further examination), but there is not much hope left. And, *pour finir,* I am once more asked to keep to purely scientific subjects, which of course is psychologically impossible.

Well, at first glance, that seems to be a fine mess. But in fact I think that things will go on, in the next future, just the same way. F. O—— does not see any reason why I should give up the Sorbonne lectures. And I will go on addressing small groups of people, and writing for a small circle, as before. Experience proves that the process is extremely efficient. And after that, God will provide, and we shall see. To be true, the weakest point of the situation just now is that I don't see how to disappear for a few months as I used to do before with China. The best escape would be America — but when, and to do what? I have written to Father L—— for an eventual shelter. And I am going to write to Mr. Fejos too, in order to explain to him the present situation. Maybe he will have some suggestion for some purely scientific work. Leaving the Order, *à ce point des choses,* would be suicidal, as far as the success of my "gospel" is concerned. In addition to the bad effect of the gesture on my "followers," don't forget that my whole spiritual construction is genuinely built on (or rather culminating into) an enlarged and "rejuvenated" figure of Christ: so that I can do nothing in the way of parting from the "Church" which is, biologically speaking, the "phylum" of Christ. The only thing I can do is to work *"from inside."* Try to understand it. And don't forget either that things are often working in the most funny and unexpected way. In addition to the real "advertisement" which the present difficulties are for my ideas, there is also the fact that the conflict helps me a lot to focus better and better the problem and its possible solution. The General is pretty narrow and strict for political reasons; but to somebody he told that I possibly was a kind of "precursor," which (true or not true) proves that he is not completely blind as far as the value of my spiritual stand is concerned. In other words, the best thing, at least presently, seems to be for me to adopt the tactic of "the mule"; just to be stubborn and sweet. . . .

One thing I did not yet tell you is that the General's stiffness is partly due to the unfortunate (and ridiculous) *compte rendu* published in *Osservatore Romano* of my lecture of September at Versailles. Would you believe that, in this *compte rendu,* I was numbered among *"les éminents théologiens"!* In Rome, these words sounded as a provocation, and a corrective note was published last week, to the effect that I was *not* a reliable theologian. We had a good laugh here, in Paris. But, in Rome, they took the matter seriously. Hence the loss of a good part of what I had gained in October in the line of a good reputation.

Too much already about these petty things. Please, believe me: Christianity is something much bigger than these *mesquineries.* As I told you in my last letter, the time has come to decide and to choose between a static or a moving Mankind. I will be proud of my life if, up to the last minute, I can use it as a proof of my belief and my faith in a converging movement of the Universe.

The news from Rome had reached me on Friday the fourth; and, since it was not good, I was not in a hurry to send it to you before I could reflect a little on the situation. Anyhow, you must by now have my lines, and know that I do not feel particularly depressed. I will not write Fejos before you tell me what you think of the possibilities in that direction. In any case I will let him know about the present situation. Maybe, after all, when I have given the Sorbonne lectures, prejudices will decrease, and the possibility reappear to talk in America. . . . Nothing else from Rome. Before a month I am expecting the final "verdict" concerning *Le Phénomène Humain* (without any hope, of course). From a letter of Gorostarzu (to whom I have sent a nice, but frank answer) it clearly appears that the note sent to the clerical press (to the effect of "correct" the article published on me in *Osservatore Romano*) was ordered by the Pope himself! Now I understand why His Holiness told Mme. de M———, exactly in January, that I had more imagination than theological knowledge. There is a very funny side to the whole business. The result (in France, at least) was to increase sympathy for the cause I am representing. Yet, it remains that Rome, in an instinctive gesture of self-preservation, is stiffening just now against any kind of really progressive thought (which of course, as far as I can see, is precisely the way to increase the danger). . . . And do believe me. Between my way of thinking and the really "orthodox" (I do not say "official" but "practical") Christian vision of the World, there is not such a big gulf as you think. The proof is the way in which the best of the Catholics are jumping on my poor essays. As I wrote a few days ago to a Superior, a good friend of mine, I do not know whether my bread is well baked: anyhow, the way the people eat it is a pathetic proof how much they are starving for a food in which Love of God does not exclude, but include, Love of the World. And that's that.

Well, the week went on much as usual. I am busy with the last preparation of my lectures (reduced to five, this first time — beginning on Friday, February 25). Day before yesterday I had a rather interesting meeting at Professor Rivet's home (on the very top of the left wing of Chaillot Palace, Trocadero) with Garry Davis and about fifteen influential men, ranging from the *Recteur de la* Sorbonne and three *professeurs au* Collège de France to a few representatives of big business. Garry Davis was carefully coached by my friends *du Front Humain,* quiet, moderate, and perfectly sympathetic: the very good American boy. I was surprised to observe how, gradually, the movement toward an international consciousness is steadily growing underneath the political turmoil. Of course, I do not particularly believe in the efficiency of many tricks used by the *partisans d'un gouvernement mondial* to awaken public opinion. But the final result (namely to develop a kind of spiritual medium in which a number of varied tendencies are bound to converge toward a general drift in the direction of a constructive peace and human feeling), this final result, I say, begins to appear, and is worth every effort.

15 Rue Monsieur, Paris VII, February 22, 1949

. . . nothing else to do (for you as well as for me) but to follow patiently, and lovingly, the thread — wherever it is leading us. More and more, I am convinced that *fidélité* to Life is the only and the highest form of *sainteté.*

Which does not mean, of course, that Life should always be perfectly clear about what we have to do. And this is the case with me, just right now. On the one hand, I do not see so far any good reason to justify a stay in America. On the other hand, how to justify either this protracted stay in Paris outside of any definite job. . . . I feel, in a confused way, that I should perhaps *do* something — but what? To which you would probably answer that, waiting for an opportunity, I have enough to do with daily business of meeting people and the fundamental work of writing down whatever is still in my head. And this is probably true. . . . Still, I would like something to happen, to show me the way on. In the meantime, I am rather busy preparing my lectures. The first one (to be delivered next Friday 25) is mostly written down; and the second one (the following Friday) is rather advanced. I rather like the work which obliges me to get my ideas more definite on many points.

Besides, the days are passing and flowing the same way. Sunday, I went to a cocktail party . . . a certain Mr. G—— was there, who claims to have discovered treasures of wisdom (well buried, I must say!) in a Negro tribe living along the Niger; we had a long discussion together, as a relief from too many very solemn people, ex-ambassadors, and *académiciens*.

From Rome, nothing more; except that, from private, but particularly reliable, reports, I heard that the last affair of *Osservatore Romano* was largely due to the fact that some people, somewhat *alarmés* by the favorable way in which I had been received in Rome last October, took this chance to sink me before my position should become too strong. I did not yet get the final decision concerning the *Phénomène Humain*. But you know that I have no hope left. Better, as you say, to think of something else, and still better.

15 Rue Monsieur, Paris VII, March 1, 1949

This week the most noticeable event was certainly that I delivered my Sorbonne lecture No. 1, last Friday. As I will tell you, I was far from being in a naturally good shape (a bit of flu . . .). Yet, things went sufficiently well; and people (a fairly well-packed amphitheater, of small size) seemed really satisfied. Now, to No. 2. But the flu (or whatever it is) still hangs unpleasantly on me. No fever, but some cough — and this dreadful feeling everybody knows of being in a tasteless world. *La nausée*, as Mr. Sartre says: but not of metaphysical origin. . . . Hope that in three days I will feel more enthusiastic about the development of Life, from its beginnings to the higher primates. In the meantime, my talk is sufficiently ready, I think, for rendering enthusiasm less necessary. Yet, there is nothing like the spark, when one has to address a good public.

Besides, nothing new. I wish the presence and the sense of

God should be more efficient to counteraffect the depressing effects of a cold. But after all, this is precisely perhaps the very core of the human condition (I mean "the dependency of the soul on the body") which has to be faced, accepted, and followed faithfully up to the end.

Paris, April 1949

Practically, I am now at the end of my stay in the hospital; and before Easter I hope to be, once more, *à* St. Germain-en-Laye. In fact, I do not feel particularly enthusiastic about this exile from Paris. But I cannot avoid it. I certainly need to recuperate, physically in a good "air," and with serious food. The sisters will provide. If I happen to experience the same type of reaction as two years ago (a kind of curious euphoria and mental freedom) during my convalescence, that will be all right. There are many ideas I should like to write down: some deeper vision of the same things. . . .

This last month seems to me, in many respects, a perfect blank; and the future too. . . . But, in any case, I feel that I must more and more concentrate on an ever greater and loving God. You know, this shock after the one of two years ago is something like a warning.

Paris, April 13, 1949

I am still writing you from the hospital; not because I am not getting better, but because there is no room for me at St. Germain before the first days after Easter. So much the better, in a way: since, after these supplementary days at Rue Oudinot, I will certainly feel stronger and fitter for the move from here to St. Germain. To be true, this last week in the hospital room is not particularly amusing. But I begin to write a little; I am reading more serious books; and also I begin to go to the garden, under already green horsechestnuts. As I told you in my last letter, the future still seems to me rather "a blank." . . . But God and Time will provide. In the meantime I have collected and adjusted, during the last months, a good number of new-old ideas, which will keep me busy and alive this summer. If only I could feel more quiet (less "anxious," physically) internally! Apparently the best cure is to "take it easy," and to try to transform anxiety into some overwhelming feeling of hope and active relaxation in God — which, after all, is the logical climax and core of my whole *Weltanschauung* and Philosophy.

Read yesterday a curious booklet by my friend Julian Huxley on "A Religion Without Revelation," very sincere, and half-true in my opinion, but only half. Evidently the concept of Revelation has to be carefully clarified. But Huxley's idea that Man can achieve his internal organization without a kind of Cosmic Love seems to me biologically and psychologically impossible and *ruineux*. Man is bound to revolt, or to dissolve, except in a "loving World" — to be discovered: that is the great and beautiful task.

15 Rue Monsieur, Paris VII, April 20, 1949

In fact, I am still at Rue Oudinot, which I shall leave most probably tomorrow, or the day after, for St. Germain, according to the facilities for getting a friend's car. In the meantime, we have enjoyed since a week (not today: gray sky, but no cold), a marvelous weather: so beautiful that I spent most of the time in the garden, or even Rue Monsieur, where I went several afternoons in order to sort out my various belongings, chiefly papers. I cannot yet foresee exactly what is going to be my life and my degree of *vitalité* when I am in St. Germain. But certainly I will have plenty to do to keep me pleasingly busy. The first thing I should like to do is to write a "printable" article (for the *Revue des Questions Scientifiques*) the plan of which has developed and matured in my mind during the past weeks; namely to show to everybody how we are once more in the same position as the men of the sixteenth century, but facing a still more revolutionary problem: not only to decide whether the Earth is revolving in Space, but whether Humanity is biologically drifting ahead *biologically,* on itself. I have already mentioned the subject to you. But now the whole thing has taken shape, structure, and life in my mind in an ever more vivid and convincing way, I think. Really I cannot understand any more how people do not perceive more distinctly the first manifestations (and try to determine the significance and possible value) of the tremendous economico-scientifico-social "maelstrom" where we are unavoidably driving to.

In addition to this relatively short paper, I would like to write a quite new "version" of my old *Comment je crois,* stressing precisely the biological necessity (in order not to be drowned in the approaching "maelstrom" of "human totalization") of developing both a human Hope and a human *Unanimité* (Hope and Love) based on the belief (a well-criticized belief) in a super-personal Focus of Evolution. And then I still have to complete the text of my Sorbonne conferences (half-ready): but, for that, I can wait until autumn. In St. Germain, I guess, I will work quietly in the morning, and walk and read during the afternoon. Visiting people, of course, will be much rarer than here; but still they will come. St. Germain is very easy to reach. And the site is really beautiful.

Excuse me for all these ideological developments. But you understand easily how all these questions concerning Man are really alive for me (much more alive than the fossils of the precedent period of my life), so much more easily that for you too tomorrow begins to be inseparable from today. I have been much interested by your awakening to the essence of modern art. I think you are right: socially, intellectually, and artistically, the same problem of human transformation recurs, so that you cannot awake along one line only, but along all together. Still, I will need your help to discover the meaning, experience the thrill of the nonrepresentational colors.

This time I write you from St. Germain, in the most pleasing and beautiful site you could find so close to Paris. The forest is full and fresh green, with plenty of owls singing during the night, and of cuckoos during the day (the nightingales are still silent or absent, apparently). This time, I am not in the clinic itself (a much better arrangement, since now I am in a perfect physical condition), but in a little villa, on the very border of the forest, and yet in a perfectly sunny place. My room has got two windows facing south, and a third one facing east, so that I get light and heat practically the whole day. Down below a large and very comfortable dining-drawing room, with a good radio set. In the same house just now (in addition to the most attentive nuns) there are three (clerical) guests, in addition to me: a quite pleasant priest and two relatively young colleagues of mine both recovering from diseases developed when they were in China (one of them was several years with me in Peking). Since we are quite free not to mix outside of meals, the association is quite pleasing. In addition, and so far, since almost a week I am here, every afternoon I had several visits (almost too many for my peace of mind). So that, you see, I am far from being lost here. On the whole, and except for a rainy day (not enough water for the fields!), the weather has been beautiful; so that I can spend a large part of the day in the garden, or in the forest. Usually, I spend the morning (or rather, two hours of the morning) writing. During the afternoon, when no visiting friend is there, I read. A good opportunity to get acquainted with the last productions of Mr. Sartre and others. In fact, although these books interest me, none of them brings me anything deep or new. As if I were living in another world.

In this other world of mine, I try to advance further and further, following my private thoughts. I have finally started writing the short (and printable?) article I told you of concerning the "new question of Galileo," and our present position right at a crossroad where we cannot wait any longer to decide whether we accept or refuse to believe in the value and the future of human totalization. The work keeps me pleasantly busy, because I am here (just like in a boat) in the favorable condition of not having to hurry up, whatever I do. Of course I am not yet as quiet as I should be "internally." But I suppose the best way to handle the situation is to remain calm and interested in a creative way.

I have read twice (because I did not trust my eyes) the place in your last letter where you announce to me that I—— is finally married. Would you believe that, just before leaving Rue Oudinot, I decided to write her a long letter, urging her (since this affair gave every evidence of deteriorating from month to month) *not* to insist, but to give A—— back his word, and to end the whole business in a dignified and aesthetic way. . . . Well, now, that the thing is over, I do *not* give up the hope that things will arrange themselves. If you happen to see I——, tell her how much (in spite of the fear expressed in my letter) I am glad to hear that she is settled, and that now she must go ahead, completely fearless. No hesitation any more, no regret, no question, no retreat: this is the way of salvation for A—— and for her.

Besides, nothing special. What you say about my "future" is probably true (meaning that I will find a new line of activity). But life still remains terribly vague before me. But I do not care so much, as long as I feel that I have something to say and to write — in other words as long as the internal fire keeps there.

Clinique des Soeurs,
Place Louis XIV,
St. Germain-en-Laye, May 4, 1949

Once more I am writing you from my sunny room in St. Germain, facing and smelling the always thicker foliage of the oaks and of the *charmes.* Right in the garden *un hêtre pourpre* looks a vivid red under the rays of the sun. Certainly an exceptionally pleasant place for recovery, chiefly if you could see our lunch and dinner! And so close to Paris that, since almost two weeks I am here, I received some visit (or even several visits) every day!

Well, in spite of these visits, I try to do something along my own line. This morning I have finished typing my short paper (some fifteen pages) on *La nouvelle question de Galilée*, which I will try to have published *dans la Revue des Questions Scientifiques*. I have the feeling to have expressed approximately in the right way, and chiefly with the right *tonalité*, not only what I saw (this is relatively easy), but what I felt (which comes much closer to the risk and the difficulty of art). And now, I am just curious to see whether the paper will be accepted by the review, or not. Because if they do not accept it, it will not be for any philosophical or theological reason: but simply because they do not see the world as I think it is (and as I think everybody will see it tomorrow). Just a human test! Besides, I am reading a lot, mostly easy-reading books, in order to fill my literary gaps. These last days I was much impressed by *Les mains sales,* of Mr. Sartre. I do not think much of the Sartre philosophy. But I must say that, as far as the gift is concerned for conceiving and developing a dramatic (and "representative") situation, he is a first-class man.

Among my favorite visitors is George Le Fèvre, a citizen of St. Germain (and, as you know, *l'historien de la Croisière Jaune*). Since the most part of his money is invested in Shanghai, he is somewhat (although quite philosophically) concerned with the development of Far Eastern affairs. A few days ago he got a cable from his daughter-in-law (she is in Shanghai) rather reassuring. But the most dangerous element, under the present circumstances, are the Chiang Kai-shek soldiers in the town. Everything may (or may not) explode every minute in this accumulation of people.

St. Germain-en-Laye, May 11, 1949

My article on the "new Galileo question" must be in the hands of the critics, by now. More and more, I think that I have really hit the point, in these few pages. But the difficulty is to have the paper widely spread. If only *La Revue des Questions Scientifiques* would take it, I will ask for a lot of reprints. That the problem No. 1, just now, is certainly to decide what means (from an objective and biological point of view) scientific socialization gets a fresh proof from the reading of *Ape and Essence,* which I finished yesterday. Of course, Aldous Huxley is a humorist; and furthermore he warns us that "the Thing could not have happened" if only the men of the after-second war had correctly directed the human ship toward a correct combination of Personal and Universal (a statement which is suprisingly correct, and *not* in the usual vocabulary of Aldous H.). But in spite of this small concession to an optimistic view of Man, one cannot escape the feeling, reading the book, that, at the depth of himself, the author believes that science leads primarily to destruction, and sex to corruption. And this is precisely the "complex" which has, by all means, to be eradicated from the modern mind, both in religious and literary circles!

St. Germain-en-Laye, May 18, 1949

In fact, the past week was particularly uneventful. Except perhaps that my friend and superior (the "Provincial" of Lyon) came directly to see me here, and behaved extremely friendly, as usual, without, however, having anything new to say concerning Rome and the future. I finished the geological note for Professor Jacob's *Livre jubilaire,* and also a short *Notice nécrologique* of Dr. Weidenreich. So that I am free now to go further on along the first writing of my conferences. I hope to finish No. 3 before ten days. I felt first some hesitation before resuming the task. But now I begin to feel caught again in the interest of the work, although it keeps me a bit too much on an old ground. When the redaction is finished (about a hundred pages), I feel rather hopeful to get the permit for printing.

Besides, I have read a lot. Just now, I have started *Le Sursis* of Mr. Sartre (Vol. II *des Chemins de la liberté*): about the days of

Munich, as lived by some ten (or more) groups of completely different people — a rather difficult book to read, since all the ten groups are moving together (in the same chapter, or even in the same paragraph), a process which allows some curious effects, but which is rather unpleasant on the whole. A most brutal and pessimistic picture of Mankind, as is usual with Sartre: clever, strong, so that it is difficult to stop reading. But, at the end, you discover that nothing positive remains, out of the whole thing, neither in your heart, nor in your mind. In my last letter, if I am right, I told you about *Ape and Essence* of Aldous Huxley (plenty for the Ape, nothing for the Essence!). Is it not strange, I have reflected, that such a modern man as H. should fall into such an old-fashioned trap: to see science as a primarily destructive power, and sex as a primarily corruptive force, and consequently human evolution as the natural Belial's kingdom? . . . Back (as he says himself) to 900 years B.C.! I have developed a very simple method (by two questions only) to test people with regard to their "humano-evolutive index." (I shall explain you.) According to this test, I am afraid Aldous would not pass, but Julian certainly.

St. Germain, May 25, 1949

Here, nothing much new. Days are passing fast, according to the same routine: work in the morning and visits in the afternoon. No news, so far, of my article (on the *Question de Galilée*); but, as I told you, this is rather a proof that the paper is accepted and sent to the editors of the review, in Belgium. In fact, I have completely lost contact with the Rue Monsieur since more than a fortnight. In the meantime, I have finished this morning (but not yet typed) Lecture No. 3. The work was longer than I thought, because, this time I gave to the text what I hope to be the final touch. Lecture No. 4 (concerned with the historical *expansion* of Man, now succeeded by a *compressive* phase, Lecture 5) is not particularly easy to master in a renewed and arresting way. Still I hope to have it more or less completed soon.

On June the ninth (that is, at the time when I plan to be back at the Etudes) I may have to deliver a small talk, before an audience of anthropologists, on the following subject: *Le sens de l'espèce chez l'Homme*. The choice of the subject was mine. That would be the place to bring and to discuss the problem of a new conception of sex.

I was much interested by what you told me about the German women. But it is so hard to appreciate the average state of mind of a big country like Germany. Last Sunday I had the visit of a quite sympathetic German *bénédictin* (in charge of starting a new monastery near Santiago, Chile); and I was happily surprised to discover how modernistic was, in the big monastery of Beuron (Wurtenberg) the philosophy and the theology of the monks. Something is decidedly moving on, in Christianity.

St. Germain, June 1, 1949

For me, last week went on rather quietly. But now my staying in St. Germain approaches its end. In a way, I feel something like a regret to leave the calm and the forest. But for many reasons I think it better to start again the ordinary life. It makes one shy to be always treated as a semi-invalid.

Otherwise things are the same. O—— told me that he had liked my article on the new Galileo problem. So that, even if *La Revue des Questions Scientifiques* does not take it (for some reason concerning its policy) I can always have the thing printed in *Psyché*, with as many separates as I like. I had to write a short Note (some five pages) for a meeting to be held in Paris next week on the following subject: *Le sens de l'espèce chez l'Homme*. Since the Note is going to be published in the Reports of the meeting, I decided that it might be worthwhile to throw one seed more in the wind. Today, I am expecting a bunch of youngsters who have decided to associate a talk with me together with a picnic in the woods.

More and more the main and almost only core of my *Weltanschauung* is that the best and only way to find one's way in life is to stick stubbornly to a loving *confiance* in the "Heart of the Universe in and around us."

Les Moulins par Neuville
(Puy-de-Dôme), August 17, 1949

. . . life here has easily taken its old routine, except on Saturday last when we went to pay a visit to some friends, at some forty kilometers from Les Moulins, in one of the wildest parts of Auvergne I know: rather high (about a hundred meters) in a hilly and densely forested country; but the fine little castle where we were received and treated with a magnificent lunch was certainly worth visiting. Everything inside (up to the curtains and the bed covers) date right back from the seventeenth century. And, all around, the trees (especially the linden) are older and bigger than at St. Germain. So funny to find this old-fashioned refinement in the deep of the wilderness. . . .

Otherwise, I did not move, so far. The weather keeps rather cool, but so dry! At least the spring near the house was luckily fixed up last spring, so that we have water. Usually, at 8:15 A.M. I say mass in the little chapel for the more pious members of the family. Then, after breakfast, I retire to my room (facing the volcanoes) and I work, practically up to lunch. Afternoon, I still write, or I take a walk, and mostly I read (just started today the book of Hemingway, which begins extremely well). As far as my work is concerned, everything is progressing satisfactorily. Correcting my two first lectures takes a bit more time than I supposed. Yet, Lecture 1 will be finished typing tomorrow, I think; and Lecture 2 does not require so much effort.

Les Moulins, August 19, 1949

Nothing much new since two days. Lecture 2 (the last one to be corrected) will be finished before a week, I think. And then I shall have the pleasure to start something new.

Today, I have received from a Benedictine Father of Beuron (Bavière), four long pages which made me very proud by the way he (a professor of theology, soon on his way to start a new convent in Chile) is thinking about my "new" conception of Humanism and Christianity. Such an appreciation, coming from a very able man (so different from me by birth and training), is for me a big "encouragement," and a strong proof that I have hit something; just as well as another letter, received two days ago, a very pathetic SOS in fact, sent to me by a man whose faith is sinking because he cannot see the way to bring together both his visions of God and of the Universe.

Les Moulins, August 25, 1949

Nothing new, except that, two days ago, we had a thunderstorm and a little rain — very little, but it was so nice and new to smell the damp earth. I did not move outside the fields and woods, around the house. And, at last, I wrote this morning the last page of the lectures (some one hundred pages, rather dense, on the whole). It just remains to renumber the pages, and to make the "Table of Contents," and also to combine a few drawings (almost ready) for the text. After a while, I will attack the "report" for Rome. . . .

Finished reading *The Sun Also Rises* (but why this title?). It reads exceedingly well. But, when you come to the end, you are surprised to discover that there is not a single idea nor "incentive" in the whole thing. Just a pathetic situation (physical still more than moral); and a lot of drinking. Still I enjoyed reading it. . . . The stories of Farrell are reaching deeper, I think; and I like them, partly maybe because the author is writing from a familiar (although disabused) Catholic point of view.

September 1, 1949

Here, life goes smoothly on. Nothing particularly exciting: but this country acts on me in a curiously soothing way. Last Sunday we went to see my sister-in-law, not far from here, along the River Allier. This is the place where I spent so many happy holidays, when I was a child; and each time I go there I enjoy, in some strange way, remembering the old days. Youth! . . . Most of the trees are the same as before; and the house did not change at all since fifty years. We spent an afternoon only there. But the day was fine, and the road perfect, among the densely wooded borders of the Limagne Plain.

Besides, I am more or less finishing what I described to you rather ambitiously as a retreat. I hope that I am closer to God. In fact, if I believe to perceive more and more clearly the main trend of my "gospel," I must confess that the possible content of the coming year seems to me a riddle, just as before. But maybe something will happen, to give some positive object to my life. . . .

No news, so far, of the article sent to Belgium; but I keep optimistic in that direction. On the other hand, I hope to write down the "report" for Rome, in the course of the next week. If so, I shall have fulfilled my holiday program.

Les Moulins, August 12, 1950

. . . reflecting, yesterday, in the train, I came to the conclusion that the best occupation I could select for this month was to try to write at least an outline of my essay *sur Le Coeur de la Matière*. And now I see better that the whole thing has to be woven with four (and not only three) threads, namely: *Le Cosmique, L'Humain, Le Christique and Le Féminin,* although I do not yet perceive exactly how to place the fourth element which, to some extent, seems to me to act less as a distinct element by itself than as a sort of subtle essence of the three other ones: "the spirit of Union."

Here, the country is somewhat greener than last year. Yet, the "natives" complain that the soil is still drier inside (most of the springs are supplying less water than a year ago). Grapes were to be splendid: they may be a failure if the rain does not come. A much darker prospect, of course, than any Korean War.

August 14, 1950

Yesterday I drew the first sketch of the foreword of *Le Coeur de la Matière*. Now I am completely decided to write a first outline of the thing, without knowing, of course, whether this outline will be final, or perhaps the nucleus of something bigger. Finally, I think that the *Féminin* will be presented and discussed as a kind of Conclusion or *Envoi:* not so much as an element by itself than as a kind of light illuminating the whole process of universal concentration: *vraiment,* as I wrote you, "the spirit of Union."

August 17, 1950

Here, the weather is pretty cool since the fifteenth. But no appreciable rain. My brother spends his time looking for the slightest indications of moisture and hitting the barometer in the hope that the finger of the dial will go down.

No news from Rome; except that I have seen in the papers that they are decided, down there, to *définir, en Novembre, le dogme de l'Assomption.* I have nothing (on the contrary) against any "magnification" of Mary in Christianity. But I stick to my idea that, in the present state of theology such a "definition" is somewhat a challenge to physics and biology.[1] Maybe we need this excess of blind conservatism to make the Christian people realize how far we have secretly advanced in the recognition of a new face of *God.*

And, also, I am slowly progressing in my "book" (or rather essay) *sur Le Coeur de la Matière.* But it takes time to start (*démarrer*), because everything depends, in the case, on a correct understanding of the problem and of the psychological elements of the problem.

---

1 This reaction on the part of Father Teilhard was provoked by the articles of some journalists who indulged the taste for the marvelous in their descriptions of the Assumption of the Virgin. When the bull *Munificentissimus Deus* was promulgated on November 1, 1950, it confined itself in fact to the most sober terms. (R.d'O., s.j.)

In spite of the drought, the country is lovely, and I am drinking the native air as a rejuvenating water. . . . I have added a few lines to my paper. So far, I do not yet foresee exactly how big the thing is going to grow. But one thing is sure: even if it remains relatively short, this first trial will have brought plenty of light into some relatively obscure corners of my mind (or, if you prefer, of my soul). I am doing my best, just now, to recapture and to express my feelings, as a child, toward what I have called, later on, *la sainte Matière*. A rather delicate and critical point, since it is unquestionably out of these early contacts with the "essence" of the World that my whole internal life has sprung and grown. In this case, at least, nobody can say that I am intruding on the grounds of philosophy or theology. A personal psychological experience: nothing more, but also nothing less.

Received two more letters from people who want to see me: but one of them seems to be rather a poet, and the other is a Rumanian prince — both of them, I am afraid, of the "illuminated" (or at least "subilluminated") type which I am decided to avoid like fire. Maybe I am wrong.

These last days have not been particularly progressive, as far as my paper is concerned. Too many visits and drives — rather pleasant and relaxing, I must confess, so that I do not regret them, but still I did not have much time for writing (thinking is always possible, face to a beautiful landscape, even in a car). Two days ago, we went some sixty miles from here to a famous old *abbaye* (La Chaise-Dieu), in the fir forest halfway between here and Le Puy. Yesterday, we spent the day at my native place (Sarcenat, near the Puy-de-Dôme), now belonging to my sister-in-law, Marguerite.

In the trip to La Chaise-Dieu what I liked most was the drive through a very wild country, densely covered by black and deep woods. The *abbaye* itself (extremely majestic and massive, with famous tapestries and paintings, such as *La danse macabre,* death dancing with every kind of young or old people) did not impress me. As usual in such cases, I only felt the surge (stronger than ever, distinctly) of a kind of revolt and anger: the utter impossibility for me to adjust myself any more to a medieval form of faith and worship; as if I got choked by being immersed in a "rarefied" God. The same kind of impossibility that I felt yesterday, *à* Sarcenat, to reenter my former "myself." Which does not prove, obviously, that I am denying the vital value and function of the medieval stage of religion and mystics, any more than I could deny the importance and the "persistence" in my present spiritual structure of my native make-up (when I was a child): but the germ is not the tree, that's all.

Yes, on the whole, I was glad to revisit Sarcenat yesterday. But the two main things I brought back from this driving in the past were: (a) the confirmation that the psychological analysis (such as I have sketched it these days in my essay) of my mystical trends (when I was a child) is correct; and (b) the final evidence that an entire previous circle of myself is completely dead (because the wave is by now much deeper inside).

August 25, 1950

Day before yesterday, we went to a lunch, in the rather *seigneurial* castle of a cousin, surrounded by most extensive and most beautiful forests. We were twenty people and I was cornered to discuss the present religious situation (not the external one, of course, but the internal one, concerning our modern vision of God). And yesterday I had to do the same. All this excitement is due to the double gesture of Rome, publishing a rather fundamentalist *encyclique* and announcing the "definition" as the dogma of the Assumption of Mary. Since a week I spend my time answering people about the subject. On the whole, the "faithful" of some intellectual caliber feel completely lost when confronted with a series of statements which seem to fall on our modern earth as from a long ago disappeared world. . . . I will explain to you later on (*en conversation*) my own position. I believe I see what is in the minds of the Roman theologians, and I agree with them. But their views are expressed in the most impossible language. I have nobody here with whom to exchange my impressions. But I am sure that a large majority of French intellectual Christians are reacting like myself. The most funny consequence of the Assumption's dogma is that, by its mere affirmation, the fundamentalists express the view that the dogma is *still evolving* (since there is not a word of it in the Scripture): they are becoming *évolutionists sans le vouloir!*

Les Moulins, August 28, 1950

Here, we are in the midst of continuous thunderstorms (with hail), which luckily did not hit Les Moulins (so far . . .), but came very close. As a compensation the meadows turn green again. But the country people are still wondering whether drought was not safer, after all. Otherwise, the house is extremely calm; so calm, in fact, that I have decidedly taken my chance, and started doing *ma retraite.* Which means, as you know, that, for a week, I will try to concentrate on the Presence of God. I don't like particularly to interrupt the writing of my essay. And I must confess that both the retreat and the essay are still somewhat conflicting on my mind. But after all, the conflict is not very serious, since both are finally concerned with the same thing, namely the research for a better vision of God. In any case, I could not hope to finish the paper before September 15. The main point is that it should be started in such a way that I *feel* I can finish it all right. And I was quite interested of course by the quotation of Aldous H.: "The quintessence of otherness is yet the quintessence of our singleness." Very good. But I still prefer your phrase concerning the bees: "It was a sort of working, and loving, and feeding, all in one fine gesture." Exactly what I have tried to express *dans Le Milieu Divin.*

I've still had a certain number of reactions about (against) the Pope's *encyclique*.[2] . . . And I have written rather strongly to O—— today. But, as I told you, I am not surprised, nor embittered, nor depressed: rather excited. Rome would be in such a better position to express whatever good they have in mind there if they would only listen to what I have been trying to tell them since years. And they will, I am sure. In the meantime, as I told O—— in my letter, *je ne peux pas prendre au sérieux des gens qui en criant, pensent empêcher la Terre de tourner*. And that's all.

Les Moulins, September 6, 1950

After a most rainy night, the sky is blue again. Everything is green, wet; the mushrooms are swarming in the meadows; and (I hope) the grapes are turning more and more juicy for the coming *vendanges* (next Sunday, perhaps).

My retreat being over, I have resumed (successfully enough) the writing of my essay on Matter, Love, and Christ. And now I am practically sure to have finished the first of the three main parts before next week. The most difficult part, as I told you, since it deals with the rather intricate roots of my present state of mind. Finally, it turns out to be a piece of psychological analysis rather than an "effusive" or "poetic" description of my youth's experience. But I am just going on, following my instinct and *mes souvenirs*. Decidedly, the parts are: (1) *Le Cosmique (ou L'Evolutif)*; (2) *L'Humain (ou Le Convergent)*; (3) *Le Christique (ou Le Centrique)*; with a "conclusion" on *Le Féminin (ou L'Unitif[?])*.

As usually, I write during the morning; whereas, in the afternoon, I take a rather long walk in the woods, or I read, or I listen to the radio. Speaking of reading, I am just finishing *The Idiot*, which I do not find particularly good, except for a few remarkable pearls ("Exactly as is a mother's joy when her baby is smiling into her eyes for the first time, so is God's joy when one of his children turns and prays to him for the first

2 Encyclique *"Humani Generis"* (August 12, 1950).

time . . ."). Really, these Russians are too much chaotic for me. And still they are worth reading.

Les Moulins, September 8, 1950

I had also noticed, last Sunday, the lesson: "Do not worry about material things . . . God will provide." I generally do not like especially this part of the Gospel, because too many people interpret it as a warning that the further development of Earth and Man is not in the genuine line of Christianity. But, taken as you took them (that is, meaning that God will provide for those who care for Him more than for themselves), these words are the best you could find at this particular moment.

Here, nothing much. The "pilgrims" are expected this evening to the greatest joy of everybody here, including the dog (who feels completely lost since five days) and myself. Yesterday my sister-in-law, her son and little Chantal (the granddaughter) dropped in for a short visit, followed by a carful of rather remote *cousins* and *cousines* — very nice people, but who make you painfully realize how much, for so many human beings, life is completely uneventful (they do not seem to be conscious of it, luckily).

Otherwise nothing much, except that my essay is progressing, slowly, but regularly. In fact, I feel the need not to go too fast, so that things should have time to ripen in my mind.

PIERRE TEILHARD DE CHARDIN

AS A SCIENTIST

BY THEODOSIUS DOBZHANSKY

Only a minority of those who read the works of Teilhard de Chardin remain indifferent, neutral, or even judiciously impartial. More usual reactions are either glowing admiration, often bordering on hero-worship, or angry rejection and sometimes abuse. A scientific colleague whom I greatly esteem both as a scientist and as a person reproached me for having quoted Teilhard in my book on human evolution, and thus "having succumbed to that mushy mysticism of Teilhard de Chardin." Another acquaintance considered it presumptuous to suggest that Teilhard's biological philosophy is in need of revision.

A writer who elicits reactions so impassioned and so antithetic in so many intelligent readers surely must have said something of interest and importance. He has said probably also something rather novel; mature intellects are seldom aroused by things *déjà vu*. What made Teilhard's views novel and controversial was that he refused to pattern his thinking to fit it into any one of the recognized academic or intellectual categories. He was too much a scientist to set forth his conclusions in a manner wholly to please the theologians, and too much a theologian to make himself altogether a scientist. He was too much a mystic to be convincing to those who demand verifiable evidence for every idea, and too familiar with the canons of scientific procedure to give free rein to his prophetic visions. He was a poet who often wrote in symbols and metaphors; one of his followers found it advisable to construct a dictionary for this private language. At the same time, Teilhard was eager to communicate his insights and endeavored to make them assimilable and unambiguous. These at least seeming inconsistencies have made his views controversial and his writings happy hunting grounds for fault-finders. And yet it is precisely Teilhard's unprecedented many-sidedness that has raised him to a position of one of the foremost thinkers of our time. He defied those who regarded science and mystical vision no more blendable than oil and water. In an age of analysis he dared to essay a synthesis.

Nonconformists, rebels, and heretics have a powerful romantic appeal to many people. Among artists, and even among scientists, there exist not a few personages who value "originality" so much that they would rather be wrong than "orthodox." Rebellions, in science at least, are meaningful, however, only if they lead to some kind of new orthodoxies, which provoke a new generation of rebels. In science, a rebel or a nonconformist differs from a crackpot in that he has mastered the very orthodoxy against which he rebels. Teilhard was anything but a rebel by temperament, and he became one in spite of himself. He saw his hand forced by the intellectual climate of his (and of our) age; as he writes in one of the letters published in this book, "it becomes more and more evident every day that no religion will satisfy Man henceforth, unless it combines together both the faith in Heaven *and* on Earth." And yet, in another letter he says, "I cannot fight against Christianity; I can only work inside it, by trying to transform and 'convert' it."

Teilhard's grandiose vision of the Universe was a fruit of his scientific research and reflection, leavened by his mystic insights. The depth of his discernment, as well as its limitations, were conditioned by the circumstances of the scientific career and of the biography of the author. Born in 1881, Teilhard graduated from a Jesuit college in 1897 and entered the novitiate in 1899. He devoted himself to a broad program of studies — theology, classics, natural history, and especially geology. In 1905–1908 he taught physics and chemistry in a college in Cairo, Egypt. From 1912 on he became a student of the eminent paleontologist Marcellin Boule; the war years 1914–1919 were spent mostly close to or on the battle lines, and were for Teilhard years of spiritual tension and maturation. In 1922 he obtained his doctorate at the Sorbonne, under Boule, and became a professor of geology at the Institut Catholique in Paris. In 1923 he embarked on his first expedition to China, making geological and paleontological studies in the desert of Ordos and in the region of the lake Dalainor in Manchuria, in cooperation with another geologist, Dr. Licent. He was back in Paris from 1924 to 1926, working on his collections and publishing numerous research papers, as well as some more general papers on evolutionary problems. These latter led to his first difficulties with his religious superiors, difficulties that intensified and continued to the end of his life. In 1926 he went back to China (Peking and Tientsin), where he remained until 1946, except for several visits to France and expeditions to various parts of China, Burma, Indonesia, India, and Ethiopia. After 1946 he resided partly in France and partly in the United States, where he died on April 10, 1955. During most of his scientific life, Teilhard was thus away from the world centers of scientific activity. This gave him ample opportunities for reflection and contemplation, but limited those for give-and-take discussions with scientific colleagues in his specialty and even more so with those in neighboring fields.

Between 1908 and 1949, Teilhard published sixty-seven major scientific papers on geology, between 1907 and 1952 a total of fifty-three papers on paleontology, and between 1913 and 1955 a total of thirty-nine papers on paleoanthropology. His complete bibliography amounts to some five hundred titles. His geological work covers a wide field; his studies on the geology of China stand out as a fundamental contribution to the understanding of the geological history of the heartland of Asia. As a paleontologist, Teilhard has concentrated his attention on the study of fossil mammals, again chiefly on those of China. A whole generation of Chinese geologists and paleontologists had him as one of their mentors and leaders. Together with Davidson Black, W. C. Pei, and F. Weidenreich, Teilhard worked on the famous fossil remains discovered in the Chou-kou-tien locality near Peking, and named Peking Man (*Homo erectus pekinensis*). Teilhard was not the actual finder of the skull of this most ancient Prometheus (Peking Man is the earliest known user of fire), but his was nevertheless a key role, since he studied the geology of the locality and the associated fossil animals, making it thus possible to arrive at an approximate geological age of the Peking Man.

Teilhard's work as a research scientist brought him ample honors and recognition from his scientific colleagues. Among his other publications, *Early Man in China* (1941), *Chinese Fossil Mammals* (1942), *New Rodents of North China* (1942), *Le Néolithique de la Chine* (1944), *Les Félidés de Chine* (1945), and *Les Mustélidés de Chine* (1945) may especially be mentioned as having established his reputation. After his return from China to France in 1946, he was invited to become a candidate for a professorship at the Collège de France in Paris, one of the most prestigious positions to which a scientist can aspire in that country. His ecclesiastic superiors discouraged him from accepting this position; some of the letters in the present collection refer to this melancholy event, as well as to the still heavier blow that fell on him, in 1950, when a permission to publish his major works (*Le Phénomène Humain* and *Le Groupe Zoologique Humain*) was withheld by the authorities in Rome. His greatest honor, election in 1950 to membership in the Académie des Sciences (Institut de France), came however at about the same time. In 1951 Teilhard accepted the invitation of the Wenner-Gren (Viking) Foundation for anthropological research to move to its headquarters in New York, where he spent the remaining years of his life.

The eminence of Teilhard de Chardin as a scientist is indisputable. His posthumous fame, and also the polemics that rage around his name, have however rather little to do with his technical contributions in the fields of geology, paleontology, and paleoanthropology. Teilhard occupies a place of honor in the history of intellectual currents of our time not as a scientific specialist but as a synthesizer and a writer. He is the author of what should, I think, be called the Teilhardian synthesis. The relations between these two sides of his activity were stated clearly by Teilhard himself in an early letter (October 12, 1926), one of the most revealing letters in this volume: "I seem to have, deep inside myself, something that needs to emerge and to be disseminated: a certain enthusiastic vision of the immensity and promise of the World, a certain relish, a certain intoxication with real concrete 'being' as it is revealed to us in the Universe. In the end, if I have come to China, if I am burying myself in my masses of fossils, if I am playing the part of the 'Knight Errant,' it is in the hope of better feeding this inner flame at all the great sources of inspirations of the Earth, and of acquiring, through a bit of notoriety or foreignness, the power to make myself heard, if only for one brief moment, before I die."

This "one brief moment" did not arrive during the twenty-eight and one-half years intervening between the date of the above letter and the death of its author. His major writings have been published posthumously. He is being "heard" all over the world. Even in Russia, I am told, his works circulate in a more or less clandestine fashion — how would this please those ecclesiastic authorities who for such a long time prevented publication of Teilhard's books?

The Teilhardian synthesis is patently not a work of a scientific specialist. Does this mean that it is "unscientific"? Could this synthesis have been created by someone who was not, among other things, a scientist? The answer is, I believe, an emphatic No! The synthesis is a work of an author who knew science from the inside, not only from the outside. It is, however, just as obviously a work of someone who was a theologian, and moreover of someone who had the gifts of prophetic vision and of poetic inspiration. The Teilhardian synthesis is not only science. But it includes science. Without science it would, indeed, become "vaguely inspirational musings," as it was branded by one of its numerous critics. Just as surely, without the "musings" it would lose its interest and become one more piece of antiquated popularization, among many such pieces that clutter the shelves of scientific libraries.

It is easiest to criticize books for not being what their authors did not intend them to be. By the same token, it is most unwise for overenthusiastic supporters to claim for their favorite authors achievements which these authors were not aiming for. A lively discussion was going on in France, during the autumn of 1965 (chiefly in the pages of *Le Figaro Littéraire*) concerning the validity of Teilhard's theory of biological evolution. The chief protagonist was Jean Rostand, a distinguished biologist, brilliant writer on scientific subjects, and, like Teilhard, a member of the Académie des Sciences. Rostand has shocked some admirers of Teilhard by saying that there is simply no such thing as Teilhard's theory of biological evolution. Now, Rostand is right that "Teilhard deliberately ignores embryology and genetics; he is not interested in chromosomes, in genes, in nucleic acids, and he leaves aside all the specific questions which face all biologists who care, using modern methods, to clarify the mechanisms of evolutionary phenomena."

The simple truth is, however, that Teilhard left aside all these questions for the good reason that he had nothing to contribute toward answering them. He lived in quasi-isolation and quasi-exile for almost a quarter of a century, which happened to be the time of most intense activity in biological sciences. This was the time of gestation and birth of the biological (synthetic) theory of evolution, and the time of the discoveries that paved the way toward such achievements as the "breaking of the genetic code." Yet *The Phenomenon of Man* was written in 1939–1940 in the scientific seclusion of Peking. This is Teilhard's sublime masterpiece, written however in a difficult and occasionally obscure language. Biological evolution as an historical occurrence is briefly but accurately described. (Rostand is not right in alleging that Teilhard "passes directly from boulder to man.") How this evolution occurs, what causes bring it about, how these causes operate, is however left puzzlingly equivocal. What little is said about these problems is dated — it is what some people accepted, for want of better explanations, in Teilhard's student days. And the matters here involved are not technicalities of interest only to specialists. They are pregnant with meaning for the Teilhardian synthesis. Fortunately, as I have tried to show in my own volume in *Perspectives in Humanism* (*The Biology of Ultimate Concern*), the present-day views concerning these matters happen to be even more favorable for the Teilhardian synthesis than were the views that he himself accepted.

Rostand is no detractor of Teilhard's reputation, since he admits that "the work of Teilhard, in which are strangely mixed scientism and mysticism, respect toward things of the earth and aspirations toward heaven, has given splendor in French literature to a curious spiritual compound that was hitherto unknown." Science is evidently an essential ingredient in this novel "spiritual compound." Evolutionism is its cornerstone. Science is however cumulative knowledge; it grows and changes with time. The "spiritual compound" must grow and change likewise. Teilhard had no intention of establishing anything resembling a new orthodoxy. His admirers, scientists and nonscientists, are called upon to develop the work to the beginning of which he devoted his life.

INDEX

Grand Khingan mountain, 74
Granger, 34, 71–72
Granite, 27
Great Wall of China, 76
Greene, Graham, 187, 190
Grew, Ambassador Joseph C., 181

Hanoi, 27
Heart of the Matter, The (Greene), 115, 187, 190
Hedin, Sven, 57–59, 67, 71–72, 84
   expedition, 61, 64
Hemingway, Ernest, 210–211
Heredity, 186
Herriot, Mme., 35
Hitler, Adolf, 131, 133, 145
Hoffman, Malvina, 181
Honan expedition, 36, 82, 84
Hooton, Earnest Albert, 136
Hope, 14–15, 42, 71, 113
Horses, fossils, 31, 46
Houochan mountains, 37
"How I See," essay, 107
Human energy, essay on, 93, 96
"Human Front," 10, 91, 199
Human Phenomenon, 163, 165–166, 196, 198, 200
Human relations, 57
Human stratum, 54, 66, 68, 70, 91
Human totalization, 205
Humanism, xiii, 17, 91, 185
   new conception of, 211
   scientific, x
Humanitarian ideas, 54
Humanities, xi
Humanity, 10, 34, 41, 58, 71, 77, 91, 100, 102, 106, 108–109, 168
   Church as servant of, 17
   faith in, 77–78
   interpretation of, 66
   movement of, 11–12
Humanization, 110
   science of, 103
Huxley, Aldous, 207–208, 216
Huxley, Julian, 116, 159, 165, 170, 186, 208
Hwang Ho River, 33, 35, 36, 51, 82, 84

Ideas, diffusion of, 69, 165–166, 168, 177

Ideograph, Chinese, xviii
Immortality, 104, 195
India, 70, 85, 223
   prehistoric finds, 85–90
Individuals, 34, 41
Indochina, 27
Indonesia, 223
Institut de Paléontologie Humaine (IPH), Paris, 94, 122
Institute of Geobiology, Peking, 8, 98–99
Intellectualism, 59
Intelligence, 32; *see also* Mind
Internationalism, 51, 57–58, 131, 199
Intuition, feminine, 13

Jacob, Professor, 95, 207
Janssens, Rev. Father, S.J., 11
Japanese occupation of China, 3, 8–9, 28, 95
Java, 89–90, 107
Jehol, China, 74, 76, 77
Jesuit Order, 80, 97, 105, 141, 154–157, 169, 171
   censorship of books, 146, 152, 155, 158, 163
   Father General, 11, 155, 177, 189–190, 192, 197
   restrictions imposed upon Father Teilhard, 4–16, 56, 58, 62, 66, 79–80, 101, 106–108, 113, 126, 129, 131, 171, 177, 196, 223–224
   Father Teilhard's visit to superiors, 11, 107–108, 124–126, 131, 183–189
Jesus Christ, 13, 18, 24, 48, 94, 109, 185
   World perceived through, 40
Joy, 45
Justice, 101–102

Kafka, Franz, 188
Kailan, coal mining center, 61
Kalgan, expedition to, 38, 41, 43, 52–54
Kansu (Lanchow), 30, 33, 37
"Knight Errant," 7, 44, 225
Knowledge, prescientific, xiv
Kuominchun (army of the people), 30, 36–38, 41, 47, 51
Kuomintang, 69

Nationalism, 51, 59, 71
Negroes, 68, 193, 200
New York City, 8, 102–103
    Museum of Natural History, 100, 103
    1940 Congress on Religion and Science, 152, 154–155, 157
Nietzsche, Friedrich, xvii, 18, 113
"Noosphere," 56–57, 63
Nouy, Lecomte de, 101
"Noviates," notes on, 91

Ordos, desert of, 5, 65, 69, 223
Osbourne Expedition, 71
Osservatore Romano, 192, 197–198, 200
Ou-pei-fou, Marshal, 28, 35, 37, 41

Paleoanthropology, 223–224
Paleolithic strata, 46, 60–61, 65
Paleontology, 60, 88, 116, 137, 172, 175, 223, 224
Paleozoic, 40, 42
Panhuman affinities, 51
Pantheism, 128
Paris, 50, 52, 55–56, 59, 61–63, 65, 70, 75, 91–92, 106
    friends and milieu, 6–7
    Laboratoire des Haustes Etudes, 94, 121
    prestige of Father Teilhard, 7, 11
    visits to, 7, 9–10, 77–78, 85–86, 163–172
Parker, Professor, 52
Pascal, Blaise, 109
Patience, 104
Peace, search for, 9, 12, 18, 57, 83, 142, 146
Peasants, 36, 39, 75
Pei, W. C., 85, 223
Peking, 28–29, 33, 76, 84, 93
    American expedition, 9, 31, 150
    Geological Society, 48, 57, 61, 63
    Imperial Palace, 49, 52–53
    Research Institute, 136
    war years, 9, 134–135, 154, 161–162
"Peking Lady," 72
Peking Man, 72, 141, 223–224
Peking Union Medical College (P.U.M.C.), 52, 84, 86, 96–97

Personalism, 91, 113, 115
Personality, 149
Personalization, 104
Perspectives in Humanism, xi, xii
Phenomenon of Man, The, 8–10, 98–99, 106, 111, 226
    submitted for censure, 8–9, 11, 111–112
Philadelphia symposium, 91, 92, 155
Philips, Wendell, 101
Philosophy, 43, 44–46, 51
    biological, 221, 225
Planning function, 186–187
Pleasure, 47
Pleistocene period, 31, 34, 36, 42, 46, 85, 112
Pliocene, 60, 85, 91
Pope Paul VI, 17
Pope Pius XII, 198, 217
Prayer, 103–104
Prehistory, 105, 112, 180
Prejudice, antihumanist, xiv
Program, socialist, xvi
Progress, 99, 102, 144, 161
    faith in, 154, 156–157
Psyche (periodical), 105, 193, 209

Quaternary, Chinese, 38, 41, 81–85

Races, articles on, 130–131
Reality, 31, 40
Rebellion and rebels, 62
Religion, 125, 132, 152, 194
    of tomorrow, 18, 58
Renaissance, the, xv
Revolution, 145, 160
    spiritual, 160
Rivet, Professor, 15, 199
Rock specimens, 26–27, 40, 74, 76, 116
Rockefeller Foundation, 52, 71, 167
Rome, 61–65; *see also* Jesuit Order
    visit to, 11, 107–108, 183–189
Rostand, Jean, 225–226

St. Germain-en-Laye, 10, 173–177, 204–209
St. John, 18, 48
St. Paul, 18, 48, 52, 104
Sangkan Ho strata, 38, 41, 46–50, 55

About the Author

Pierre Teilhard de Chardin was a Jesuit priest and a scientist whose lifework was the reinterpretation of Christianity in the light of evolution. When he died in 1955, his work was known to only a privileged few among his fellow Catholics, for during his lifetime, publication of his key works had been forbidden by the Vatican's Holy Office. Soon, however, they were being issued: first, *The Phenomenon of Man*, next *The Divine Milieu*, then others. Since publication of his seminal works, Teilhard is now widely acknowledged as one of the most important Christian thinkers of our century.

About the Editor

Ruth Nanda Anshen, philosopher and editor, plans and edits Perspectives in Humanism, World Perspectives, Religious Perspectives, Credo Perspectives, and The Science of Culture Series. She writes and lectures on the unity of knowledge in relation to the unity of man.